WITHDRAWN
NDSU

THE APPEAL TO THE GIVEN

THE APPEAL
TO
THE GIVEN

A Study in Epistemology

BY

JACOB JOSHUA ROSS

London

GEORGE ALLEN AND UNWIN LTD

RUSKIN HOUSE   MUSEUM STREET

PRINTED IN GREAT BRITAIN
in 11 on 12pt. Ehrhardt
BY C. TINLING AND CO LTD
LONDON AND PRESCOT

PREFACE

This book has taken a long time to reach its present form. It started out as a doctoral dissertation. But twelve years have gone by, during which much has happened in contemporary philosophical discussions to render commonplace what was then considered novel. In particular the *rapprochement* with traditional modes of philosophy, now an ever more prominent feature of the development of philosophy of the so-called analytic school, has rendered unexceptionable what I then thought its most original feature, the thesis, namely, that the appeal to the given, so characteristic of epistemological discussions in England and America in the period between the two world wars, was simply the intrusion of unacknowledged metaphysical features into the apparently pure analytic treatment of the problem of perception.

The changing climate of opinion has made the rewriting of the original work especially difficult, and the whole enterprise was abandoned on at least three occasions. Much new material has been added and the structure of the argument has been altered, but the central thesis of this study remains the same as that of the original dissertation on which it is based. After all the toil and effort expended I should have remained unconvinced whether what I have to say is either sufficiently original or important to merit publication, were it not for the fact that the notion of the 'given' has been made topical once more by the attempt of contemporary epistemologists in America to restate the idea and defend it as sound and even basic to the whole epistemological enterprise. I shall attempt to take issue with this view in the present study.

In the first chapter the debate concerning 'the given' will be reviewed and I shall show that contemporary discussions of 'the given' fail to take into consideration the fact that there are at least three different theories about the nature of 'the given'. In Chapter 2 these theories are distinguished and a certain view of the issue between them, which I call 'the Naive View', is suggested. This Naive View is rejected by the discussion of the three theories of 'the given' in Chapters 3, 4 and 5, and by a more careful examination of the notion of 'the given' in Chapter 6. In Chapters 7 and 8 the attempt is made to provide a better evaluation of the argument about the nature of 'the given' by showing how certain other issues are involved, and in Chapter 9 several plausible explanations of the dissension are finally united in what is offered as the true explanation. In Chapters 10, 11 and 12 this explanation serves as the basis for the discussion of the task and methods of the epistemologist. The newest defence of 'the given' is discussed as part of a wider examination of the aims of the philosophy of perception, and the relationship between scientific studies of the topic, Epistemology and Metaphysics.

As a result of the long period of incubation within which this work assumed its present shape, I have had the benefit of the advice and counsel of many former teachers, colleagues and friends too numerous to mention, whose assistance I should like to acknowledge with gratitude. I single out for particular mention my debt of gratitude to Dr A. C. Ewing, formerly Reader in Philosophy at Cambridge University, and Prof. R. M. Chisholm, Chairman of the Department of Philosophy at Brown University, Providence R.I., the former for his never-failing assistance and courtesy, the latter for the opportunity he gave me of sitting at his feet and discussing with him some of the views expressed in this book. Of course it is I alone who am responsible for the views expressed here, and for any mistakes and errors which may have been made.

London 1967

CONTENTS

CONTENTS

Contents

Chapter 1

THE GIVEN IN MODERN
PHILOSOPHY

(1) INTRODUCTORY REMARKS

'The whole notion of the construction of objects out of the given is simply a metaphor which we are all of us liable at times to take seriously.'

> F. Strange, *Bradley's Doctrine of Knowledge*,
> *Mind*, 1911, pp. 459–60

'Ascertaining is not a process which bases upon a fund of certainties a superstructure of guesses; it is a process of making sure. Certainties are what we succeed in ascertaining, not things which we pick up by accident or benefaction. They are the wages of work, not the gifts of revelation. When the sabbatical notion of "the Given" has given place to the week-day notion of "the ascertained", we shall have bade farewell to both Phenomenalism and the Sense-Datum Theory.'

> Gilbert Ryle *The Concept of Mind*
> (London: Hutchinson, 1949) p. 238.

Both of the above statements seem to me to contain a great deal of truth. But neither individually nor together do they tell the whole story. Both Strange and Ryle were critical of the notion of 'the given'. But they were attacking different theories, and the grounds of their criticisms were largely different. Strange addressed himself to the nation of the given which he found in F. H. Bradley's writings. Ryle was thinking of the concept of the given associated with the Sense-Datum Theory, which reached the zenith of its popularity in the period between the two world wars. Unfortunately the older concept of the given has been largely neglected by contemporary philosophers, and no effort has been made to evaluate the newer concept in the light of the older. Such an attempt will be undertaken here. We shall find, if I am not mistaken, that much light is thrown on the function that the notion of the given has covertly been fulfilling in modern philosophy.

(II) C. I. LEWIS ON THE GIVEN

The expression 'the given' became an accepted term of significance in contemporary philosophical vocabulary largely because of its use by C. I. Lewis in his *Mind and the World Order*.[1] In that work, which came to be regarded as one of the classics of modern epistemology, C. I. Lewis drew attention to what he called 'one of the oldest and most universal of philosophical insights', the fact, namely, that

'There are in our cognitive experience, two elements, the immediate data such as those of sense, which are presented or given to the mind, and a form, construction, or interpretation, which represents the activity of thought'[2]

Lewis confessed himself disturbed by certain tendencies in the philosophical discussions of the day which seemed to be denying this insight. Some philosophers were asserting that there was no element of interpretation at all in knowledge, while others were maintaining that there were no given data at all and that cognition consisted entirely of interpretation. Lewis thought such tendencies dangerous, for to deny the distinction between the given and its interpretation in knowledge would be to betray obvious and fundamental characteristics of experience. If nothing were given to the mind, he argued, then knowledge must be contentless and arbitrary, for there would be nothing of which it must be true. On the other hand, if there were no interpretation offered by the mind, then thought would become superfluous, the possibility of error inexplicable, and the distinction between true and false almost meaningless.

So he went on to argue that a closer examination of the views to which he was referring would reveal that the distinction between the given and its interpretation was still recognized even by those

[1] New York: Scribner, 1929.
[2] ibid pp. 38 ff.

who appeared to reject it and was merely observed by preoccupation with other issues.

In a vague sort of way it is not very difficult to understand what Lewis meant by his distinction between the given and its interpretation. But unfortunately he omitted to make this distinction as precise as one could have wished, and in particular failed to distinguish between:

(1) The metaphysical issue of the relation between knowledge or thought and reality, which might be called the problem of 'the nature of thought'.[1] This is connected with the controversy waged so relentlessly during the first quarter of this century between supporters of the Correspondence and Coherence Theories of truth.
(2) The issue which arises out of the attempt to analyse sense-perception in terms of sensual appearances or 'sensations' usually with a view to explaining perceptual illusions, hallucinations, etc.
(3) The question of whether our knowledge could be regarded as a structure resting upon certain foundations.

It would seem that Lewis associated these issues closely together. The context in which he introduced the distinction between the given and its interpretation indicates that what was uppermost in his mind was the problem of 'the nature of thought'. But the way he phrased this distinction, to make it depend on the fact that immediate data are connected with sensation while interpretation is connected with the mind, shows that Lewis supposed the metaphysical issue of 'the nature of thought' to be intimately connected with the problem of the analysis of sense-perception. I shall later on be maintaining a similar view and hope, in particular to be able to formulate just what the connection between the two issues might be.[2]

[1] Following the title of Paul Blanshard's well-known book *The Nature of Thought* (London; Allen and Unwin, 1939).
[2] See below Chapters 8 and 9. What Lewis says (pp. 39–48) about the other issues which preoccupied philosophers and led them to try to deny the distinction between the given and its interpretation is suggestive, and particularly the remarks about Bergson may be set side by side with my own comments. I think Lewis is wrong when he suggests that the distinction between the given and its interpretation is implicitly implied by everyone. He fails to realize that his distinction between a sensory given and interpretation as a result of thought constitutes a specific theory regarding the relationship between sense and thought in perception, and that his espousal of this theory reflects a certain commitment regarding the issue of "the nature of thought".

It has required a contemporary treatment of the subject[1] to elicit the clarification that what is central to the doctrine of the given is (3), i.e. the notion that our knowledge may be regarded as a structure or edifice, resting upon certain foundations. When this is taken together with the notion that the foundation of knowledge consists (at least in part) of the apprehension of what have been called variously 'sensation', 'sense-impressions', 'appearances', etc., which are concepts that emerge from a discussion of issue (2) above, we have what is essential to the doctrine of the given.

In this way the expression 'the given', which has gained currency partly on account of Lewis's exposition, can be seen to be part of a much older tradition. In the twentieth century the notion was popularized in the English-speaking world, subsequent to 1910 by the work of Russell and Moore. The very technical term 'sense-datum' which these thinkers invented round about this period betrays its dependence on the concept of something 'given' to sense, and as has been remarked, 'the notion of epistemological order is central to all of Russell's major writings on the theory of knowledge'.[2]

The notion of the given was consequently bound up with the epistemological discussions concerning the Sense-Datum Theory which were so widespread right till the period of the Second World War. Since the Sense-Datum Theory admittedly had its historical analogues in the 'ideas' of Locke, Berkeley and Hume it has been claimed, with some justice, that the doctrine of the given is essential to the empirical tradition in Western Philosophy.[3]

(III) THE APPEAL TO THE GIVEN

The intimate connection between the Sense-Datum Theory and this concept of the given was illustrated graphically in H. H. Price's

[1] R. M. Chisholm in 'Philosophy, Essays by R. M. Chisholm, H. Feigl, W. K. Frankena, J. Passmore and M. Thompson' in *The Princeton Studies, Humanistic Scholarship in America* (Englewood N. J., Prentice-Hall, 1964). I am indebted to Chisholm's essay for some of the historical material mentioned in this section.

[2] R. M. Chisholm 'Russell on the Foundations of Empirical Knowledge' in *The Philosophy of Bertrand Russell*, Library of Living Philosophy vol. 5 (Evanston and Chicago; North Western University, 1944) p. 421.

[3] R. M. Chisholm in 'Philosophy', *The Princeton Studies*, p.261, n.l; also J. Wild in 'The Concept of the Given in Contemporary Philosophy—Its Origins and Limitations', *Philosophy and Phenomenological Research* vol. 1 (Sept. 1940).

work on 'Perception',[1] one of the culminating expositions of the Sense-Datum Theory. The first chapter of that book was entitled 'The Given', and in it, after arguing that no scientific theory of any sort could possibly throw doubt on the validity of normal sense-perception, Price concluded that pure inspection must be the basis of any acceptable account of perception. He therefore proposed to give an account, based on pure inspection, of what it is to see or hear something. In seeing a tomato, for example, there was much that could be doubted about the veracity of one's perception, but one thing remained indubitable, namely

. . . that there exists a red patch of a round somewhat bulgy shape, standing out from a background of other colour patches, and having a certain visual depth, and that this whole field of colour is directly present to my consciousness. What the red patch is, whether a substance or a state of a substance. . . we may doubt about. But that something is red then and there I cannot doubt.

We could doubt whether this something persisted before and after it was present to consciousness, but we could not doubt its *present* existence. This something was directly present, in the sense that

. . . consciousness of it is not reached by inference, nor by any other intellectual process (such as abstraction or intuitive induction), nor by any passage from sign to significate. There obviously must be some sort or sorts of presence to consciousness which can be called 'direct' in this sense, or else we should have an infinite regress.

This peculiar and ultimate manner of being present to consciousness which is incapable of doubt, instantaneous and direct, Price called 'being given', and that which is present was 'the datum', or simply 'the given'. We were given sense-data in any case of perception, and our corresponding mental attitude which accompanied the presentation of the data was called 'acquaintance', or 'direct apprehension' or 'intuitive apprehension'.

Since sense-data were 'given', Price confessed himself unable to understand how anyone could doubt their existence. The only way to convince unbelievers would be to answer their arguments and leave them to appeal to the deliverances of their own consciousness.

[1] H. H. Price *Perception* (London, Methuen, 1932)

'It is impossible from the nature of the case to prove that there are sense-data, or data of any other sort. The utmost we can do is to remove misunderstanding which prevent people from searching for them and from acknowledging them when found.[1] And this is what Price attempted to do in the remainder of his chapter on 'The Given'.

The concept of the given that formed the basis of H. H. Price's appeal was widely accepted and played an important part in philosophical discussions during the 1930s and early 1940s both in England and America. On the one hand, it was crucial to the epistemological discussions of the Sense-Datum Theorists (Russell, Moore, Broad, Price, etc.) whose work at that time was very influential. On the other hand, acceptance of this concept was reinforced by the writings of the Vienna Circle of the late 1920s who initiated a movement known as 'logical positivism' or 'logical empiricism'. Philosophers influenced by this movement dealt with such topics as the logic of probability and confirmation, and attempted to set up an adequate 'language of science'. This was connected by them with the 'empiricist' thesis that our knowledge of reality was derived from the inspection of the 'appearances' of reality. Thus there was much talk about the status of *Protokolsätze*, and Rudolf Carnap (and also others) held that the 'protocols' which embodied 'given, direct experiences' constituted the basis of the entire scientific edifice.[2]

This concept of the given has lost considerably in popularity since the Second World War, and many have come to think of 'the myth of the given'[3] as a classical case of bad philosophy. The main reason for this disenchantment is probably the influence of the later philosophy of Ludwig Wittgenstein as represented in the writings of G. Ryle, J. L. Austin and similar philosophers in England, and in the writings of O.K. Bouwsma, Max Black, Alice

[1] ibid. Quotations from pp.3–6. For an appraisal of Price's concept of 'the given' see R. J. Hirst, *The Problems of Perception* (London, Allen and Unwin, 1959) pp. 28–31, and G. M. Wyburn, R. W. Pickford and R. J. Hirst, *Human Senses and Perception* (Edinburgh and Toronto, 1964) pp. 268–78.

[2] R. Carnap, *Unity of Science* (London, Kegan Paul, 1934) pp. 76 ff., and R. Carnap, *Logische Aufbau der Welt* (Berlin, Schlachtensee, 1928) p. 93.

[3] An expression used by W. Sellars in 'Empiricism and the Philosophy of Mind' in *Foundations of Science and the Concepts of Psychology and Psychoanalysis* ed. H. Feigl and M. Scriven, Minnesota Studies in the Philosophy of Science Vol. I (Univ. of Minnesota, 1956) pp. 255–329.

Ambrose Lazerowitz, Morris Lazerowitz, Norman Malcolm and others in the USA. These philosophers have pointed out the confusions associated with such terms as 'doubt', 'certainty', 'appearance' and 'immediate experience'. The main criticisms have been directed at the Sense-Datum Theory and have led to this theory being abandoned by perhaps the majority of the newer generation of epistemologists. The notion of the given has been regarded as characteristic of some of the worst faults of the Sense-Datum Theory, and it too has consequently been repudiated by most epistemologists.

There has been a return to the situation in the first quarter of the century, when the newer ideas in epistemology, which were later propagated in the Sense-Datum Theory, were fought unsuccessfully by the representatives of the Absolute Idealism which had dominated British philosophy till then, and by the Pragmatists (especially the 'instrumentalist' wing associated with John Dewey) in the United States. The criticisms then brought to bear on the Sense-Datum Theory were similar in some respects to the criticisms which have now been so widely influential, and the notion of 'sensory atomism', which was associated with the concept of the given, was repulsed with particular vehemence. Representatives of the Idealist[1] and Pragmatist[2] schools, as well as one or two thinkers associated with some of the more classical approaches to philosophy, have, throughout the period of the rise of the Sense-Datum Theory, been expressing dissent, and some of them have singled out the concept of the given for particular opprobrium.[3] But their voices were not heard with much sympathy.

Now all is changed. What Moore could refer to as 'the accepted theory'[4] is now the rejected theory. And philosophers of many different schools have come to regard the notion of the given as completely discredited.

It is, therefore, refreshing to find this notion of the given newly expounded and defended.

[1] H. H. Joachim in his *Logical Studies* (Oxford, Clarendon Press, 1948).

[2] 'Instead of trying to provide 'Foundations for Knowledge' the philosopher should apply what is known to the intelligent conduct of the affairs of human life.' John Dewey, *Problems of Men* (Philosophic Library, 1946) pp. 6–7.

[3] See the paper of J. Wild referred to in p. 14 note 3 above.

[4] G. E. Moore, *Some Main Problems of Philosophy* (London, Allen and Unwin, 1953) p.44.

(IV) THE NEW DEFENCE

According to R. M. Chisholm,[1] most of the recent criticism of the doctrine of the given has missed the point since it has been based on a rejection of the notion that our knowledge of physical things is 'inferred' from any kind of antecedent knowledge about the appearances, and on a rejection of what has been said about 'knowledge' 'doubt' 'certainty', etc. by some of the protagonists for the notion of the given, in associating this notion with the traditional 'scepticism with regard to the senses'. But both the notion that our knowledge of things is somehow 'inferred' from antecedent knowledge about appearances and also 'scepticism with regard to the senses' are not really central to the doctrine of the given even although they have in fact been associated with this doctrine by many philosophers in the past.

Essentially all that this doctrine states is that[2]

(A) The knowledge which a person has at any time may be regarded as a structure or edifice, many parts and stages of which help to support each other, but which as a whole is supported by its own foundation.

(B) The foundation of one's knowledge consists (at least in part) of the apprehension of what have been called, variously, 'sensations', 'sense-impressions', 'appearances', 'sensa', 'sense-qualia' and 'phenomenon'. These are 'the given' elements in knowledge.

Many of the exponents of the doctrine of the given might agree that there are also additional 'foundations' to our knowledge in the form of truths provided by 'sources of knowledge' other than sense-perception. Such sources may include memory, 'inner consciousness' or the apprehension of one's own states of mind (e.g. our awareness of our sensations, beliefs, feelings, desires, undertakings), reason (as the source of our a priori knowledge of necessary truths such as some of those of logic and mathematics) 'moral consciousness', 'intuitive understanding' or 'religious

---

[1] Chisholm has expounded his epistemological views in various articles and in his *Perceiving : A Philosophical Study* (Ithaca, Cornell University Press, 1957). His views on the doctrine of the given are expounded specially in 'Philosophy', *The Princeton Studies* (1964) and in *The Theory of Knowledge*, Foundations of Philosophy Series, (Englewood N. J., Prentice-Hall, 1966).

[2] 'Philosophy', *The Princeton Studies*, pp. 261 ff.

consciousness'.[1] But some exponents of the doctrine of the given have restricted the basis of the structure of knowledge to the given in sense-perception only (i.e. 'sensations', 'appearances', etc.) This is what Chisholm calls 'the phenomenalistic version'. Chisholm believes that though 'the phenomenalistic version' is false, the doctrine of the given as summarized in (A) and (B) is true.

In this version, all that the doctrine asserts is that our knowledge may be thought of as a structure which rests upon a sure foundation provided (at least in part) by what is given in sensation. There is thus a distinction between 'basic' or 'primitive' knowledge (which perhaps cannot strictly be called 'knowledge' at all) and 'derivative' or 'inferred' knowledge, and the latter is, in some sense 'based upon' or 'presupposes' the former. In speaking of the latter as 'inferred', however, we need be saying nothing about the genesis of our knowledge or be casting doubts upon its validity. The distinction between 'basic' knowledge and 'inferred knowledge' arises only because the philosopher finds two sorts of truths which are known, the sort which when he asks himself 'what is the justification for my supposing I know this?' he will answer by referring to something else that he knows, and the sort which he finds when, in putting this same question repeatedly, he is unable to point to anything else which he knows and which would justify his claim to knowledge.

Hence it is not essential to the doctrine of the given to regard derivative knowledge as ever being actually inferred from primitive knowledge in some process of reasoning. The critics who have based their rejection of the given mainly on the non-existence of such a process of inference have been barking up the wrong tree. When it is said that the belief that there is a table is inferred whereas the assertion of how the table appears is not inferred, all that is meant is (1) that the assertion about how the table appears refers to immediate experience alone, whereas the belief about the table refers beyond it, and (2) if the observer were to doubt whether it was really a table, he would appeal to the way the table appears.[2] The way things appear and the way we feel, think, believe, are the sort of things which serve as *evidence* for assertions of knowledge which are derivative. The primitive truths themselves are what *confer* the

---

[1] ibid pp. 245–6.
[2] 'Russell on the Foundations of Empirical Knowledge', Library of Living Philosophers Vol. 5. p. 429.

evidence, and they themselves may be regarded as 'pre-evident' (or perhaps 'self-evident'). It is not essential to regard these pre-evident truths as being 'known', and so, once more, those critics who have laid great stock on the point that such truths (e.g. 'I feel a pain' or 'it looks red') cannot be said to be certain at all since they cannot be said to be *known*, have been on the wrong track. It is sufficient that these primitive truths be what confers the evidence on which our claim to knowledge is based; they need not themselves be 'known'. The pre-evident truths are like the Prime Mover of Aristotelian cosmology which is itself unmoved. The given can confer evidence without itself being evident. If it were possible to construct rules of evidence describing the ways in which the given, or pre-evident, confers evidence upon all other things we know, then the structure of our knowledge will have been demonstrated.

It is to the establishment of these rules of evidence that the efforts of those epistemologists who have spoken of the given have been dedicated, although some of them have been misled into not realizing clearly the task on which they were engaged.[1]

(v) REOPENING THE QUESTION

Chisholm's defence of the doctrine of the given can be fully appreciated only when we have considered in more detail some of the points that have been made in previous discussions about the given. Since these points will be dealt with in subsequent chapters, a discussion of Chisholm's defence must be postponed till later on.

But it should be noted that an evaluation of what has been involved in the appeal to the given by past philosophers, Chisholm's defence tells only part of the story since it relates only to the sort of doctrine that has been connected with the Sense-Datum Theory. As we shall see below, there are other theories concerning the nature of the given, and these theories clearly regard themselves as being at issue with each other. Chisholm ignores the existence of rival theories and this results, as we shall see, in a serious lack in his account of the 'doctrine of the given'. No defence of the doctrine of

---

[1] For this view of the task of the Epistemologist see especially C. I. Lewis *The Ground and Nature of the Right* (New York, Columbia University Press, 1955) and R. M. Chisholm, *Perceiving*. For criticism of this view see Chapter 11 below.

the given can be complete which does not take into consideration the rival theories as to the nature of the given and evaluate the issue between them.

It is, therefore, necessary to reopen the issue of the given and examine the appeal to the given in the light of the different theories that have been put forward regarding the nature of the given and the issue between them.

It is to this task that the following chapters will be devoted.

Chapter 2

THE NAIVE VIEW

(1) THREE VIEWS REGARDING THE GIVEN

H. H. Price purported to discover what was given in sensation by discounting everything in the perception of an object which could possibly be doubted. The residue, the existence of which is indubitable, he found to be a given particular—in the case of sight a coloured 'patch' standing out from a background of other coloured patches—and it is to sensible particulars of this sort (i.e. coloured patches, sounds, smells, etc.) that Price and other theorists gave the name 'sense-data'.

I wish to distinguish two additional views which, together with the view that what is given are sensible particulars called 'sense-data', form what seem to me to be the three chief views regarding the nature of the given. These are not the only possible theories; there are philosophers who have held views differing from any of the three views with which we shall be dealing. But when I say they are the *chief* theories, I mean that the three theories are *archetypal*, in the sense that they are the most distinct and clearly formulable views to hand, dividing up the possible relationships of 'the given' and its interpretation in a particularly simple and straightforward way.

In addition to (a) the Sense-Datum Theory of the given (which I shall refer to hereafter as the SDT) we must take note of the following two:

(b) The Object Theory of the given (referred to hereafter as the OT) and

(c) The Immediate-Experience Theory of the given (referred to hereafter as the IET)

There are, finally, also many philosophers who deny that there is a given at all.

Of the SDT, the first (a) of the three theories regarding the nature of the given to be discussed, little more need be said, since the idea

22

that sense-perception provides the raw materials of knowledge in the form of sensible presentations, called 'Ideas' and 'Impressions' by most European philosophers since the sixteenth century, called phenomena by some of the ancient Greek writers, and called 'sensa', 'sense-data', etc., by twentieth century philosophers, is one that is very familiar indeed. Whether these sensible particulars form a starting point from which our apprehension temporally originates (The Discursive Inference Theory) or whether they are distinguishable only upon later examination (The Sensory Core Theory), the sensible particulars are in any case much smaller points of contact with the perceptible world than the 'things' or 'objects' with which untutored common-sense supposes itself to be directly presented in sense-perception. There is a certain fragmentariness pertaining to these sense-particulars which gives some urgency to the problem of seeing how our knowledge of the world of things is related to raw material provided by sensation.

The second (b) of the three theories regarding the nature of the given to be discussed, the OT, maintains that we are presented in perception with the 'things' and 'objects' themselves, and not with any such sensible particulars as 'ideas', 'impressions' or 'sense-data'. C. D. Broad, though himself one of the leading exponents of the SDT, gave what is perhaps the clearest expression to the phenomenon upon which the OT is based when he wrote that

' . . . the object (or, at any rate, a literal part of it) seems to be "given" bodily and the perceptual judgments which we make about it seem to be "read off" from the object itself.'[1]

The view that things or objects are what are given in sense-perception has appeared heretical and naive since the beginnings of modern philosophy. But investigation shows that it has been maintained by many great philosophers both in antiquity and in modern times. Since the later thirties of the twentieth century a growing volume of thinkers argued for the view that it is objects and not sense-data that are given and it came to be as acceptable as the SDT which had been the dominant view during the first quarter of the century.[2]

[1] *Scientific Thought* (London, Kegan Paul, 1963), p. 248.
[2] R. Firth in his articles on 'Sense-Data and the Percept Theory', *Mind*, 1949 (Part I) and 1950 (Part II) has provided a short account of some of the main stages in the reaction against the SDT during this century. See Part I, subsection entitled (c) criticism of the Traditional Concept.

By the fifties a large number of epistemologists had given up the SDT and some of them did so while adopting the OT. Others came to reject the claim that there was anything given in perception. Of the latter we shall speak presently. The OT is thus a theory which commands considerable explicit and implicit support among contemporary philosophers.

The third (c) of the three views that have been expressed regarding the nature of the given, the IET, is an unusual one of whose existence many contemporary philosophers are hardly aware. According to the IET what is really given is neither sensible particulars such as sense-data, nor 'the world of things'. Cognition starts from a unity of experience in which everything is a blur and in which subject and object have not yet been discriminated. This is the view maintained by such philosophers as F. H. Bradley, B. Bosanquet and H. H. Joachim in the first decade of the century. It may be regarded as being in some respects implied, even though rarely expounded, by many of the contemporary heirs to the 'Absolute Idealist' tradition such as C. A. Campbell, P. Blanshard and others. Similar though by no means identical views of the given are to be found in the works of W. James and A. N. Whitehead. The IET view of the given is an important one. But since it has been so widely neglected, we shall subsequently have cause to expound the view at greater length, selecting the version of F. H. Bradley as our example of a clearly worked out IET. Bradley's view of the given is admittedly bound up with his metaphysical opinions, but it is with his concept of 'immediate experience' alone that we are here primarily concerned. There seems no doubt that with this concept Bradley offers a clear third alternative to either the SDT or the OT. Bradley realizes this explicitly, and a résumé of his fundamental criticisms of the SDT and the OT may serve as the best short introduction to the IET.

(II) THE IET AND ITS OPPOSITION TO THE OTHER THEORIES

In one of his essays on the subject,[1] Bradley expounds his concept of 'immediate experience' and then argues that an acceptance of the notion that perception originates in an undiscriminated 'blur' of

[1] F. H. Bradley, *Collected Essays* (Oxford, Clarendon Press, 1935) pp. 376 ff.

experience must lead to a rejection of what we have called respectively the SDT and the OT:

(1) Let us consider the SDT first. If the notion of 'immediate experience' is correct, Bradley says, then the immediately experienced is not a collection of pellets or a cluster of things like grapes, together with other things called relations served as a kind of stalk to the cluster. On the contrary, what is experienced at any time is a whole and each of these wholes is an event. But they are not discrete events, for every whole has a certain duration, and it has some qualitative identity through different times actual and possible. The duration that is experienced at one time is continuous with that which is experienced after it and before it; and so, in a sense, our 'immediate experience' is always the *same* 'immediate experience'.

If what appeared at any moment were as discrete as the sense-datum has generally been proclaimed to be, then we should be lost, because

'The idea of a Self or Ego joining together from the outside the atomic elements, and fastening them together in some miraculous way not involved in their own nature, is quite indefensible. It would be the addition of one more discrete to the former chaos of discretes, and it would still leave them all discrete.'[1]

Therefore Bradley concludes that this atomistic conception of 'the Given' must go. We must get rid of the idea that our mind is a train of perishing substances that are coupled together by another sort of existence called relations.

'If we turn to what is given this is not what we find, but rather a continuous mass of presentation in which the separation of a single element from all context is never observed, and where, if I may use the expression, no one ever saw a carriage, and still less a coupling, dividing from its train.'[2]

(2) With regard to the OT Bradley points out that this distinguishes absolutely between the act of experiencing and the object which is experienced.

On the one side we have the self on the other its objects; and the self is not an object. Besides the self and its objects, we also have

---

[1] ibid., pp. 376–7.
[2] ibid., p. 209.

feeling in the sense of pleasure and pain. But, Bradley argues, this is a vast oversimplification, which will by no means do justice to the complexity of the facts. For example, the account it gives of pleasure and pain is hopelessly obscure; they are not objects and cannot be made into objects. Hence it would seem that they cannot be remembered, nor can we even have an idea of them. Then again 'the Given' at any moment will not break up without remainder into objects and a self; for the self feels itself, which is not an object, and yet is experienced. Moreover, emotion will not permit of being broken up into objects, a self and pleasure or pain; nor will desire and conation. Thus '. . . this whole view is a construction which for certain purposes may seem convenient, but which from first to last is really in sharp collision with the facts'.

The view does not work and finally breaks down on the question of self-consciousness. It cannot become an object; but in that case how can we even become aware of it?

'Here is a fact—a very large and most important fact surely which on a certain theory seems explicable, and which, so far as we see, would on that theory be impossible. . . I sumit that with so much any theory must be taken as disproved.'[1]

We need not concern ourselves with the question of the validity of these criticisms of the SDT and the OT. It is sufficient for our purposes to note that Bradley's remarks reveal (a) that he clearly regards his view as an alternative to the SDT and OT, and (b) that whereas the latter views fragment our experience, his own view, the IET is said to be the only one that adequately expresses the complexity of sensory experience when it maintains that the experience from which perceptual knowledge originates is unitary, undiscriminated and undifferentiated.

(III) THE CLAIM THAT THERE IS NO GIVEN

Right throughout the twentieth century (and perhaps before) there have been philosophers who have asserted that there is no given. In the first quarter of the century these philosphers were mostly representatives of the Absolute Idealist tradition in British philosophy.

[1] ibid., pp. 378-80.

Thus we find F. H. Bradley, warning that

'we must refuse to allow that experience comes from an operation on a *datum*, or yet is a *datum* without an operation and so independent. Both assertions would suppose that something is given where nothing is yet given.'[1]

And again:

'At a certain stage we should all admit that our presentations show marks of intellectual activity. Well, as you follow backward these presentations to the earliest rudiment which you can say is given, at what point will you draw your dividing line? Where will you say, We have here the crude material, which would be exactly what it is now, though there were nothing like comparison, reproduction or abstraction? And non-success in finding the proper place for this line, may lead to the belief that no place is proper, and that no material is wholly crude. . .'[2]

Bernard Bosanquet puts the claim this way:

'. . . it is vain to attempt to lay down boundaries between the given and its extension. The moment we do this we are on the wrong track. . . the so-called 'given' is no less artificial than that by which it is extended.'[3]

These statements suggest a view of knowledge according to which cognition may be understood by analogy with a spider spinning his web and drawing the raw materials for his labours solely from his own body. Thought is held to create the 'real world' that we profess to know from its own 'body', with no given raw material other than itself. This analogy misrepresents the views of Bradley, Bosanquet and others sharing the same opinion, in a number of important respects, but it illustrates graphically the basic position these philosophers adopt with respect to 'the nature of thought', which is that cognition is a constructive creative process throughout.

In answer to these extreme views we find other philosophers who adopt the equally extreme view that in knowledge 'all is given'.

---

[1] F. H. Bradley, *The Principles of Logic*, 2nd ed., (London University Press, 1922) p. 483.

[2] ibid., p. 482.

[3] B. Bosanquet, *Logic*, 2nd ed., (Oxford, Clarendon Press, 1911) Vol. I, p. 72.

According to them, the activity of thought is represented as selective only: it may determine what is included or excluded in cognition and perception, but does not supplement or modify the given data. The mind is merely a spectator of reality. All thought is thus, basically, just description;

'. . . it only uses argument in order to help you see the facts, just as the botanist uses a microscope.'[1]

Samuel Alexander argues that while knowledge and science are indeed, in a sense, 'artificial', this does not mean that in cognition we construct a coherent system of symbols which stand for sensible experience and through it for the real things of the world of which we can know nothing directly. All that happens is that, in pursuit of our theoretical purposes, we move away from a too close contact with the 'brute given'.

'What happens in science is comparable to what happens when we go up into the air and see the landscape below us, not in all its detail, but in certain determining outlines. These are still the outlines of the same landscape out of which we rose. . . the data remain still in view though reduced to compendious form, and represented not by symbols, but, as it were, by delegates and plenipotentiaries.'

Cognition thus consists solely of a judicious selection from 'the given' for theoretical purposes. But essentially knowing something is simply the passive acceptance of what is given.

The argument between the two schools of philosphers whose views I have here sketched as to whether 'everything is given in knowledge' or 'nothing is given in knowledge' is exceedingly perplexing. It is indeed the case that the question at issue is whether knowing is more like 'finding' or like 'making'.[3] But then this does not mean that the argument proceeds by each side pointing to respects in which knowing resembles the one or the other, and that all we have to do is to make complete lists and see which list is

[1] S. Alexander, 'Some Explanations', *Mind*, 1931, p. 423.

[2] S. Alexander, 'The Historicity of Things', *Philosophy and History* (Oxford, The Clarendon Press, 1936), p. 24.

[3] See A. C. Ewing, *Idealism*, (London, Methuen, 1933), p. 440; also J. Laird, *A Study in Realism*, (Cambridge, University Press 1920).

longer. This is not the way the argument has in fact been carried on; nor is it likely that either of the parties to the dispute would be satisfied with the irenic solution that there were respects in which it resembled both, but also respects in which it differed from both. Both sides regard their positions much too seriously to find such a suggestion acceptable.

It was to reject such extreme and one-sided views that C. I. Lewis affirmed his previously mentioned distinction between the given and its interpretation and argued that although these philosophers seemed to be denying 'the old and universal insight' that there are both given and interpretive elements in our cognition, closer examination would reveal that this insight was still recognized by them, though in a blurred form.

I think he was clearly right with regard to these philosophers who maintained that there was no given in knowledge. Closer examination does indeed show that when they say there is no given, they deny only the given as conceived by the SDT (and sometimes as conceived by the OT, though few of them give any thought to the OT). This they do because they are convinced that perception is a different sort of process than is represented by the Sense-Datum Theory. Such philosophers nonetheless accept the fact that sensation in some sense provides the raw material for thought. It is only that they conceive this in some manner similar to Bradley's notion of 'immediate experience'. So that it is quite natural to interpret them to mean (as Bradley in fact explicitly says) that there *is* something given, namely 'immediate experience'.

The more recent critics of the given (such as Ryle, Austin, Sellars, etc.) who have maintained that there is no given have also, like the 'Absolute Idealists' of a previous generation, primarily been intending to reject the 'sensory atomist' view associated with the SDT. It is tempting to interpret them too as not meaning quite what they say and to regard them as tacit supporters of the OT, i.e. as meaning that objects, not sense-data are what are given in sense-perception. I think that we must exercise caution and not follow this temptation uncritically. We must accept the fact that these thinkers are to be distinguished from other explicit supporters of the view that objects are given, such as John Wild, for example, for the latter regards the notion of the given as legitimate, whereas it is against the legitimacy of the very notion of the given that the former are arguing. However, we shall see later on,[1] that to the extent that some of these critics are supporters of the common-sense view which they regard as opposed to metaphysical interpretations of the world, they may well be regarded as tacit supporters of the OT.

(IV) VIEWS OF THE GIVEN AND THEORIES
OF PERCEPTION

There seems to be a prima facie connection between the three views of the given we have distinguished and the more familiar 'theories of perception' which have been listed and discussed in the standard works on perception. These theories of perception are offered as rival ways of analysing perception in terms of sensual appearances or 'sensations', usually with a view to explaining perceptual illusions, hallucinations, etc. In modern philosophy it has become customary to distinguish three alternatives regarding 'the problems of perception': (1) Realism (sometimes called 'Naive', sometimes 'Direct'), (2) The Causal Theory (sometimes called 'Representationalism') and (3) Phenomenalism.

H. H. Price has in addition distinguished three modified versions of Realism, namely 'The Multiple Location Theory', 'The Theory of Compound Things' and 'The Appearing Theory'.

Both (2) and (3) have been related to the Sense-Datum Theory and to its predecessors in modern Philosophy called variously The 'Theory of Indirect Perception' or the 'Representative Theory of Perception'.

Thus it would seem that Realism and its versions are related to the OT, The Causal Theory and Phenomenalism to the SDT.

But though it is true that there has been a widespread association between the different views of the given and the various theories of perception, there has not been, nor need there be any one-to-one correspondence between them. This may be seen (a) from the fact that the IET has no corresponding theory of perception with which it may be associated. In fact, it may (and has) been combined with either the Appearing Theory or the Sense-Datum Theory. Moreover, (b) Realism has been stated by Price himself (as by Moore) in terms of the assumption that sense-data are given, the problem

[1] See Chapter 12.

then being phrased as whether or not sense-data are identical with parts of the physical objects. It may be argued that the unsuccessful and unplausible face that Realism presents when so formulated is in fact due to the unwarranted assumption of the SDT, but in any case it surely becomes clear that the SDT and the Sense-Datum Theory in either its Phenomenalistic or its Causal or Representationalist form are not identical. Finally (c) it may be noted that though many supporters of the Sense-Datum Theory's explanation of the problems of perception (e.g. Moore, Price, etc.) have also maintained, quite naturally, the view that sense-data were given (i.e. have endorsed the SDT), others (e.g. Broad, Ayer, etc.) have professed to avoid any commitment regarding this.

In brief, then, the SDT, the OT and the IET are different views about what is given in sense-perception, while Realism, Representationalism and Phenomenalism are theories which offer an explanation or analysis of the facts of sense-perception. The two lots of theories are related but different. A supporter of the OT may be a Sense-Datum Theorist in either its Causal or its Phenomenalist form.[1] A supporter of the IET may be either a Realist or a Sense-Datum Theorist. And a supporter of the SDT could be a Realist or Sense-Datum Theorist.

(V) THE NAIVE VIEW OF THE DISPUTE

Now that we have outlined the three chief views regarding the nature of the given, we are ready to embark upon our task of evaluating such appeals to the given. And we shall be able to do this if we can reach some conclusion regarding the nature of the dispute between these three theories. What is the dissension about and how would one be in a position to settle it?

The simplest answer to these questions is one that is immediately suggested by the manner in which H. H. Price introduced the notion of the given. Price, it will be recalled,[2] started with a straightforward case of seeing something and after discounting everything in the perception of this thing that could be mistaken he arrived at the conclusion that what was really given was a certain visual

---

[1] Hans Reichenbach, *Experience and Prediction*, (Chicago, Univ. of Chicago Press 1938) may be an example of this.

[2] See above. Chapter I (III).

coloured patch standing out from a background of other coloured patches.

The impression is here given that Price was attempting to describe what it is that he was really seeing. If this be extended to other theories regarding the nature of the given, the view that suggests itself is that all theories of the given must be regarded as attempts to describe what happens when we perceive something through our senses. Take any situation where we perceive something e.g. the present perception of the table on which I happen to be writing. Something happens here of which we give a perfunctory account when we say simply 'I see a table'. This statement is completely satisfactory for all practical purposes and for most theoretical ones. But the philosopher, who is interested in describing what happens in this present case of perception in the light of other cases, in order to give an account which will fit all the possible cases of perception, cannot be satisfied that this correctly formulates what happens, because, for example, he constantly recalls such phenomena as hallucination, double vision, and so on, all of which are cases which may, at the time they occur, be indistinguishable from ordinary perception. What makes these borderline cases of perception different from cases of perceiving objects such as tables seems to lie primarily in the fact that what is 'seen' in the former cases is hallucinatory, illusory, etc. Thus there arises the problem of formulating a theory of perception which, mindful of such borderline cases, will attempt to describe more accurately just what happens in any 'perceptual situation'. And to describe such situations more accurately we have to re-examine any particular case of normal perception with our judgment sharpened by these theoretical considerations.

This, I think, is what the appeal to the given seems to imply: if you look again, carefully this time, you will see that what you directly apprehend is not the table itself, but a coloured, spatial 'patch' which you *take* to be a table. This is what we shall call a 'sense-datum' and this it is which is given—so runs the most well-known re-formulation of what happens when we perceive something. The philosopher 'opens our eyes' to the truth.

This seems to be what Price thought he was doing, and many other philosophers dealing with the topic of sense-perception seem to have imagined themselves to be doing something similar. This is part of what seemed to be so interesting and enlightening about their talk of 'the given'. It is in this fashion that the Sense-Datum Theory was introduced into modern epistemology by such philosophers as G. E. Moore. So it is not surprising that the theorist who has had his eyes opened to what is really given finds it difficult to understand how any other theorist could possibly formulate what happens in perception in any other way. His natural reaction is that there must be some misunderstanding: either his colleague is expressing himself badly or else he cannot have borne in mind all the borderline cases of perception.

If this is the case then the existence of rival views as to the nature of the given in perception becomes something surprising and of great interest. Each of the theories appears to offer itself as an account of what the philosopher will discover on closer inspection to be really given when he re-examines any particular case of perception in the light of theoretical considerations. So that insofar as there is a dispute as to the nature of the given, this dispute must concern itself with what is really discoverable upon closer inspection. This is the simplest account of the nature of the dispute, and it fits in with the actual procedure which some of these philosophers seem to have adopted in introducing us to their theories. I shall refer to it as the 'Naive View'.

But this account, in the last resort, carries with it the implication that the dispute is insoluble. For if each party firmly believes as a result of his personal investigation that what is given is what he says, no argument is liable to disturb his conviction about the matter, for his theory has 'opened his eyes' and he now *sees* that this is what is given. The only consideration which might dispose him to argue with those who did not see clearly what was given would be to help to remove the misunderstandings and 'veils of theory' which prevent others from seeing reality as it is.

There would seem to be no way for an outsider to settle the dispute for himself except by reading through each account of the nature of the given, and then carefully inspecting his own experience to see which view fitted best.

This situation may well be acceptable to many thinkers, for there are some who will be content with a universe which is full of insoluble mysteries. But when a problem is insoluble in just this particular way, we may well suspect that something has gone wrong. The three accounts of the given, it seems, cannot all be right. And yet each is backed by arguments of considerable weight and propounded by theorists of eminent reputation whose reliability and intelligence are beyond question.

And each of the disputing theorists is pronouncing on a subject—the analysis of what he himself really sees or hears—about which he alone is in a position to know best. Are we then to say that reality presents itself differently to different people? What a strange situation that would be!

Insofar as we are convinced that such an impasse is to be avoided, we must treat the Naive View of the nature of the dispute about the given with suspicion, for the Naive View clearly implies that the dispute is not soluble, or at any rate, soluble only for each man according to his own lights. In what follows we shall fill out the suspicion of the Naive View by attempting to demonstrate that it is in fact erroneous. This will be the first stage in the argument, and will engage our attention in the next four chapters.

After that we shall attempt to explain why the three groups of theorists nevertheless consider themselves to be arguing about what it is that is given, and of what their dissension consists. In this way we shall be able to cast light upon the appeal to the given in sense-perception and assess what is involved in such an appeal.

But though I have disclosed my conviction that the Naive View of the dispute concerning the given is the wrong view, it is worth noting how very plausible this view is. For though I shall be concerned to show that it is erroneous and very misleading, the fact that the disagreement about the nature of the given in sense-perception so easily suggests this view seems to me to provide an important clue to the true evaluation of the appeal to the given.

Chapter 3

THE GIVEN AS SENSE-DATA

(1) IMPLICATIONS OF THE NAIVE VIEW

According to the Naive View of the dispute about the nature of the given in sense perception, each of the three theories we have distinguished is an attempt to describe what really happens when we perceive things. Though we generally assume that what present themselves to us are the things themselves, certain considerations engender doubts about this, and the need is felt for a more cautious examination of the facts. The different theories about the nature of the given come to formulate the findings of experts who have undertaken an examination of this sort.

If this Naive View is correct, all three theories are attempted descriptions of the facts. Thus if any of them is to be the correct description, at least one of the terms 'immediate experience', 'object' or 'sense-datum' must denote some thing empirically discoverable, for this is the most important part of what each theory means by claiming one of these terms as denoting the given. The argument between the three theories would then most simply be understood as the argument as to *which* of the three was in fact discoverable in our perceptual experience upon closer examination, i.e. it would be an argument about the facts.

There is also the possibility that more than one of the terms 'immediate experience', 'object' or 'sense-datum' denotes something empirically discoverable. All three may be empirically discoverable, and it may be the case that the rival experts are aware of this. The account to be given of the argument between the three theories would then be a little more complicated. It could no longer be regarded merely as an argument about the facts, but must also relate to the *significance* of the facts. It could be regarded, for example, as the argument about which of the three of these empirically discoverable phenomena was of prior epistemological significance. This concept of epistemological priority is one that has already been noted before. It requires careful consideration and will be discussed in greater detail in a subsequent chapter.

But whether or not each of the experts is claiming epistemological priority for 'immediate experience', 'object' or 'sense-datum' on grounds *other* than that of its being simply a discoverable fact, he must, if the Naive View is to be correct, be saying at least that what he claims to be given is an empirically discoverable fact. Hence each theory stands or falls, according to the Naive View, on the question whether or not what it claims to be given is in fact empirically discoverable.

Of course all three theories may be mistaken about the nature of the facts. But if the Naive View is correct, this is certainly not what the rival experts themselves suppose. And since we are dealing with philosophers of eminent reputation, if we can show that none of the terms 'immediate experience', 'object' or 'sense-datum' denotes something empirically discoverable in the simple straight-forward manner suggested by the Naive View, I think we can take this as evidence against the Naive View rather than against the experts themselves. This is what I shall attempt to show in this and the two following chapters.

(II) THE NON-EMPIRICAL NATURE OF THE SENSE-DATUM

I propose to demonstrate firstly how easily the pretence that the SDT is simply 'picking out' or 'pointing to' a sense-datum, which everyone who looks carefully enough may see, can be shown to be misleading. What we have here, I shall argue, is a case of the *postulation* of a theoretical entity in order to 'account for' certain puzzling phenomena of sense-perception. We shall also see that the 'accounting for' is not as straight-forward as it seems. It is not the case that we discover the sense-datum by closer inspection, and are thereby *incidentally* able to understand certain peculiarities about perception; rather is it the case that we start by noting these peculiarities, and are drawn, for a variety of interesting reasons, one of which we shall unravel by evaluating the appeal to the given, to invent sense-data to 'account for' them.

In arguing against the notion that sense-data are simply existents waiting to be discovered, I shall be covering ground which has already been well-trodden in recent discussions. For there has been a marked change in the way in which the Sense-Datum Theory has come to be understood. It used to be regarded, indeed, as is suggested by H. H. Price's appeal to the given, as the empirical discovery that there are sense-data. But there were always some who regarded the sense-datum as a postulated theoretical concept. And, finally, many came to the conclusion that the Sense-Datum Theory was nothing more than an improved language for talking about perception. Without attempting to follow and survey the history of these changes of opinion too closely, I shall try to discuss and evaluate some of the arguments that were offered by theorists in passing from one to the other of these interpretations.

(III) POINTING OUT SENSE-DATA

H. H. Price's account of the sense-datum as 'the given' follows in certain crucial respects G. E. Moore's celebrated attempt to 'point out' what sort of things he meant by sense-data. Moore's instructions were, briefly, that one need only look at one's right-hand and 'pick out' something which he would naturally tend to identify with the surface of his hand, but would also, on a little reflection, be able to see that it could be doubted whether it was indeed identical with the surface of his hand. Things of this sort were sense-data. Moore's definition left open the question whether the sense-datum was or was not identical with a part of the surface of one's hand.[1]

Critics objected, correctly, that this was merely a misleading way of asking whether one was seeing one's hand or seeing something else which was not one's hand. Moore's way of expressing this question prejudices the inquiry from the start. It *must* be the case that in any normal perception we are seeing either a hand or some other entity: if we are seeing at all we must be seeing *something*. And this something *must* be either a hand or something else; there is logically no *other* alternative. But this does not mean that Moore is using the term sense-datum in such a way that there can be no

---

[1] G. E. Moore, 'The Defence of Common-Sense' in *Contemporary British Philosophy* 2nd series (London, Allen and Unwin, 1925) p. 217. Moore's technique here (also in evidence in his contribution to the *Aristotelian Society* symposium (Proc. 1926) on 'The Nature of Sensible Appearances') for 'picking out' what he meant by sense-data is very similar to Price's method of 'pointing' to Sense-data as the given. It is likely that Price was influenced by such passages in Moore.

doubt of the existence of a sense-datum.[1] This would be the case if the alternatives which we were considering were all physical objects. For example, in Moore's case, instead of saying,'I see my right hand' and leaving myself open to correction ('No, it's not your right hand, it's a piece of wood or paper, etc. which you have wrongly supposed to be your right hand'), I can say 'I see *something*.' This claim cannot be so easily disputed; but that is only because, in such a case, no definite claim has been made. What I mean, really, is something like 'I see X', where the letter 'X' could be replaced by such expressions as 'my right hand', 'a piece of paper', etc. In this case, if instead of saying 'I see something', I said 'I see a sense-datum', it *would* be true that sense-data must exist. But the sense-datum I should then be claiming to see would be either my right hand, a piece of wood, a piece of paper, etc. that is, it would be a physical object.

But these are not the alternatives which Moore is considering. What he is doubting is whether the *something* which he is seeing is the surface of his right hand (a physical object), or some other entity which is not a physical object at all. Nor is Moore using the term 'sense-datum' ambiguously, that is, as the name of *either* an object *or* a non-physical entity. He is using the expression 'sense-datum' as equivalent to something which *could* be either part of an object or a non-physical entity. But is there something in our perceptual experience which could be either part of a physical object or a non-physical entity? Is there such a neutral entity as this?

O. K. Bouwsma has confessed that in spite of Moore's instructions he fails to be able to 'pick out' any such neutral entity. He complains that Moore has not given sufficient description of this something to enable anyone to recognize when he had 'picked it out'; nor has he indicated the sort of 'picking out' which would be necessary, since, unlike any other sort of 'picking out', Moore's 'picking out' is not amenable to any simple empirical check. Thus it seems that if once we have managed to stir up the requisite doubt, 'there is nothing to do but go on doubting. Scratching, smelling, looking more closely, do not give relief.[2]'

---

[1] This is the mistake made by C. A. Mace in his article in *The Philosophy of G. E. Moore*, ed. Schilpp, Library of Living Philosophers, Vol. 4 (Evanston and Chicago, North Western University, 1951) pp. 627–8, which Moore points out in his 'Reply to my Critics' in that volume.

[2] Article in *The Philosophy of G. E. Moore*, p. 207.

This line of attack cuts fundamentally at the notion that sense-data are things just waiting to be seen. And for this reason it is worthwhile to examine very briefly the defence which Moore offers of his original instructions. (1) Moore confesses that his original instructions were not clear and that this lack of clarity arose because he was really trying to do more than he said he wished to do'[1] If he had merely, as he professed, been giving a method of finding a specimen of a sense-datum, he could have said simply, 'Stare at an electric lamp, for a little while, and then close your eyes; the after-image which you will then see is a specimen of the sort of thing I mean by a sense-datum.' Nobody could then have doubted, he believes, that there *are* such things as sense-data, because nobody can doubt, that after-images are sometimes seen.[2]

But, in his original procedure, he had also unconsciously been trying to establish his assumption that when a person is seeing something, he must at the same time be 'seeing' a sense-object, in a special sense of 'seeing' which Berkeley called '*direct* perception' and which Moore in his 'Status of Sense-Data'[3] had called 'direct apprehension'. Moore illustrates this special sense of 'see' by giving two examples: we 'see' an after-image, although our eyes are shut, and Macbeth 'saw' a dagger which was merely a hallucination. Hence this special sort of perception called 'direct perception' can take place where there is no physical object (or part of one) that is in fact seen, and even when one has one's eyes shut.

Moore admits that he had assumed that every case of perception must involve this special sort of perception called 'direct perception'. Whenever one is seeing something, one is at the same time 'directly perceiving' a sense object. In saying that 'direct perception' *must* be involved, Moore says that he is not merely stating an empirical fact learned by observation. He means that the propositional function 'x is seeing at least two objects' entails the propositional function 'x has a direct visual field which contains at least two objects'. One can say that it is *part of the very meaning* of the assertion that a person is seeing his own right hand, that he has a direct visual field containing at least two objects. This assumption still seems to Moore evidently true.[4]

[1] 'A Reply to my Critics', pp. 630 ff.
[2] ibid., p. 644.
[3] *Philosophical Studies*, (London, Routledge and Kegan Paul, 1922) p. 173.
[4] 'A Reply to My Critics', p. 632.

Unfortunately Moore cannot tell us very much more about this special sort of perception called 'direct perception'. It seems obvious to him that in visual perception we could not possibly 'directly see' the whole physical object but only that part of its surface which is turned toward us. He is prepared to admit that his use of the expression 'directly see' may be in some respects obscure, and may even involve some fundamental mistakes.

In reply to this A. J. Ayer argued that since the occurrence of 'direct perception' in all cases of perception is held to be absolutely necessary, and indeed 'directly perceiving' some sense-object is held to be 'part of the meaning of 'perceiving some object, we might come to suppose that the only way to resolve Moore's doubt whether what is 'directly seen' is part of the surface of the physical object or some non-physical entity, is to reflect upon the actual usage of the expressions concerned. But there is no everyday usage of the expressions 'directly see' and 'sense-datum', nor any uniform usage amongst philosophers either. Hence Ayer concludes that there is really no way of resolving Moore's doubt, because the answer depends upon the meanings to be attached to the technical terms involved, and Moore has not given sufficient indication of such meanings to enable anyone to resolve the doubt. What Moore is really doing, whether he admits it or not, is 'hesitating over the choice of alternative verbal conventions'.[1]

Moore denies this, and believes he can reformulate his question in a way which does not require such technical terms as 'directly seen' or 'sense-datum'. In fact, he suggests, it simply reduces itself to the question how to explain what object we are referring to by the words 'this' or 'that' when we point with our fingers and say 'this is a penny' or 'that is a penny'.[2]

But Ayer rejects this suggestion. Moore is assuming that these demonstratives refer to one and the same object in every case where one points and says 'this is a penny' or 'that is a penny'. Assuming this, the doubt of which Moore speaks arises by invoking cases of hallucination, after-images, etc., to throw light upon ordinary perception. Ayer retorts that he cannot see any warrant in the ordinary usage of expressions like 'this is a penny' for holding that

[1] A. J. Ayer, 'The Terminology of Sense-Data', *Mind* 1945, reproduced in *Philosophical Essays*, (London, Macmillan, 1954).

[2] Addendum to the 2nd ed. of *The Philosophy of G. E. Moore*.

the demonstrative refers to an object such as Moore describes. When I look at a penny there is normally *no* object which I attempt to identify with the part of the penny's surface which I am seeing but which at the same time I have strong reasons for supposing that it cannot be so identified. When I point and say 'this is a penny', the correct denotation of the word 'this' is simply 'the penny', and not 'part of the surface of the penny' (which would, however, be correct if I had said, 'this is part of the surface of the penny'). Where I mistake some other object for a penny and say 'this is a penny', the correct denotation of 'this' is whatever it is that I have mistaken for a penny. And in the case where I am undergoing a complete hallucination and say, with a gesture that would be appropriate if I really were looking at a physical object 'this is a penny', the word 'this' really does not denote anything at all.[1]

This exchange between Bouwsma, Moore and Ayer is enlightening and illustrates the difficulty raised by Moore's profession to be able to 'pick out' a sense-datum.

(2) A second point which emerges in the course of the discussion is the technical nature of the expression 'direct perception'. Moore in his revised instructions suggests that one can 'pick out' a sense-datum by simply inducing in oneself an after-image and realising that this is the sort of 'object' which may be 'directly perceptible' in cases of normal perception as well. But it is worth insisting (though the point is obvious enough and has been made often before) that there seems no need to suppose there is anything in normal vision at all comparable to the seeing of an after-image. The suggestion seems to be that whether we are actually seeing a table or undergoing a hallucination in which we imagine we see a table, we are in both cases 'directly seeing' what may well be one and the same 'sense-datum'. But there is no necessity at all which could force us to the conclusion that normal perception is just a sort of hallucination which happens to be substantiated. The distinction between 'seeing' and after-image or hallucination and normal perception may well be an unbridgeable distinction in kind, which can by no means be overcome by stringing together normal perception, hallucination and after-image, with the latter two being regarded as a sort of subspecies of normal perception. So Moore's revised instructions too seem to be of no use to us unless we assume

[1] *Philosophical Essays*, note at bottom of pp. 78–80.

(what Moore takes to be obviously true) that every case of normal perception must involve 'directly seeing' something. But so far from assuming this to be obviously true, we may well question its truth altogether.

It may be the case, that under certain circumstances we can come to see the physical object so vaguely and indistinctly as to be in doubt whether it is really the object we are seeing at all, even though we are sure we are seeing something. And this may perhaps encourage us to speak of 'directly seeing' something in cases of normal vision as well as in the examples of 'seeing' an after-image or hallucination. But what one sees in such circumstances could perhaps be more accurately described by saying that one sees the physical object vaguely or indistinctly. It is certainly questionable whether one is here 'directly seeing' a 'sense-datum'. Hence no fresh light is thrown upon the matter by Moore's revised instructions for 'picking out' sense data in hallucinations and after-images.

(3) It is clear from Moore's attempt to 'pick out' sense data, as well as from Price's exposition of the sense-datum as the given, that only the phenomena of illusion, hallucination, perspective variation, etc., are what lead to the formation of the concept of a 'sense-datum' as something other than a physical object. It would be reasonable, therefore, to suspect, that the sense-datum is not any 'neutral entity' recognizable from the start, and concerning which consideration of the phenomena of illusion, etc., raised the doubt whether it is, after all 'identical' with some feature of the object, but rather a theoretical concept produced by the supposed necessity of 'accounting' for these phenomena. This is the sort of view to be found in other exponents of the Sense-Datum Theory, and emerges clearly, for example, in C.D. Broad's exposition of that theory.

(IV) THE SENSE-DATUM AS A THEORETICAL ENTITY[1]

According to Broad[2] the Sense-Datum Theory (or as he calls it, the Sensum Theory) arises out of the necessity of distinguishing

---

[1] This section is essentially a revised version of material used in my 'The Reification of Appearance', *Philosophy*, Vol. XL (1965), pp. 114–18.

[2] *Scientific Thought* (London, Kegan Paul, 1923) Part II, *Mind and Its Place in Nature* (London, Kegan Paul, 1925) Ch. IV.

between things as they are and as they appear to be. The difficulty is to reconcile the supposed neutrality, persistence, and independence of a physical object with the obvious differences between its various sensible appearances. We know, for example, that when we lay a penny down on a table and view it from different positions, it generally looks more or less elliptical in shape. But the penny, at which we were looking all the time, is round and not elliptical. Thus in this and similar examples, account must be given of how the same thing can be both round and elliptical. The normal way of putting the matter is to say that the penny *appears* elliptical but is *really* round. But what does this distinction between appearance and reality amount to? Out of the many appearances of the penny, why do we select the round appearance as representing the real shape?

Broad rejects the attempt to explain such facts by rules of perspective; these rules, according to him, state only that we can predict what particular appearances an object will present to the observer when we know the shape of the object and its position with respect to the observer.[1] They are a statement of the facts relating to the correlation between the different phenomena rather than an explanation of these facts. Nor will Broad accept the view that appearances are merely mistaken judgments about physical objects. We are not, for example, mistakenly ascribing an elliptical shape to what is in fact round. Sensible appearances may lead to mistaken judgments but they need not.

Broad's Sensum Theory is a suggested solution for this situation, attempting to analyse the distinction between appearance and reality. It asserts the existence of a peculiar kind of entity which may be called 'an appearance', or more technically a 'sensum', and claims that such entities really possess the characteristics which physical objects only seem to possess. Thus whenever a penny looks elliptical, one is apprehending an object which is in fact elliptical. This object is connected in some specially intimate way with the round penny and for this reason is called an appearance of a penny. The object and the penny cannot be identical for the same thing cannot be round and elliptical at the same time.[2] If we admit such entities as 'appearances' or 'sensa' in some cases, it is

[1] *Scientific Thought*, p. 235.
[2] ibid., pp. 239–41.

possible and indeed likely that we should do so in all cases. This suggestion is accepted by Broad and we thus reach the basic position taken by the best-known form of the Sense-Datum Theory, according to which we are directly acquainted only with 'sensa' and consequently have no direct perception of physical objects.

It is clear that the problem to which Broad offers his Sensum Theory as a solution is much the same as the sort of 'little reflection' which, according to Moore and to Price, leads us to doubt whether what we 'directly perceive' can ever be the physical object itself. Roughly stated, it is the 'discrepancy' between the differing appearances which we suppose the physical object to possess. There is, however, this important difference: whereas Price and Moore state the 'discrepancy' at all times in terms of what is 'directly perceived' and the existence of 'direct perception' and its object the 'sense-datum', is taken for granted, Broad conceives this 'discrepancy' as a problem which his Sensum Theory is designed to resolve. In view of the arguments of Bouwsma and Ayer regarding the technical nature and obscurity of the concept of 'direct perception', Broad's exposition seems a more realistic and accurate account of how the notion of 'sense-datum' is to be reached.

Unfortunately there is a basic difficulty with regard to Broad's exposition, which renders his version that the 'sensum' (or sense-datum) is a postulated theoretical entity suspect. If we are to regard the Sense-Datum Theory as the postulation of such an entity in order to solve the problem of the 'discrepancy' between the differing appearances which the object presents, as opposed to the constant characteristics which we suppose the object to possess, we must first be sure that there is really such a problem which requires a solution. But it has been argued that this 'discrepancy' constitutes no real problem which would necessitate any such solution as the postulation of such an entity as a sense-datum. It is the 'sense-datum' approach itself that begets the difficulties which Broad professes to find in the common sense view.[1]

Thus Broad's exposition of the problem involves a reference to what he calls 'perceptual situations'. This is a technical term which enables Broad to class together cases of normal perception and cases of illusion and hallucination. The basis for doing so is the claim

---

[1] See Martin Lean, *Sense-Perception and Matter*, (New York, Humanities Press, 1953) p.18.

that these are not internally distinguishable. At the moment of perception we are unable to say whether we are really perceiving something or whether what we see is illusory or hallucinatory. In the light of this, Broad finds two elements within 'perceptual situations', (a) what is sensuously manifested—the 'objective constituent', and (b) the conviction that what is sensuously manifested is part of a larger whole of a certain kind, namely, a certain physical object, which has qualities other than those sensuously manifested in the perceptual situation.[1] Broad then turns to the phenomena of changing appearances, mirror-images, illusions, perception through non-homogeneous media, etc., to prove that the 'objective constituent' of 'perceptual situations' is not the physical object, and offers the Sensum Theory as the best solution which will 'account for' these perceptual facts.

But first, as we have already seen, it is questionable whether normal perception and hallucination, after-image, etc., can be classed together under the umbrella of the term 'perceptual situations'. It may be true that we cannot 'internally' distinguish between normal perception and hallucination, for example, but it does not follow that the same sort of 'objective constituent' is to be found in both cases. Why should we not rather class hallucination with reports of one's states of mind rather than with normal perception?[2] Secondly Broad errs when he rules out as irrelevant for an explanation of the perceptual phenomena with which he is dealing, the principles of perspective, the behaviour of light and the nature of the human eye. These are genuine explanations.[3] A.M. Quinton has attempted to explain Broad's procedure by arguing that 'philosophers have not set out to *explain* the appearances an object presents but to interpret it in terms of them, to elucidate the logical, not the causal, relations between objects and appearances'.[4] But it is not at all easy to understand what is involved in this 'logical elucidation' or why it is necessary, unless it is already assumed, even before the Sense-Datum Theory is offered as a solution to the problem, that the 'appearance' is a distinct entity something like what the sense-datum is later claimed to be. If this is

[1] C. D. Broad, *The Mind and Its Place in Nature*, p. 151.
[2] Lean, loc. cit.; compare also J. L. Austin, *Sense and Sensibilia* (Oxford, Clarendon Press, 1962) pp. 45–54.
[3] Lean, loc. cit.
[4] Review of Lean's book in *Mind*, vol. 63, 1954, p. 548.

assumed, we can easily interpret the 'logical elucidation' to be something analogous to establishing the relation between 'microscopic' elements (i.e. sense-data) and 'macroscopic' elements (objects). But without this assumption, which puts the answer before the question, what are we to make of this phrase 'logical elucidation'?[1] Similarly, in the third place, an examination of the function that Broad's term 'objective constituent' performs in the formulation of the problem to be solved, reveals that it is meant to play the same bogus 'neutral' role which we found in Moore's concept of the sense-datum as the 'something' which we see when we look at our right hands. It seems that Broad implicitly regards the 'objective constituent', right from the outset, as a kind of photographic image which literally has properties and qualities in the same sense that physical objects do.[2]

Hence it does indeed appear that this whole 'discrepancy' between the differing appearances which the object presents and the qualities we suppose to inhere permanently in objects, arises only because the sense-datum approach is assumed right from the start. There is thus no genuine problem to which the Sensum Theory may be offered as a solution.

It might seem at first that this conclusion concerning Broad tends to support Moore's claim after all. If there is no problem about the phenomena of sense-perception unless sense-data are surreptitiously assumed, what makes people adopt this confused procedure of covertly assuming sense-data in order to produce them jubilantly as the solution to a problem which they themselves have created? Is it because the existence of sense-data is really so obvious? Aren't sense-data, after all, simply given?[3]

But this line of reasoning, however plausible, goes much further than the circumstances warrant. The alleged inconsistency ascribed to Broad and all those who purport to produce the Sense-Datum Theory as a theoretical solution to a genuine problem, shows only that there is some impelling desire or motive to espouse the

---

[1] See further in Ch. 11, (IV) and (V).

[2] Lean, pp. 171, 203–6. See also Austin, loc cit. pp. 47ff.

[3] Defending Broad against Lean's criticisms, John W. Yolton, in *Philosophic Review*, vol. 63 (1954), pp. 264–6, makes Broad's theory covertly depend upon the doctrine that sense data are given. He interprets the doctrine of the given as a 'methodology of indubitables' together with a 'dualistic ontology'. There is some truth in this evaluation. Compare my own remarks in Chapters 8 and 9.

sense-datum approach and make use of the concept of an entity like the sense-datum. It by no means supports the view that sense-data are empirically discoverable.

We are thus faced with the conclusion that neither Moore nor Broad has given us an acceptable account of the considerations which lead up to the positing of such entities as sense-data. Moore is wrong, we have seen, in thinking of such entities as existing things which we need only look for in order to discover. Broad is wrong in thinking that there is a problem the solution of which requires their postulation.

(V) THE LINGUISTIC THEORY

A third account of the Sense-Datum Theory regards it as an improved terminology for talking about the facts of perception. It is suggested to philosophers by the phenomena of illusions, differing appearances, hallucinations, etc., which are not adequately accounted for in our ordinary ways of talking about perception. This verbalist thesis associated particularly with the names of G. A. Paul and A. J. Ayer,[1] points out that the issue between the rival philosophical theories of perception (Direct Realism, the theory of Appearing, etc.) is not to be decided by an examination of the facts or by an analysis of ordinary usage. We may prefer one particular terminology to another; Ayer prefers the Sense-Datum Terminology for what he calls 'good philosophical reasons'. But he makes it clear, in expressing this preference, that for him the questions and problems regarding sense-data are not questions of fact, but verbal, linguistic questions which arise within the sense-datum language and which can only be solved by making our technical language more clear and precise.

This thesis would seem to carry with it the implication that all

[1] G. A. Paul 'The Problem of Sense-Data' *Arist. Soc. Proc.*, Supp. Vol. XV, 1936; A. J. Ayer, *Foundations of Empirical Knowledge* (London, Macmillan, 1940), and also in 'The Terminology of Sense-Data', *Philosophical Essays* (London, Macmillan, 1954). In his *The Problem of Knowledge* (London, Pelican Books, 1956) pp. 84–113, Ayer qualifies his support for the 'Sense-Datum Terminology' very considerably. He seems still to wish to defend the admissibility of its adoption, but now recognizes that the question of its admissibility is much more problematic. He insists however that the sceptic's problem of the gap between things as they are and as they seem still remains even if the introduction of sense-data is held to be inadmissible. We shall discuss the nature of this alleged "gap" a little more in Chapter 4.

talk about sense-data being what are really given would be basically mistaken. At the very most such talk could merely be a misleading way of expressing a preference for the sense-data terminology, while those who insist that objects are what are really given might be interpreted to be misleadingly expressing their preferences for the language of common sense.

This is the implication that has been thought to follow from Ayer's view,[1] and it is the implication which, in general, Ayer seems to accept (though he does not explicitly say so) in most parts of his book *The Foundations of Empirical Knowledge*. But the matter is complicated by his remarks on Carnap's views according to which the question 'What objects are the elements of given direct experience?' is really verbal, and equivalent to asking 'What kinds of word occur in observation sentences?', the answer to which depends wholly upon one's choice of language. Ayer disagrees with this. He admits that the choice of the terminology of sense-data to describe what we observe, rather than the language of Appearing, Multiple Location, etc. is indeed conventional, but he insists that it does not follow from this that the propositions which are intended to describe the characteristics of sense-data are true only by convention. For sense-data can have properties other than those which belong to them by definition, and to describe these properties is not to express a rule of language but to make a statement of fact. Thus questions such as whether the 'Gestalt' or Atomic Theory more adequately describes the nature of our visual sense-fields must be decided not by verbal convention but by an examination of the empirical evidence. In deciding to use the sense-datum language,

---

[1] In his review of Ayer's 'Foundations of Empirical Knowledge', *Mind* 1941, Price shows signs of interpreting Ayer's verbalist thesis in this way, but seems to have scorned what might then have been the easiest reply for him, namely, that the verbalist thesis must be incorrect because it implies that sense-data are not given, whereas, as a matter plain fact, sense-data *are* given. Price might have exhorted the verbalists to note that their arguments were at the very most only plausible, and to turn to their own experience to see what this reveals to them about the given. And even though Price himself seems to have hesitated to reply in this way, others such as J. W. Yolton (in his paper 'A Defence of Sense-Data', *Mind*, 1948 pp. 2–15) have had no compunctions in rejecting the verbalist thesis on the grounds that sense-data are given. Nor is there any reason, assuming that Price is correct in his remarks about the given in his book *Perception*, why such arguments should strike us as a little crude. Price's reticence was perhaps an indication of his later view (as expressed in the preface to the 1950 edition of *Perception*) that what he had said about the given was not quite so straightforward as it had originally seemed to him.

Ayer claims that he is not either assuming or rejecting any special empirical theory about the nature of what we observe.[1]

This admission that empirical evidence while not relevant to the decision whether or not to adopt the sense-datum terminology, is relevant at least sometimes in determining the correct use of this terminology, seems to be the thin end of the wedge; and if this admission is pressed, I think it should lead us to conclude that perhaps the sense-Datum Theory cannot properly be said to be merely a 'language'. If it were merely a language then to say that 'sense-data' are the objects of 'direct awareness' would not really be to imply that 'direct awareness' is a name for any sort of empirically discoverable or introspectable act. 'Direct awareness' and 'sense-data' are merely correlative terms to be used within the sense-datum language. Ayer indeed says just this. However he also admits the possible existence of such acts in fact, though he cannot himself discover these facts by introspection.[2] And he even regards it as a weakness of his position, as of Moore's, that he is unable to say anything more positive about the nature of this 'direct awareness'. He is anxious, he says, to believe that some further analysis of it can be given, but he confesses that he does not see on what lines it is to be developed.[3]

But surely this is in effect admitting that 'direct awareness' is the name of an introspectable act. And if so, then in defining sense-data as the objects of 'direct awareness' we are not *merely* introducing a language for talking about perception; we are drawing attention to the *possibility* that there are real existents, namely, sense-data. Thus there seems to be something inconsistent in the attitude Ayer takes up toward 'the given', and it is my belief that his apparent inconsistency arises mainly, if not solely, because of Ayer's insistence on calling the Sense-Datum Theory and other theories of perception 'languages' rather than 'theories'.

We may readily agree with some of the arguments which Ayer uses to show that the rival theories of perception are not what they seem to be. In calling them 'languages' Ayer is trying to stress the point that none of the various theories of perception draws attention to any perceptual situation which the others disregard or deny.

[1] *Foundation of Empirical Knowledge*, pp. 113–16.
[2] ibid., pp. 61–2.
[3] *Philosophical Essays*, p. 103.

According to him if there is to be any question of truth or false-hood, there must be some disagreement about the nature of empirical facts. But, says Ayer, there is no disagreement about the nature of empirical facts; hence, he concludes, 'these so called theories of perception are not theories at all in the ordinary sense, and therefore... the notions of truth and falsehood, which we apply to scientific theories are not applicable to them'.[1]

It is very difficult to make sense of Ayer's claim that there is no disagreement about the facts.[2] But I think we can all see how much the verbalists' thesis is illuminating in pointing out the very flimsy empirical basis for the arguments between rival theories of perception. However, to call the rival theories merely 'languages' carries the unfortunate implication that the issue between them is merely verbal. This suggests that it is of no real significance and makes no special difference whether one uses the sense-datum terminology or any of its rivals. But this is plainly not the case, as is proved by the fact that Ayer himself expresses a marked preference for the sense-datum terminology on what he regards as good *philosophical* grounds. Briefly these are: (a) the unambiguous use of perceiving words (e.g. seeing, hearing, etc.) to mean that what is perceived must exist (even in hallucination), which has the advantage, according to Ayer, of enabling us to clarify statements about physical objects by relating them to statements of a different form;[3] (b) it is useful to have a terminology that enables us to refer to the contents of our experience independently of the material things they are taken to represent;[4] (c) the possibility of applying the physical object language depends on the constancy of certain relations between sense-data which might conceivably not obtain, i.e. it is a contingent fact that the structure of sensory experience is such as to make it possible to 'construct' out of it the world of material things. Price has pointed out, and Ayer agrees, that sensory experience might well have had a eurythmic rather than a thing-like order, arranging itself in visible or tangible *tunes* rather than things. Thus it follows that the sense-datum terminology is in a certain

---

[1] *Foundations of Empirical Knowledge*, p. 28. See also Lean's objections in *Sense-Perception and Matter* to describing such views as 'theories'.

[2] See *The Problem of Knowledge*, pp. 85-6 and J. L. Austin's criticism in *Sense and Sensibilia*, pp. 59-61.

[3] *Foundations of Empirical Knowledge* pp. 25-6 and *Philosophical Essays* p. 88.

[4] *Foundations of Empirical Knowledge*, p. 26.

sense more comprehensive than the physical object language; it is logically prior, because while referring to sense-data is not necessarily a way of referring to physical objects, referring to physical objects is necessarily a way of referring to sense-data.[1]

Ayer writes as if these were reasons for preferring a terminology; but I think that closer examination shows that they are much more than this. In (a) and (b) it is being assumed that there is some sort of a philosophical problem concerning the relationship of sensory experience to the propositions about material things. Ayer admits that this problem is 'obscured' by the terminology of Appearing. I think it would be truer to say, however, that in the terminology of Appearing the problem never really arises. It arises only because of the adoption of a terminology which postulates such a thing as a sense-experience which may be isolated from the perception of the material world as such. If we postulate such a state of affairs then Phenomenalism is both reasonable and, perhaps, even the most likely solution to the problem we have raised. But Ayer should realize that if we do not admit the existence of such a division, Phenomenalism is both preposterous and senseless.

It is all very well for Ayer to say that when non-Sense-Datum theorists refuse to 'play this sort of game'[2] they are missing something. But when he says that what they are missing is the opportunity of 'getting to the root of the matter' of 'somehow getting deeper', of 'understanding better what is meant by propositions about physical objects', then it is clear, I think, that Ayer's espousal of the Sense-Datum Theory is far more serious than is suggested by his insistence on calling it a 'terminology' or 'language'.[3] Indeed, if it were merely a language then it would *not* be simply a contingent fact that 'sense-data' group themselves so as to make the physical object language possible. This would be a characteristic with which we should necessarily have to invest sense-data in order to make them applicable to the empirical facts about which we speak in ordinary language.

However, I think Ayer was, in general, on the right track and it is only the use of the word 'language' which has confused the issue.

---

[1] *Philosophical Essays*, pp. 103-4.

[2] ibid., pp. 141-2.

[3] Even in *The Problem of Knowledge*, Ayer is still maintaining that 'if the procedure which leads to the introduction of sense-data is legitimate, the naive realist, by refusing to follow it, denies us an insight into the analysis of perceptual statements' (p. 97).

It does not indeed make very much empirical difference (at least not in its practical application) whether we adopt the Sense-Datum Theory or any of its rivals, but it does make an important *philosophical* difference, as we shall see later. If Ayer would agree to the word 'theory' rather than 'language' then it would be quite consistent for him to doubt whether 'direct awareness' was the name of any introspectable act but admit the possibility that it was. For although the actual existence of a theoretical entity may not be an empirical fact it may well be a practical possibility.

(VI) CONCLUDING NOTE ON FACT, THEORY AND LANGUAGE

So, of the three ways of presenting the Sense-Datum Theory, namely, as (1) the empirical discovery of an entity, (2) as a theory involving a hypothetical theoretical entity, or (3) a special terminology invented by philosophers making use of a new locution, the foregoing discussion seems to indicate that the first and third of these interpretations are dubious and the second interpretation is the most acceptable.

What then of the criticism that there is no genuine problem to which the Sense-Datum Theory could be offered as a theoretical solution? I think we must reply that it is simply mistaken to suppose that philosophical theories come to solve genuine problems of the type Broad suggested.

We must note in this connection that the discussions regarding the Sense-Datum Theory which, as we have seen, have veered from interpreting the 'sense-datum' as an empirically discoverable existent, to treating it merely as a postulated theoretical concept, and then to the suggestion that the 'sense-datum' was merely a technical term in an artificial terminology, have very interesting parallels in the discussions in the philosophy of science that have concerned themselves with the function and nature of scientific theories. Such discussions similarly moved from the view that scientific theories are conjectures about the facts which subsequent experimentation served to confirm or deny, through a period in which it was widely agreed that they are not conjectures about the facts but 'hypotheses', whose nature required careful examination, to the view now widely prevalent that scientific theories set up a logical apparatus, usually exemplified by a model, which enables us to deduce the empirical behaviour which at present obtains, and predict subsequent empirical behaviour. Whereas theories were formally regarded as conjectured descriptions, they are now often thought of as logical instruments which enable us to deal with the empirical data. A feature of the change between these two approaches has been the circumstance that whereas theories were formerly regarded as second best to 'facts', they now tend to be regarded as something like languages or deductive systems.

Similarly, philosophical theories regarding perception were at the beginning of the century regarded as putative descriptions to be confirmed or denied by observation. The move in the direction of the verbalist interpretation may well reflect the views of a more instrumentalist-minded generation, questioning whether these different views about perception might not really belong at the uppermost limit where logical apparatus is foremost and predictive capacity of negligible importance. With the realization that each of the theories of perception is practically water-tight, in the sense that, all the usual and borderline phenomena of perception being agreed upon, a theorist has only to exercise sufficient ingenuity and adroitness in order to be able to maintain his position in spite of all criticisms, it became natural to regard the different theories of perception as barren alternative deductive systems, i.e. simply alternative ways of saying the same thing.

This parallel will interest us later on when we come to assess finally the whole question of the appeal to the given, and its significance for contemporary epistemology. Here we shall note only that if the parallel between the moves regarding the interpretation of the Sense-Datum Theory and the shift of opinion regarding the nature of scientific theories can be sustained, the question which ought to be put is whether we may reasonably demand that philosophical views should be like scientific theories. I shall argue later on that philosophical theories are fundamentally different from scientific theories.

It is plain from the foregoing discussion that the claim that the sense-datum is an entity which is empirically discoverable must be rejected. The procedure which must be resorted to in order to explain what sense-data are or how we come to speak of them makes it clear that the concept of a sense-datum arises from the consideration of the phenomena of changing appearances, illusions, etc. and is most plausibly regarded as a theoretical conception rather than as something which can simply be 'pointed out'.

We may thus conclude by noting that inasmuch as the Naive View of the dispute about the nature of the given in sense-perception involves the assertion that the Sense-Datum Theory stands or falls on the question whether the expression 'sense-datum' denotes an entity which is empirically discoverable or not, our discussions in this chapter have shown that either the SDT is quite wrong since 'sense-data' are not empirically discoverable or else the Naive Theory as a whole is wrong. The latter will be the case if we can show, as we propose to do, in the next two chapters, that neither the 'object' nor 'immediate experience' are entities empirically discoverable either.

Chapter 4

THE GIVEN AS OBJECTS

(I) OBJECTS AND PHYSICAL OBJECTS

The question whether 'objects' are or are not entities that can be discovered by simple inspection is complicated by the circumstance that in one sense it is the merest truism that we perceive objects. The term 'objects' is in fact precisely the one that is used to denote whatever it may be that we perceive. Though we might normally hesitate to regard a gas as a 'thing', for example, in the same way that the bell-jar containing it in the laboratory is regarded as a 'thing', we should feel perfectly entitled to refer to the gas as the 'object' of our observation. In this sense it is simply a tautology to say that 'it is objects that are perceived', for the term 'objects' would be used indiscriminately of whatever it might be that we could in any way perceive or conceive, i.e. for whatever it is that will serve as the *grammatical* object after the verb 'perceive' (or 'conceive') or after particular verbs of perception (or conception) in such sentences as 'I see/hear/smell/feel. . .' (or 'I think/imagine/ . . .)

The OT, however, is connected with the more restricted usage of the term 'objects', in which objects or 'physical objects' are contrasted with 'sense-data', appearances, and so on. This usage is admittedly a more technical one. We shall later on question whether it is not merely a mistaken usage, or at any rate one that is liable to mislead. But the concept of a 'physical object' is so traditional in modern philosophy and initially seems so obvious that I shall for the present assume its legitimacy. It is in connection with objects of this sort (i.e. 'physical objects') that we shall have to consider whether they are or are not entities empirically discoverable.

(II) THE ARGUMENT FROM ILLUSION

Innumerable writers have asserted that it is the view of the ordi-

nary man that we directly perceive 'physical objects' of this sort.[1]
To the uninitiated, perception seems an effortless process. We
simply open our eyes and the things or objects of the world reveal
themselves to us as they really are. The colours we see, smells we
smell, the tastes we perceive are all part of the real world which is
'external' to us. These objects of the real world are 'public' or
'neutral' as between different observers and independent of our
perception of them, both in the sense of existing before and after
our perceiving them as also in the sense that our perceiving of them
leaves them unchanged. Part of modern epistemology has consisted
of the attempt to show falsity, or at least the relative inadequacy, of the 'common-sense view' that we directly perceive
objects.

The grounds upon which this has been questioned have been
the existence of such phenomena as illusion, perceptual relativity,
hallucination, etc., as well as the scientific facts regarding the
causation of perception (which physiology shows to involve a
complicated causal chain), the psychological processes involved,
and such physical facts as the time-lag brought about by the speed
at which light travels, the phi-phenomenon and so on. These
phenomena have been described in detail in the standard philosophical texts on perception. Some are known from the writings of
the Greek Sceptics and their use in epistemological discussions
dates back to the pre-Socratics. Others, particularly the scientific
phenomena which derive from the study of physics, physiology
and psychology, are of more modern origin, and have formed the
background to the interest in epistemology which has been characteristic of modern philosophy.

These phenomena have been used by writers on epistemology
to prove that we do not perceive objects directly, as we ordinarily
suppose, but only indirectly. What we do perceive directly has been
called, at different times, by such names as 'appearances', 'ideas',
'sense-data', etc. Although epistemologists have phrased their
proofs in different ways, the general line of their arguments has
become so standardized that they have been grouped together by
modern writers in order to form different phases or variations of

[1] See specially H. H. Price, *Perception* (London, Methuen, 1932) and R. J. Hirst,
The Problems of Perception (London, Allen and Unwin, 1959).

what has come to be known as the 'Argument from Illusion'.[1] We have already come across parts of this Argument in watching Moore 'pick out' sense-data, and in following Broad's introduction of the 'sensum' as a theoretical concept to account for the problems to which he drew attention. Roughly stated, the purpose of the Argument from Illusion is to get people to accept 'sense-data' as the proper and correct answer to the question what they perceive on certain exceptional occasions (e.g. in any of the cases mentioned above) and to follow this up with arguments intended to show that they always perceive sense-data, since, e.g. we cannot really distinguish between those of our perceptions which are veridical and those which are delusive since veridical and delusive perceptions may form a continuous series.

Very different evaluations have been given to this Argument from Illusion by different philosophers. Some have accepted it at face value; others have held that it proves something, though not as much as it claims; others still have held it to be worthless. A. J. Ayer who once accepted the Argument from Illusion at least as pointing to the need for the introduction of the sense-datum terminology[2] has now virtually given it up altogether.[3] J. L. Austin's *Sense and Sensibilia*[4] provided a sustained attack on the Argument from Illusion and rocked it to its foundations. But there have been other philosophers since then who have rushed to its defence and purported to find that it has not yet been completely demolished, and that what is left standing is still sufficient to support the claim that it cannot be the physical object as such that is directly perceived.

One of the most important of these defences[5] maintains that while Austin has shown that the Argument from Illusion cannot be used to support the Sense-Datum Theory, it can be nonetheless used to support the Adverbial Theory. This rejects the act-object analysis of sense experience which is the basis of the Sense-Datum Theory and advocates an adverbial analysis, in accordance with which, for example, when it is said that 'the thing appears white',

---

[1] H. H. Price, *Perception*, and all subsequent books on the subject.

[2] In *The Foundations of Empirical Knowledge* (London, Macmillan, 1940).

[3] See *The Problem of Knowledge* (London, Penguin Books, 1956) Chapter 3.

[4] Oxford, The Clarendon Press, 1960.

[5] Roderick Firth, 'Austin and the Argument from Illusion, *Philosophical Review*, LXXIII (1964), 372–82.

the word 'white' is to be regarded as an adverb telling us about the *way* in which the object appears. The Adverbial Theory seems to be based on interpreting these 'Appearings' or 'looks' in an experiental sense, and the experience which can be described in these terms is an example of 'a sense experience'. The argument from Illusion, it is suggested, should be regarded as no argument at all, but rather as a method for *the ostensive definition* of terms which are supposed to denote the sensory constituent of perceptual experience (i.e. 'sense-experience').[1]

I do not myself think that this defence of the Argument from Illusion succeeds, since it seems to me very doubtful whether the experiental interpretation of 'appearings' or 'looks' can be sustained.[2] Instead of interpreting 'the ways in which the objects appears' relationally, i.e. as denoting a relation between a real object and a percipient, I suspect that the Argument from Illusion is inducing its would-be 'adverbial' defenders to interpret these 'ways in which the object appears' as non-relational *parts* or *contents* of our perceptual awareness. How else could we explain Macbeth's seeing of a hallucinatory dagger being used by the Argument from Illusion in order to ostensively define 'sense experience' even in cases of non-hallucinatory perception?

But whether or not this criticism is valid, I think it is clear that all those who have in any way accepted the Argument from Illusion have been committed thereby to some form of Epistemological Dualism, which draws a distinction between the perceptual awareness of the object itself and the direct perceptual experiences upon which this awareness of the object is based. Most epistemologists in the past who have used the Argument from Illusion have assumed some form of act-object analysis of their perceptual experiences and spoken of the objects of direct perception as 'appearances', 'ideas', 'impressions', 'sense-data', 'sensa', percepts', etc. But even the modern epistemologists who offer an 'adverbial' analysis of their perceptual experiences will, if they accept the Argument from Illusion, be compelled to distinguish between 'sense experiences' such as the object's 'looks' which are the direct deliverences

---

[1] An interesting return to the Naive View of the appeal to the given.

[2] A similar assumption seems to be involved in R. M. Chisholm's interpretation of 'The Theory of Appearing' in M. Black, *Philosophical Analysis* (Ithaca N.Y., 1950) and in his exposition of the 'Adverbial Theory' in *Theory of Knowledge* (Englewood, Prentice-Hall, 1966) pp. 95 ff.

of perception, and the perceptual awareness of the object, which is somehow indirect or derivative.

This distinction between 'direct' (or 'immediate') and 'indirect' ('mediate' or 'derivative') perception has served as the basis for the three theories that have become the stock-in-trade of modern epistemological discussions: Direct Realism, The Causal (or Representative) Theory, and Phenomenalism. In general the conclusion drawn from the acceptance of the Argument from Illusion in any form has been that Direct Realism, which maintains that we are in direct perceptual contact with physical objects, is mistaken. It has therefore often been referred to by its critics as Naive Realism. This nick-name reflects also the association of this view with the opinion of the ordinary naive man that we directly observe a public external world.

(III) COMMON-SENSE AND DIRECT REALISM

The opinion that the common-sense view is identical with Direct Realism has been very widely held. Certain writers have expressed reservations about whether the ordinary man can be regarded as maintaining any epistemological theory whatsoever since he has never thought about the matter systematically in such a way as the epistemologists have done. Yet these writers too have been inclined to say that *if* the ordinary man were to make his every-day assumptions explicit the theory he would be found to be assuming would be Direct Realism. If this association between common-sense and Direct Realism is accepted, then the acceptance of any form of Epistemological Dualism would seem to involve the rejection of common-sense. This has been the view of a great many philosophers in the past.

A second group of philosophers has suggested that in accepting the Argument from Illusion epistemologists do not overthrow common-sense but merely refine it. It is in this spirit that many have distinguished between an uninstructed common-sense and an instructed or enlightened common-sense, the implication being that though the ordinary man might at first find the arguments of the epistemologists surprising, he could easily come to recognize that their views were merely a more accurate and subtle formulation of the same facts roughly summarized in his own unthinking view of the matter. The more accurate formulation could now become the sophisticated ordinary man's common-sense view.

In this century the second view has been complemented by a third view stemming from philosophers who have suggested that the common-sense view cannot really be superseded or rejected, since it is the view from which we all start and to which we all naturally return. The epistemologists are, therefore, not to be interpreted as attempting, self-defeatingly, to overthrow common-sense, but only to offer rival *analyses* of common-sense.[1] According to this interpretation we cannot appeal to common-sense in order to settle the issue between rival epistemological theories, since it provides the common *analysandum* from which they all start and which they at no time leave behind. When, therefore, it is claimed to be a matter of common-sense to say that we directly perceive objects, this cannot be held to pre-judge the philosophical issue of whether objects are or are not what are directly or immediately perceived. For this latter question, for the purposes of analysis, uses the concept of 'direct' or 'immediate' perception in a special *technical* sense which has nothing to do with the common-sense view about our being directly aware of objects.

This last view which maintains that the views of the ordinary man are irrelevant, has had wide currency in contemporary philosophy. But it has also been disputed by other philosophers who have held that the issue between Direct Realism on the one hand and any form of Representationalism or the Causal Theory on the other is simply whether or not objects are perceived in the ordinary sense, to which Direct Realism has been taken as true but trivial while its opponents have been saying something absurd and unacceptable. Philosophers who have taken this line have done so on the grounds that the special sense in which the epistemologists have alleged themselves to be using the expression 'directly perceived' was entirely obscure and unrealistic, and could be made meaningful, if at all, only for the exponents of the Causal Theory and Phenomenalism. The Direct Realist must therefore be interpreted as maintaining that we do directly perceive objects (in the ordinary sense of 'direct perception').

I am in sympathy with those who have argued that the special

[1] G. E. Moore, 'The Defence of Common-Sense' in *Contemporary British Philosophy*, 2nd series (London, Allen and Unwin, 1925).

technical sense of 'directly perceive' is obscure and that the argument between the traditional theories has been expressed in a very misleading manner. But the special technical sense of 'directly perceive' seems to me to be connected with the claim that what is 'directly perceived' is given. We shall therefore be in a position to give a more complete assessment of the value of the common-sense view when we have provided an evaluation of the appeal to the given.

(IV) THE GAP BETWEEN SENSATION AND PERCEPTUAL AWARENESS

Whatever we may think of common-sense, it is also a plain fact of experience widely attested that in perception we seem to be immediately conscious of the object as such. Thus, H. H. Price has written that

'Somehow it is the *whole* thing and not just a jejune extract from it, which is before the mind from the first. From the first it is the complete material thing, with back, sides and insides, as well as front that we 'accept', that 'ostends itself' to us, and nothing less; a thing too, persisting in time both before and after. . . and possessed of various causal characteristics . . . Already in this single act in a momentary glance we take all these elements of the object to be there, all of them . . .'[1]

It is this seemingly intuitive character of the perception of the object rather than any consensus of common-sense that would seem to constitute the factual basis of the OT. There seems here, therefore, to be prima facie evidence for the claim that the object is something empirically discoverable in our experience.

To the extent, however, that the Argument from Illusion has in any way been accepted, a doubt has been raised regarding the proper evaluation of the seemingly intuitive awareness of objects. It is convenient to phrase this doubt in terms of the distinction between 'immediate' (or 'direct') and 'mediate' (or 'indirect') perception which is characteristic of Epistemological Dualism. We shall use the term perceptual awareness to stand for the mode of consciousness in which we perceive or think we perceive a material object. If we regard intuition as a form of knowledge, the apparent

[1] H. H. Price, *Perception*, pp. 151-2.

immediacy of the perceptual awareness of objects cannot, according to H. H. Price, be truly intuitive (it is therefore called by him 'quasi-intuitive'), since the Argument from Illusion shows that the only thing of which we are sure in perception is what we *sense*. To say that objects were given or intuited would imply, according to him, that perception yields knowledge of these objects. But this cognitive claim must be mitigated by the two factors to which the Argument from Illusion has drawn attention, namely:

(a) the lack of certainty attaching to our claim to knowledge, which arises from the fact that perceptual consciousness may be mistaken. We may think we perceive an object, but we may be in error. It may be a counterfeit, an illusion, even a hallucination. (b) The gap which examination seems to reveal between the features of the object actually perceptible and the necessary minimum qualities which serve to define any particular object and which must be instantaneously revealed to the observer if his perception is to be said to constitute a knowledge of the object. Such knowledge must include an awareness of the object's spacial completeness as a three dimensional whole, with back, top and bottom, as well as front, inside, and outside. It must also include an awareness of its continued persistence in time, and the object's public accessibility to many observers at the same or different times, of its possession of certain indispensable causal characteristics, etc. But such features of objects are certainly not momentarily revealed to perceptual consciousness. Hence there is a gap between the features of the object actually perceptible and the perceptual consciousness which seems to reveal the whole object right from the start. The gap exists not only initially, at the first instant of perception, but even finally, after the observer has perceived as much as he possibly can of the object. Certain features of an object, for example, its continued existence in time both before and after being perceived, its public accessibility, and so on, do not seem to be perceptible at all. Hence the doubt raised concerning the quasi-intuitive character of perceptual awareness of objects may be expressed as the question whether the apparently intuitive awareness of physical objects is genuinely intuitive, or, if not, of what this perceptual awareness really consists.

The question of the certainty of our claims to perceptual knowledge of physical objects (a) is an important part of the Argument from Illusion and will be discussed in a later chapter.[1] Concerning the gap referred to in (b), it is to be noted that I have phrased the question of this gap in such a way as to lend support to the plausible view that this gap between what is revealed in perception and what is implied to be known in any awareness of the object as such, is independent of the Argument from Illusion.[2] This view has been contested by some philosophers, who have claimed that this alleged gap which is basic to the central epistemological problem of exhibiting the relationship between what we perceive and what we know, is in fact *created* by the conclusion, drawn from the Argument from Illusion, that there are such entities or existents as 'appearances', 'sense impressions' or 'sense-data'.[3] Once the existence of such entities is rejected, the gap disappears.

But in answer to this it has been maintained that the gap between what is perceived and what is known of the object remains even where the existence of such sensuous particulars is denied. Even if 'appearances' are regarded as *ways* in which objects appear, the gap remains, though in the different form of the question of the relationship between the way things appear and our perceptual awareness of the things themselves. And if 'appearances' are identified, as in the more classic versions of Direct Realism, with actual features or parts of physical objects, the gap remains as that between knowledge of the particular features revealed by perception and the knowledge of the whole object as such.

This issue I regard to be crucial. But I have stated the nature of the gap in such a way as to be initially neutral with respect to this question, for I wish to consider several classic theories which explicitly or implicitly recognise the existence of the gap and attempt to overcome it. I shall, however, proceed to argue that this gap is indeed artificial and is created by the acceptance (in whole or in part) of the Argument from Illusion.

(v) INTUITION VERSUS THOUGHT

The traditional alternatives regarding the interpretation of per-

[1] See Chapter 9 (v).
[2] See A. J. Ayer, *The Problem of Knowledge*, p. 112.
[3] M. Lean, *Sense-Perception and Matter*, (New York, Humanities Press, 1953) and others.

ceptual consciousness are (1) that in perception the observer is stimulated by sensation to the *thought* of the object, and (2) that in perception the observer somehow becomes intuitively aware of the whole object as such so that even though not consciously aware of its non-perceived features, he none-the-less is aware of them by *intuition*. The former alternative is the one most closely associated with the Sense-Datum Theory; the latter alternative is traditionally associated with Direct Realism.

But in the course of the arguments between the Sense-Datum Theorists and supporters of the Direct Realist Theory, there was a movement away from the two extremes of 'intuition' and 'thought', and an attempt to effect a compromise between these two alternatives. Thus whereas in the more primitive versions of the Sense-Datum Theory the perceptual awareness of the object is regarded as the product of a process of inference which follows upon the 'sensing' or intuiting of a sensible particular, in the extremely sophisticated version of the Sense-Datum Theory to be found in H. H. Price, a distinction is drawn between 'perceptual acceptance' (or 'taking for granted') which is the quasi-intuitive basis of our awareness of physical objects, and which is present right from the start in the 'sensing' of sensible particulars, and 'perceptual assurance', which is the state of consciousness which is achieved when the original 'perceptual acceptance' is complemented in subsequent observation by a process of 'specifying the unspecified'. Price tends to use the expression 'perceptual consciousness' to refer to the resulting 'perceptual assurance' rather than to the complete process of perception. Hence for him the observation of an object is equivalent to 'sensing' plus 'perceptual consciousness'.[1]

In Price's version the dichotomy between 'intuition' and 'thought' has somehow been overcome. Certainly the gap between the sensing of sensible particulars and the perceptual awareness of the object as such cannot be said to be overcome by a process of inference or thought in the simple meaning of these terms. It should nevertheless be noted that the vocabulary which Price invents in order to give his analysis of perceptual awareness (i.e. 'perceptual acceptance', 'taking for granted', etc.) makes use of terms which are ordinarily associated with processes of thought.

If we wish to find a discussion where the gap between the simple

[1] Price's views are expounded at length in his *Perception* (1932).

alternatives of perceptual awareness of objects and perceptual experience is still phrased in terms of 'intuition' and 'thought' we have to go back to the early part of this century to find Samuel Alexander maintaining that the problem how we can pass from immediately experienced sensible appearances to external objects, is based on the false assumption that the sensible appearance is an existent *distinct* from the external object. The problem vanishes, he thought, the moment we realize that whenever we perceive some object, the sensible appearance is simply some feature either of the thing perceived or of some other thing previously perceived. At length and with great ingenuity he attempted to account for all those cases of illusion and hallucination in which it seemed difficult to understand how the sensible appearance could be identical with the features of a perceived object.[1] Wherever appearances seem to differ from the known characteristics of the object, Alexander attempted to show that this is because these features were revealed to the percipient only partially or else in a distorted fashion.

G. F. Stout[2] charged that Alexander was ignoring the distinction between experiencing sensible appearances and being aware of the object as such. He was assuming that in perceptual knowledge all that we know primarily is what we immediately experience as a sensible appearance. But this assumption overlooks the vital distinction between what is immediately experienced and what is immediately known. Objects are immediately known, though not immediately experienced, whereas sensible appearances are immediately experienced. This distinction is amplified by Stout, who explains that we know of the object by *thought*. This thought has its source in the essential incompleteness of immediate experience. Strictly, objects are known *by* experience rather than experienced as such. If Alexander wished to call the thought a kind of experience the issue would reduce itself to an argument about words. The essential point was that the immediacy of sense is transcended to yield knowledge of matters of fact. More is immediately known than is immediately experienced.

Alexander protested against the word 'thought' in this context.[3]

[1] S. Alexander, *Space, Time and Deity*, (London, MacMillan, 1920) Vol. II.
[2] G. F. Stout, 'Prof. Alexander's Theory of Sense Perception', *Mind* 1922.
[3] S. Alexander, 'Sense Perception, Reply to Mr Stout', *Mind* 1923.

Stout was saying, in effect, that thought informs us of an object different in kind from sensible appearances. It was true that perception contained more than the mere sensing of sensible appearances. But the remainder, said Alexander, was not 'thought' but *intuition*. When someone perceived a sensible appearance this was not merely a sense-quality, a 'greenness', for example, but a bit of space-time that possessed the quality of greenness: a *patch* of green, rather than greenness as such. One was intuitively aware of the patch of space-time, and this intuition was a 'lower experience than sensation' which occurred simultaneously with the sensing of a sensible appearance. Thus there was no question of *passing* in perception from an immediate experience of the sensible appearance to an awareness of the object. The awareness of the object was as immediately revealed by intuition as the appearance is revealed by sensation. Both intuition and sensation occurred simultaneously. If the two were at all distinguished, they were distinguished only upon later examination by the philosopher. The ordinary man did not distinguish between them at all.

Both Alexander and Stout are in agreement that there are such things as sensible appearances. The argument between them concerns the question whether we pass from the experience of these appearances to a knowledge in *thought* of the object, or whether no such transition takes place, the awareness of the object being grasped in *intuition* as part of the process of sensing the sensible appearance. The gap between the sensing of the appearance and the awareness of the object as such is recognized by both Alexander and Stout. But Alexander attempts to overcome this gap by means of his theory that the intuition of the object forms part of the sensing of the appearance. His Direct Realist position therefore rejected the implication that such considerations as those marshalled by Price cast doubt upon the genuinely intuitive character of perceptual consciousness. Alexander admits that the intuition of the object may be erroneous. It may be as variable as the sensible appearances, in the sensing of which the intuition is contained. But this is a regrettable circumstance of fact rather than one casting any theoretical doubt upon the nature of intuition. The intuition as such is infallible. Sensible appearances deceive us, however, because we can only have our intuitions through the functioning of the senses. If we could strip off the sensations and be purely intuitive, all intuitive perceptual consciousness of objects would be incorrigible.[1]

(VI) ARMSTRONG'S THEORY

Awareness of these alternatives may help us to understand more clearly the Direct Realist position that has recently been maintained by D. M. Armstrong in *Perception and the Physical World*[2].

According to Armstrong the question 'What is the *direct* or *immediate* object of awareness when we perceive?' is a genuine question, and the correct answer to this question is that 'The immediate object of awareness is never anything but a physical existent'. However, the *mediate* objects of perception are also physical objects. Hence it turns out that the very same thing may be the object of either mediate or immediate awareness. Armstrong therefore rejects the Epistemological Dualism which distinguishes between two sorts of epistemological object, and replaces it by a dualism which makes a distinction between two kinds of *awareness* of objects, mediate when one makes 'inferences' (page 20) or allows 'suggestions' (page 21), and immediate when one does none of these. It turns out that the 'sense impressions' of which the traditional epistemological dualists have spoken are nothing but our 'acquiring of beliefs or inclinations to believe'. To perceive itself is *nothing but* to acquire knowledge of, or at least an inclination to believe in, particular facts about the physical world by means of the senses (page 105). To perceive immediately, then, is to acquire such knowledge without inference or suggestion.

Armstrong's account of perception therefore attempts to overcome the gap between sensing the sensible appearances and the awareness of the object as such by: (a) maintaining (in disagreement with Alexander and Stout) that there are no such things as 'sensible appearances'—these, according to him, are only worth distinguishing where we wish to speak of illusions and hallucinations; (b) cutting away the distinction between sensing or perceiving, on the one hand, and having perceptual knowledge or belief on the other. Perceiving, according to Armstrong, does not involve acquiring *evidence* for beliefs about physical things; it is simply *having* such

[1] ibid., p. 5.
[2] D. M. Armstrong. *Perception and the Physical World* (London, Kegan Paul, 1961).

beliefs. In this respect Armstrong comes near to Stout's view that objects are immediately known to thought on the occasion of experience. However Armstrong does not admit that there is such a thing as an immediate experience of sensible appearances which can be contrasted with the thought of the object. Hence Armstrong, unlike Stout, will not allow us to speak of this knowledge of objects as being acquired *by* experience; it is itself the immediate experience.

There is a difficulty here in ascertaining what precisely the difference might be between the thought of an object which arises as a result of perception, and which according to Armstrong is precisely what perception means, and a thought of an object which arises spontaneously, as in the case of hallucination. Armstrong says there is a difference between perceptual beliefs which are acquired in the presence of an object, and beliefs about the object which are held without its being present. The former are acquired 'by means of the senses' whereas the latter are not. But he gives no account of what it is like to acquire beliefs 'by means of the senses'. No doubt he regards this process as having to do essentially with the physiological mechanisms of the percipient, and being of no significance to the epistemologists. Yet the whole notion of the acquisition of perceptual knowledge remains obscure. The knowledge is simply there. But why we should be 'inclined to believe', in the sense of being entitled to give some credence to our perceptual knowledge, is not explained.[1] Armstrong suggests only that we treat the reports of those on the spot as authoritative, since they are in the best position to know. But in what way, on his view of experience, can experience teach us this fact? Armstrong vaguely suggests that we know it from our individual experience: if we are in the presence of an object we are in the best position to know it. But this suggestion is nowhere worked out in any detail, and in any case does not seem capable of bearing the weight placed upon.

Armstrong's attempt to overcome the evils of Epistemological Dualism by eliminating such things as 'sensible appearances' seems to be a step in the right direction. His removal of the distinction

---

[1] It has been suggested that for Armstrong 'beliefs about the object' turn out to be a sort of 'representative' coming between the mind and the object. See M. Deutscher in The *Australasian Journal of Philosophy*, vol. 41, 1963, pp. 80–91. This is probably quite unfair, but reflects the lack of clarity in Armstrong's account of the genesis of perceptual beliefs.

between perceiving and having perceptual awareness or knowledge is a radical move which might have enabled him to do away with the gap we have been discussing at one fell swoop. Unfortunately he has not succeeded in explaining how perceptual awareness arises. Nor does his retention of the distinction between 'direct' and 'indirect' awareness of objects, and his equation of the former with the acquiring of beliefs without inference, enable us to interpret perception in a manner which would be in any way credible, as it might have been if the 'acquiring of beliefs' had, at any level, been regarded as a process of judgment.

(VII) INTUITION AND DIRECT EXPERIENCE

Before proceeding with showing how the gap might be eliminated in the Judgment theory, it will be worth noting, first of all, that even so extreme view as that of Alexander which attempts to overcome the gap by saying that the perceptual awareness of the object is identical with an intuitive awareness of a patch of space-time which is somehow contained within the sensing of sensible appearances, fails in its attempt. And its failure is due to its admitting the existence of such things as 'sensible appearances'. For even if the latter are regarded as identical with perceived features of the actual physical object, neither the awareness of this identity nor the awareness of the object as something solid, durable and public is borne on the face of the sensible appearances. So that even if sensible appearances are held to be 'directly experienced' in the sense in which sense-data have been alleged to be 'directly experienced', the object *as such* cannot be regarded as 'directly experienced' in this sense. When Alexander tells us that there is an 'intuition' of the object as such, he is suggesting the existence of a *second* process parallel to and simultaneous with the 'direct experiencing' of the sensible appearance. Thus, in the same way as Sense-Datum Theorists subscribing to the Sensory Core Theory would maintain that perception consists of sensing together with interpretation, both of them occurring simultaneously and the former being a 'core' which may be later discriminated within the perceptual process, so too for Alexander perception consists in the intuition of a patch of space-time together with the 'direct experience' of a sensible appearance, the former being a sort of 'core' contained within the latter which may be discriminated in subsequent analysis. According to either view perception is a two-fold process.

But why then need Alexander maintain that the sensible appearance is identical with some feature of the physical object? Is the gap not already overcome by the notion of the intuition of the patch of space-time of which the object consists? It seems that Alexander is here implicitly meeting a second objection, which is, 'If there are both sensings of sensible appearances as well as "intuitings" of patches of space time, what is the relation between the appearances which are sensed and the patch of space-time which is intuited?' This is the same old problem of the gap re-appearing in different form. But is this problem really answered by Alexander's view that the appearance is identical with some real feature of the object? Alexander says there is no contradiction in saying that in sense knowledge one knows the independent existence of the sensible appearance as a fact and yet that this sensible appearance is a feature of the thing perceived. The two are different experiences, the first that of the man innocent of philosophy who apprehends an object, a sense-appearance which is not himself, and the second that of the philosopher who, when he has 'synthesized' many sensible appearances and percepts into an object and has learnt to distinguish a particular sense-appearance from the object, can say that what he was originally aware of was a feature of some physical thing which has an independent existence. The ordinary man does not experience the part of the object which he perceives *as* a part. This is the knowledge of the philosopher.[1]

Alexander is here saying that the identification of the sensible appearance with part of the object is not part of the consciousness of the ordinary percipient, but is revealed to the philosopher as the result of his analysis. But how this revelation takes place is not explained. What is it that the ordinary man thinks he is perceiving? If he thinks he is aware of only a part how does he ever come to the knowledge of the object as a whole, even after all the philosophical training in the world. But if we say that he is vaguely aware of what he experiences as a whole object (as indeed it seems more likely that Alexander will say) then when later discrimination tells him it was only a part that he was directly experiencing, how does he account for his having taken it to be the whole? The actual identity

[1] *Mind* 1923, p. 8.

of the sensible appearance with part of the real object will not help us to answer this question, for this identity is the judgment of the philosopher resultant upon his analysis of the facts of perception. If this identity were also intuitively experienced by the ordinary man, then the criticism would be that knowledge of the whole is implied in the knowledge of the part as a part.

Hence, the gap between what is revealed in perception and the perceptual awareness of the object as such seems to remain in any form of Epistemological Dualism, any view, that is, which will allow of the distinction between sensible appearances and the objects themselves.

(VIII) THE PERCEPT THEORY

This conclusion is explicitly confirmed in the theory developed by R. Firth.[1] According to Firth, the objects of 'direct perceptual inspection' are not sense-data but 'ostensible physical objects'. Since the investigations of William James, Edmund Husserl and leading psychologists of the Gestalt school have shown that the traditional distinction between sense-data and physical objects is untenable, the only way of making any sense of the claim of Sense-Datum Theorists to have 'discovered' such things as 'sense-data' is by interpreting them as having unconsciously made use of a second method called 'perceptual reduction' rather than the method of 'direct inspection'. In 'perceptual reduction' a special effort of attention has brought about a radical change in which a new object of consciousness appears, and is called a 'sense-datum'. The new state of consciousness destroys the state of perceptual awareness which it replaced. Firth disputes the opinion of the Sense-Datum Theorists that 'perceptual reduction' constitutes a better method for discovering the facts than 'direct inspection'. Such theorists are really assuming the 'exposure hypothesis' according to which 'perceptual reduction' merely serves to 'expose' what was contained in ordinary states of perceptual awareness. However, the psychologists have shown that perceptual awareness is not divisible into a sensuous part (the 'sensing' of a sense-datum) and a non-sensuous part (the 'interpretation' which yields a mediated perception of

[1] R. Firth, 'Sense-Data and the Percept Theory', *Mind* Vol. LVIII 1949 (Part I) and Vol. LIX 1950 (Part II).

objects), but is on the contrary (as William James put it) 'one state of mind or nothing'. This is the Percept Theory according to which perceptual awareness is a single act in which no distinct sensuous and non-sensuous elements can be discriminated.

Thus, 'perceptual reduction' may be legitimate for some purposes. But it cannot be regarded as part of normal perceptual awareness; it is a new and specialized form of awareness. Hence the Percept Theory leads to a rejection of the 'exposure hypothesis'. It supports the normal phenomenological method of 'direct inspection' which reveals that 'ostensible physical objects' are given.

The only possible argument in favour of the 'exposure hypothesis' might be that without it epistemological analysis becomes impossible. But Firth sets out to demonstrate that epistemological analysis is possible even by reliance on the ordinary method of 'direct inspection'. This is so because what is revealed to us by 'direct inspection' are not the objects themselves but only 'ostensible physical objects'. These are distinguishable from physical objects in at least one important respect. Some of the properties of 'ostensible physical objects' can be discovered by the 'direct inspection' of a single state of perceptual awareness, whereas a physical object transcends any one of the states which might be called a perception of it. According to Firth the epistemological problems revealed by the analysis of perceptual awareness remain, except that they are no longer the problems regarding the relationship between 'sense-data' and objects, but rather regarding the relationship between 'ostensible physical objects' and objects.

In arguing that what he calls 'epistemological analysis' remains possible even after the rejection of the view that sense-data are given, Firth is in fact maintaining that the gap between the awareness of the particular appearances of the object and the awareness of the object as a whole remains. It is this gap which forms the problem that the epistemologist must analyse. According to Firth's Percept Theory, the gap appears not as that between sense-data and physical objects but as between 'ostensible physical objects' and 'physical objects'. The problem of the relationship between the two is, however, almost exactly the same.

Both sense-data and 'ostensible physical objects' are regarded as discoverable by a single act of perception, whereas physical objects are known only as the result of a more complex process. Thus according to Firth, the basic epistemological question considered by traditional epistemologists will not be affected by the outcome of the conflict between the Percept Theory and the Sense-Datum Theory. We may still be exercised by the problem whether our general concept of a physical object is in some sense 'derived from' the presentation of 'ostensible physical objects' in perception, or whether it is, in one sense or other, *a priori*. We may even come to the phenomenalist conclusion that physical objects are composed of 'ostensible physical objects'. In fact, Firth takes pains to demonstrate that 'ostensible physical objects' can fulfil exactly the same epistemological function that sense-data are supposed to do. Like sense-data 'ostensible physical objects' are causes, clues, signs, etc., or at any rate, perceptual beliefs are based on 'ostensible physical objects'. Morever, 'ostensible physical objects' are the evidence which justify our belief in the physical world in the same manner as sense-data have been held to be.

Firth concludes, therefore, that the epistemological implications of the Percept Theory are important (namely, that 'ostensible physical objects' are epistemologically basic rather than sense-data) but not revolutionary, for the fact that 'ostensible physical objects' are given does not solve the problems of epistemological analysis which the Sense-Datum Theory has also to solve.

It is difficult to avoid the conclusion that Firth's 'ostensible physical object' is a distinct particular entity in much the same way as the sense-datum is regarded by Sense-Datum Theorists as a distinct particular entity. Firth denies this. In his original article he insists that 'ostensible physical objects' are not to be conceived as sensible particulars. He suggests that supporters of the Appearing Theory may speak instead of perceptual experience 'ostensibly manifesting' a physical object. But surely his own remarks undermine the truth of this reservation. If 'ostensible physical objects' are merely the ways in which a physical object 'ostensibly manifests itself' then how can we possibly entertain the idea that physical objects are 'composed of' ostensible physical objects? An object can surely not be 'composed of' or 'consist of' the *ways* in which it appears.

In 1965 Firth adds a note[1] in which he insists once more that all

[1] *Perceiving, Sensing, and Knowing*, ed. Robert J. Swartz (New York, Anchor Books, 1965) p. 270.

the phenomenological and epistemological issues discussed in his essay are entirely independent of the act-object terminology and can be formulated in any terminology which allows us to describe a sensory constituent which may occur in hallucination as well as in genuine perception. Here Firth clearly betrays an acceptance of the Epistemological Dualism which distinguishes between sensory appearances and objects, and which regards hallucination and normal perception to be classified together. There seems to be a partial acceptance of the Argument from Illusion, and this it is which serves to explain why it is that the gap between sensing the sensible particular and observing the object as such nonetheless reappears in the Percept Theory.

(IX) THE JUDGMENT THEORY

A theory similar in some respects to Firth's Percept Theory is the Judgment Theory associated with exponents of the Absolute Idealist tradition in philosophy, and expounded with particular clarity by R. G. Collingwood.[1]

Like the Percept Theory this theory denies the possibility even in principle of distinguishing between a sensuous part of perception and an interpretative part: the perceptual act is a unitary rather than a two-fold process. But whereas the Percept Theory seems to imply that this unitary act is unique or, at any rate, does not specify the nature of this act, the Judgment Theory maintains that this unitary act of perception is, in fact, a rudimentary form of judgment. Thus, according to this view, all perception necessarily involves judgment, and this judgment alone is the condition determining whether the object is perceived at all, and if perceived, how it is perceived. There can, therefore, never be any such thing as an uninterpreted acceptance of particulars such as the apprehension of sensible appearances would have to be in most forms of the Sense-Datum Theory. The so-called 'sense-impressions', 'looks', or 'appearances', are nothing but entities produced for the purposes of discussion and explanation by a deliberate supposition that conditions obtain which do not, in fact, obtain in any normal case of perception. For example, the appearances which the painter must train himself to

[1] See specially 'Sensation and Thought', *Proceedings of the Aristotelian Society*, 1923–4.

observe are based on the supposition that his whole visual field has been projected upon a flat pane of glass held at right angles to his line of vision. Such a way of interpreting his field of vision is necessary to the painter who has to transcribe his field of vision by projecting it upon a flat piece of canvas. Similar artifices are involved in the formation of all other 'looks' or 'appearances', what is sometimes called 'experience'. Since we almost always do not perceive things under conditions in which these circumstances prevail, we are certainly not aware of the details of our 'experience' at the time we are perceiving things, and the perceptual act can therefore in no way be regarded as consisting of two forms of awareness.

The gap between the recognition of appearances, and the awareness of the object as such would seem to disappear in the Judgment Theory. Since the perception of the object as such and the perception of some feature of the object equally depend upon attention, discrimination and perceptual judgment, the difference between the two becomes simply the difference between whether we are attending to the feature as a particular feature or attending to the object as a whole. Normally it would be more usual to attend to the object as a whole rather than to any of its particular features. But we may, of course, attend to a particular feature, just as we may view our visual field supposing circumstances to prevail which in fact do not. In neither case, however, will the appearance produced be anything which might be said to be 'epistemologically basic' and so constitute an epistemological gap between itself and the object as such.

As between the Percept Theory and the Judgment Theory the latter has the advantage of completely avoiding the gap which the former still admits, albeit in somewhat different form than in the Sense-Datum Theory. A second advantage which the Judgment Theory possesses consists in its making the unitary nature of perceptual consciousness more comprehensible. It may be argued that the mistake of the Sense-Datum Theory in dividing perception into a sensuous part and an interpretation is not rectified by the claim that perception is a unitary process differing from both sensing and interpreting. For surely the Sense-Datum Theory is correct in basing itself on the insight that perceptual statements regarding the observation of objects are not different in kind from other statements. All statements involve interpretation or judgment.

If, then, perception is not to be divided into a sensory core and an interpretation, as suggested in most forms of the Sense-Datum Theory, it must at least be recognized that a perceptual act bears a certain likeness to an act of interpretation or judgment. Perhaps the Judgment Theory over-states the matter in suggesting that perception is simply a rudimentary judgment; it will have to explain in what way it is 'rudimentary'. But the Percept Theory seems to be neglecting entirely the interpretative element which psychologists have demonstrated to be so important a function of any act of perception.

(X) IS THERE REALLY A GAP?

As we have seen, the gap between awareness of the way things appear and the awareness of the object as a whole tends to vanish once the process of perception is no longer regarded as a simple case of 'accepting' something but rather as a process akin to discrimination. But even if we hesitate before characterizing perception in this way, we are now in a position to see what was at fault in the original statement of the gap.

The main factor involved in creating the illusion of a gap is the assumption that we can somehow legitimately speak of something that is instantaneously and comprehensively perceived at a particular moment. It is supposed that something reveals itself more or less completely and what we do is to add new revelations bit by bit until we have absorbed all the details that are perceptible and 'synthesize' them to form the concept of the object. The difficulty then arises by pointing out that somehow we are aware of many other things about the object even before we have had time to actually notice them, and that there are certain qualities (e.g. its continued existence before we began to perceive it and after we stop perceiving it) which cannot be perceived at all.

What should be questioned is both (a) whether what is perceived is simply accepted, and (b) whether one can legitimately divide up the process of observation into instants of time at the end of each of which something is accepted by the mind. It is surely wrong to conceive of perception as something like a camera's taking a rapid series of snapshots. To absorb anything at all by means of perception will take time, and just how much time it takes may vary from occasion to occasion, depending upon the observer's readiness, his familiarity with the circumstances, the quality of his perceptual organs, the nature of the background, etc. Interesting psychological studies have been made of the varying aspects of perceptual performance in differing conditions. It is at any rate clear that the momentary character of perceptual 'acceptance' is a myth. How long, for example, does it take to sense a 'sense-datum'? It may take as long or as little to become aware of some feature of the object as it does to become aware of the object as a whole. The temporal basis of the gap is, therefore, certainly completely misleading. The 'what' that is seen at any particular moment depends, among other things, upon what we are looking for.

The gap is also illusory in another way. From the fact that certain features of the object may not be perceptible at all from one particular vantage point, or from any vantage point, it does not follow that we do not see the object as a whole. One may see the object while failing to discern or discriminate certain of its parts. In fact, every part that we see may itself have parts which we do not see except through a microscope. Whenever we perceive an object by means of any one of the senses there are certain features of that object which we perceive and certain others which we do not. But to conclude from this that we do not see the objects at all, is like arguing, as Chisholm points out, that since the butcher does not cut every part of the roast, therefore strictly speaking he does not cut the roast at all.

How we become aware of the continued existence of objects and how we can justify our belief in such continuity or in the 'neutrality' and independence of objects, are interesting questions to which there may be partial or complete answers from psychology, physiology, and physics. But the gap between the perceptual consciousness of the object and the awareness of the ways in which it appears is an illusory gap.

It is surprising that H. H. Price should have come so near to describing adequately our experience of the acquisition of knowledge about physical objects with his account of the transition from 'perceptual acceptance' to 'perceptual assurance' by 'specifying the unspecified',[1] and yet maintained that the 'intuitive' character of the awareness of objects was illusory on the basis of this alleged

[1] H. H. Price, *Perception*.

gap. It would appear that in formulating the existence of this gap the question of certainty and corrigibility has played the crucial role. The two factors mitigating the cognitive claim of the intuitive awareness of objects, i.e. (a) the lack of certainty and (b) the gap, turn out to be internally connected with one another. The gap, it would seem, is really created by the acceptance of the Argument from Illusion, at least insofar as it distinguishes between an incorrigible sensuous object and the physical object, the awareness of which is other than identical with the former. This gap, then, does not exist independently of Epistemological Dualism; it is created by it.

(XI) THE NON-EMPIRICAL NATURE OF OBJECTS

Our examination has thus led to the conclusion that insofar as the intuitive awareness of objects has been thought to be discounted by the existence of the gap between actual sensual experience and our perceptual beliefs concerning the object, it has been quite needlessly discounted, since the existence of the gap is itself very problematic. Does this mean, then, that we are to regard the intuitive awareness of objects as a secure basis for the statement that objects are simply discoverable within our experience?

The answer to this is that it can be regarded as nothing of the kind. We are aware of objects when we see them, and when these objects are permanent, public and possess qualities that are not immediately perceptible, we can usually become aware of all these things given time and experience. But this is true of anything of which we can in any way have perceptual experience, including after-images, illusions and hallucinations; given time and experience we can usually come to realize what they are and become perceptually aware of them 'intuitively' as they are on most subsequent occasions. This by no means implies, however, that we are intuitively aware of 'physical objects' every time we perceive anything. We have already remarked on the technical nature of the term as opposed to the vacuous and uninteresting usage in which 'object' refers indiscriminately to anything that may be the grammatical object after verbs of perception. We are undoubtedly intuitively aware of objects every time we perceive. But we are not always aware of 'physical objects'.

Most writers on epistemology in recent times have used the

terms 'physical object' and 'material object' as synonyms. Both expressions reveal that it was the growth of science, particularly in the seventeenth century, that brought into prominence the problem of defending the ordinary man's belief in the fact that the world was very much as it appeared to be in the face of the attacks of the new physics. The growth of natural science was largely due to the abandonment of the medieval concept of irreducible qualitative differences between kinds, in favour of a concentration upon their observable and quantitatively measurable properties. The laws of science could then be formulated in purely mathematical terms, connecting the variations in the properties.

It has often been told how the mechanical measurable qualities came to be regarded as the only properties which were 'real', leading to the discussions concerning the unreality of the so-called 'secondary qualities' such as colour, taste, smell, etc. which dominated the philosophy of these centuries. It was here that the need to defend the common-sense view was thought to arise. The idea of the 'physical' or 'material' object, i.e. the colourless, tasteless, mass of atoms possessed only of real 'primary qualities' had to be reconciled with the view of things held by the ordinary man. This led to a revival of interest in the ancient problems of phenomenal variation in perception, which were now discussed in a sharper and more contemporary form. Historically, therefore, the notion of a 'physical object' functions in modern epistemology not merely as a foil to the notion of a sense-datum—something which J. L. Austin has correctly observed. It also reflects a predicament that was created by the rise of modern science.

But the concept of a 'physical object' becomes no more ultimately comprehensible when we have realized its historical origins. What is included in the class of 'physical objects' is unclear. As Austin says, chairs, tables, pictures, books, etc., clearly are held to belong there. But what about rivers, voices, flames, rainbows, shadows, vapours and gases; are all these 'material objects'? If not, which are not and why? It does indeed seem that

'. . . there is no one kind of thing that we perceive but many different kinds, the number being reducible, if at all, by scientific investigation and not by philosophy.'[1]

[1] J. L. Austin, *Sense and Sensibilia*, p. 4.

Thus the concept of a 'physical object' involves the notion that the 'things' we perceive are somehow basically all like chairs, tables, etc., and this view, a clearly mistaken one, is produced by the attempt to give expression to the concept of matter central to the new science (i.e. of a mass of atoms possessed only of 'primary qualities') in such a way as to relate it to the traditional problems concerning perceptual variations, illusions, etc. This is, of course, not the whole story. There are other motives and interests which have led to the formation of the concept of 'physical objects'.

But the point clearly emerges that the adoption of this concept as basic to one's ontology is certainly a decision in which metaphysical considerations play an important part. It is, therefore, plain that 'physical objects' are not simply empirically discoverable entities which we need only examine our experience in order to find, and which are the invariable or even usual 'objects' of our perception.

Chapter 5

THE GIVEN AS IMMEDIATE
EXPERIENCE

(I) THE PRESENTATIONAL CONTINUUM

The theories we have been dealing with hitherto, i.e. the SDT and OT, both agree in maintaining that although whenever we perceive things, there is always something given, what is given in any case is not necessarily the same as what is given in other cases. There are many different 'sense-data', just as there are many different 'objects'. Our perceptual lives consist in the presentation at different times of different givens, and very often we are presented with many different givens at one and the same time, sometimes through a single avenue of sense (such as sight or touch or smell), and sometimes by different avenues of sense. In the most simplified statements of the SDT we are regarded as 'seeing' a patch-work of visual sense-data while at the same time hearing various aural sense-data, tasting and smelling various tastes and smells, and being subjected, at the same time to many different feelings. All these data 'come in upon us' through our various senses, though, at any particular moment, we may be attending only to comparatively few of them, and perhaps to only one particular datum.

With the OT comes a slight modification of this account, for it is now maintained that all the smells, noises, tastes, feelings, and patches of colour we experience are not to be regarded as so many isolated units of sense-experience which reflection must piece together; each is a smell *of* something, a sound *of* something, a feeling *of* something, a visual appearance *of* something. Thus we are presented, according to this view, with objects, people, buildings, vehicles, etc. which we apprehend in various ways, at the same time smelling, seeing, hearing, and feeling them; and of course, again it is obvious that we may be attending at any time only to a few of the objects with which we are presented, and perhaps to only one of them.

F   81

The first step away from the above accounts is taken when it is admitted that no separate act of apprehending is required for every sense-datum or object. This is the theory of the 'presentational continuum'. We begin to see that the process of perception is much more like a segmentation of what is originally continuous than an aggregation of elements at first independent and distinct. If we now start from this 'continuity of consciousness' and work back, we are led to the idea of an objective continuum which is gradually differentiated and then gives rise to what we call distinct presentations. James Ward, the foremost exponent of the 'presentational continuum' view, rejects the notion that knowledge begins with a confused manifold of sense-impressions, devoid of logical and psychological unity, which '... coming out of nothingness admit of being strung upon the "thread of consciousness" like beads picked up at random, or of being cemented into a mass like . . . bits of stick and sand. . . .' On the contrary, at any given moment we have a certain whole of presentations, a 'field of consciousness', psychologically one and continuous, and a new sensation is really a partial modification of pre-existing and persisting presentational whole which thereby becomes more complex than it was before. But this increasing complexity never gives rise to a plurality of discontinuous presentations, having a distinctness and individuality such as the atoms or elementary particles of the physical world are supposed to have. Even if we could attend to a pure sensation of sound or colour by itself, there is much to justify the suspicion that even this is complex and not simple, and owes its clearly marked specific quality to this complexity.[1]

It would seem at first glance that a presentational continuum view is incompatible certainly with the SDT and perhaps also with the OT, for if sense-data or objects become discernable only through a segmentation of a continuum of presentation, in what sense can these be said to be given?

But, as a matter of fact, the presentational continuum view (or something like it) has been maintained both together with some versions of the SDT as also with some versions of the OT.[2] The

[1] James Ward, *Psychological Principles* 2nd. ed. (Cambridge, University Press, 1933) Ch. 4, especially section 2.

[2] See C. D. Broad, *Scientific Thought*, (London, Kegan Paul, 1923) p. 216 ff; G. Dawes-Hicks, *Critical Realism*, (London, MacMillan, 1938) pp. 60-7; and J. Laird, *A Study in Realism* (Cambridge, University Press, 1920).

reasoning behind this, I suppose, lies in the fact that although the presentational continuum view constitutes a step away from the more naive versions of those theories, it may still be maintained that the given in sense-perception, though it always comes to us as part of a 'presentational continuum', is nonetheless itself unaffected by this circumstance. What is given is the sense-datum (or object) and not the continuum itself. The continuum is a sort of framework which holds together what we are given; and though the recognition of the existence of this framework may solve many a difficulty concerning our knowledge of the external world, we are never acquainted with, immediately aware of, or presented with, this framework as such.

(II) BRADLEY ON IMMEDIATE EXPERIENCE

When the IET-ists ask themselves what it is that is actually given in experience,[1] they find their eyes opened to the fact that it is neither a sense-datum nor an object which is given but only a 'blur' of feeling, a 'One', a unity of experience, in which Subject and Object have not yet been discriminated. This 'felt totality' is what Bradley calls 'immediate experience'; and the illustration that is sometimes given of the sort of thing to which Bradley is referring is the case of someone lying out on an open hillside on a fine summer's day completely absorbed in his own thoughts. All sorts of sights and sounds and smells assail his senses, but they 'mean nothing' to him; so far as his awareness of the physical surroundings is concerned, he might equally as well be sitting in his easy chair before the fire. Suddenly something occurs to awaken him abruptly from his reverie—perhaps a sound in the distance. He 'comes back to life' and begins to notice his surroundings. What he previously 'looked at' without being aware of anything now registers in his mind and has some meaning for him.

Whether this is an actual example of 'immediate experience' is doubtful.[2] But there is no doubt that this case illustrates the general nature of cognition according to the IET. We start with a vague

---

[1] As F. H. Bradley explicitly asks himself in *Essays on Truth and Reality*, (Oxford, Clarendon Press, 1914) p. 201.
[2] See Bradley, loc. cit. p. 174 and also F. H. Bradley, *Collected Essays*, (Oxford, Clarendon Press, 1935) pp. 622–3, 654.

'feeling' which is an awareness of the totality of things, and out of this, primitive discriminations arise, which gradually take the form of intellectual activity.

We may sum up briefly the main elements of Bradley's theory in the following points:

(1) Bradley argues at length that all cognition is judgment. 'Judgment' is here a technical term, standing for an act of analysis and synthesis, which is not however always an 'inference', for 'inference' is an experiment performed on a datum, whereas in judgments of perception, says Bradley, there is properly speaking no datum. He says:

'I do not mean that, like the Deity of our childhood they create their world from nothing at all, and exert their activity on a void externality, or their own inner emptiness. What I mean is, that the basis from which they start is *for the intellect* nothing. It is a sensuous whole which is merely felt and which is not idealized. It is not anything which, as it is, would come before understanding, and hence we cannot take it as the starting point of inference, unless we are ready to use that term in a somewhat loose sense. We first must begin our voyage of reasoning by working on something which is felt and not thought. The alteration of this original material, which makes it first an object for the intellect is thus not yet inference because the start has not been made from an ideal content. Before reasoning exists, there must come an operation which serves to transform this crude material; and this operation is both analytical and synthetical. But it is not an inference, for, though its result is intellectual, its premise, so to speak, is merely sensuous.'[1]

In a sense then Bradley holds that 'nothing is given'; and this is the burden of his reply to the SDT and OT. But, on the other hand, it is he himself who speaks of 'immediate experience' as 'the Given', though he makes it clear that he does not mean the relation of an object to a subject.[2]

(2) 'Immediate experience' is synonymous with 'feeling' in

---

[1] F. H. Bradley, *Principles of Logic*, 2nd ed. (London, Oxford University Press, 1922) pp. 479, 482.

[2] *Essays on Truth and Reality* p. 200 and elsewhere; *Collected Essays*, p. 632; *Principles of Logic*, pp. 44-5, 102, 297 n.4; and especially *Collected Essays*, p. 218.

Bradley's terminology.[1] This 'feeling' is '... a sort of confusion, and ... a nebula which would grow distinct on closer scrutiny'. But there is no distinction between what is felt and that which feels. It is experienced all together as a coexisting mass parted and joined by no relations. This 'feeling' comes first in the experience of each of us. In it the distinction between cognition and other aspects of our nature is not yet developed. Feeling is not one differentiated aspect, but, on the contrary, holds all aspects in one.[2] (3) As a 'blur of feeling', the given, for Bradley, is something in which the distinction between subject and object has not yet arisen.[3] He insists that in the beginning of our experience no such distinctions are discriminated. Nor is there any aspect of self-feeling.[4] Subject and Object are later discriminations within this immediate experience which arise when the discursive thought-process begins. This is not to say, however, that they suddenly appear at a certain stage, prior to which they had been nothing. In his earlier version of the theory, Bradley explained that they existed from the start as 'dim feelings' which were 'aspects' within the 'blur of feeling' which were felt, but of which we were not conscious. In his later version Bradley preferred to speak of Subject and Object as felt differences, present from the start, but not connected with specific 'dim feelings'. In either version the main point was that Subject and Object existed as vague feelings from the start but were not yet discriminated.[5] In 'immediate experience' the 'felt relation' of two things is not yet experienced *as* a relation. We have a feeling which is altered but still remains one and the same feeling.

[1] 'I use, in brief, immediate experience to stand for that which is comprised wholly within a single state of undivided awareness or feeling', *Essays on Truth and Reality*, p. 173.
[2] *Appearance and Reality*, (Oxford, Clarendon Press, 1951, 9th impression) pp. 198, 419; *Collected Essays* p. 216; also *Essays on Truth and Reality*, p. 157. 'Feeling' is not the same as 'pleasure or pain'. Bradley considers the identification of feeling with pleasure or pain to be a perversion of 'the older view' that feeling is immediate experience. Of course, pleasure and pain, too, are given from the very beginning. 'If we take "given" or "presented", not as implying a donation or even a relation to an Ego, but rather for that which is simple, and becomes as it is, then in this sense pain and pleasure must be called presentations.' *Collected Essays*, pp. 217, 220.
[3] This view of 'feeling' Bradley claims to have learnt from Hegel's *Encyclopedia*. sections 399 ff; he refers also to Volkmann's *Psychologie* (ed. II or III Section 127), For further comments on this view see 1922 note to *Principles of Logic*, p. 515.
[4] *Essays on Truth and Reality*, pp. 159–60; *Collected Essays*, pp. 218, 222–8.
[5] *Principles of Logic*, p. 503. See 1922 note pp. 516–17.

(4) This 'immediate experience' which is equivalent to 'feeling' not only transcends the distinction between Subject and Object, but is also, in a sense, beyond time. Its presence is not simply confined to a single here and now. If the given were so confined, then, according to Bradley, we should be faced with insuperable difficulties. It would be impossible to guarantee the truth of universal judgment or the truth of any proposition which extends beyond the instant.

The given is indeed present, admits Bradley. But it is a mistake to suppose that the present is a part of time, indivisible and stationary, and that here and now can be solid and atomic. In one sense the 'present' is *no* time; it is a point we take within the flow of change. Reality is not present in the sense of being given in one atomic moment. The real is that with which I come into contact, and the content of any part of time, any section of the continuous flow of change is present to me if I directly encounter it.

Hence the given is not confined within simply discrete and resting moments. Every 'now' and 'here' is a portion of that continuous content with which we have come into direct relation.[1]

(5) Though Bradley regards the Self as an abstraction which we later discriminate within our 'immediate experience', he recognizes the existence of 'finite centres of feeling and experience', which, while they last, are not pervious to one another. However, such a centre of experience is not a Self; in every centre the *whole* of Reality is present. This does not mean that every other centre of experience as such is included there. It means that:

'every centre qualifies the whole, and that the whole, as a substantive is present in each of its adjectives. Then from the immediate experience the self emerges, and is set apart by a distinction. The self and the world are elements each separated in, and each contained by experience.'[2]

It is very difficult to conceive the relationship of 'the finite centre of experience' to the whole experience which Bradley attempts here to describe. But it seems clear that it is by means of these

---

[1] *Principles of Logic*, pp. 51–55.
[2] *Appearance and Reality* pp. 524–5.

'finite centres' that he wishes to distinguish one 'immediate experience' from another.

(6) G. F. Stout accused Bradley of holding that thought was 'mutilated feeling', and concluding therefore that whatever was thought was unreal. He said that for Bradley the whole development of thinking consciousness resolved itself into an endeavour to reconstitute the unity which it itself had destroyed.[1] Bradley strenuously denied both accusations. It was impossible, he said, to think of anything unreal. Furthermore the unity at which thought aimed must lie beyond that from which it started for otherwise the absurd conclusion would follow that the more one thought, the more one would remove oneself from reality.[2]

But the issues in this exchange between Stout and Bradley are more subtle than they appear at the surface. Bradley himself noted that they depended on the sense in which 'reality' was being spoken of, and I think it is clear that it was the 'degrees of reality' doctrine which was at stake. Roughly Bradley's position was that although relational thought inadequately gave expression to our 'feeling' or 'immediate experience', it was nonetheless partially true and real. In the last resort no possible truth is quite true, for it is an inadequate expression of the 'immediate experience' which it professes to give bodily. But it may be utterly true in the sense of not being *intellectually* corrigible. Absolute truth is only attained by passing outside the intellect and taking in the remaining aspects of experience; but in this passage the proper nature of truth is, of course, transformed and perishes.

This is not to say that 'feeling' is what is ultimate. On the contrary, 'feeling' is the starting point, not the final unity. The ultimate reality must hold within itself every variety of fact and experience. It must contain thought no less than feeling. In one sense, indeed nothing can pass beyond feeling or 'immediate experience', because everything that is real must be felt. But in our experience this felt content is developed in such a way that it goes beyond and conflicts with mere immediacy or feeling by being mediated in the process of thought. It is in the character of this ideal content too that the full nature of the real must be sought.

[1] G. F. Stout, *Studies in Philosophy and Psychology* (London, Macmillan, 1930). See also Bradley's comment on Strange's criticism, *Collected Essays*, p. 696.

[2] *Essays on Truth and Reality*, p. 275.

'We must conclude to a higher Reality which at once transcends' and yet re-includes the sphere of mere feeling.'[1]

(7) Thus Bradley holds that 'immediate experience' or feeling, though transcended by relational thought, ultimately combines with the latter in the Absolute. This Absolute is an experience which is the complete realization of all our desires. It is not in detail knowable, and remains inexplicable. But, as the fulfilment of every end and the complete reality of all partial existence, it is both knowable and certain. It is beyond any one kind of experience, whether this be feeling, thought, intuition, sense, activity or will, though it positively must include each and all of these. However it is clear that Bradley regarded feeling or 'immediate experience' as more ultimate and closer to the Absolute than thought. What is more, 'immediate experience' is the chief source of our knowledge of the Absolute, for in this mere feeling we have the experience of a whole, which though it contains diversity, is not parted by relations.[2]

(8) But in the transition from 'immediate experience' to thought and then to the ultimate or 'Absolute Experience', in which both find their satisfaction, 'immediate experience' is never at any stage left behind. In this sense feeling can never be transcended, and we never at any time, pass beyond 'immediate experience'. In the growth of discursive knowledge, all that is removed is the *mereness* of immediacy. Every distinction continues to rest on an immediate background of which we are aware, and is felt to belong to an immediate totality. This felt background remains always immediate, but its content may show mediation, for parts of the content may at some time have been elements in the objects and internally distinguished into relations and terms. Conversely we may find tracts of immediacy in the object which are still felt and have never been analysed.[3]

Thus, at any moment, however relational its contents, actual experience is always, in the end, non-relational and felt; no analysis into relations and terms can ever exhaust its nature. 'Immediate experience' not only escapes, but also serves as the basis on which

[1] ibid., p. 157.
[2] *Collected Essays*, pp. 630–1, 653; *Appearance and Reality*, pp. 159–60.
[3] *Appearance and Reality*, 1st ed. pp. 544–5; and *Essays on Truth and Reality*, pp. 175–8.

the analysis is made. Every analysis proceeds from, and on the basis of, a unity. Analysis and abstraction are the substitution, at the level of thought, for a certain end and purpose, of another kind of synthesis. The unity of 'immediate experience' is ultimate in the sense that no relational thinking can adequately reconstitute it, and no relational thinking can ever get free from the use of it. An attempted unity of 'one and many', at a higher remove, is the ultimate goal of all our knowledge and of every endeavour. The aspects of coherence and comprehensiveness are each a way in which this principle appears and in which we seek to realize it.[1]

Moreover, we cannot speak of the relation between 'immediate experience' and that which transcends it, except by license. It is a convenient mode of expression, but not ultimately defensible, because a relation exists only between terms which must be objects. And thus 'immediate experience', taken as the term of a relation, becomes a partial object and ceases, to that extent, to preserve its nature as a felt totality. The relation must simply be taken as a fact. It can neither be explained nor, properly speaking, described, since description necessarily means translation into objective terms and relations. We directly feel and experience this relation as a fact. But in attempting to describe it, we half negative it. The attempt is justified when the description rings true, that is, does not jar, in spite of being inadequate.[2]

The above summary depicts a very striking view of the given, in which all knowledge and activity are regarded as only partly real discriminations within the 'immediate experience' of a finite 'centre of experience', which reflects the whole of reality and bears a relation, which is really no relation at all, to the timeless Absolute. The given is 'immediate experience', the goal 'Absolute Experience', and the path from the given to the goal is traced by a process of discursive thought which grows ever more comprehensive and coherent until it takes up into itself all those felt elements from

[1] ibid. p. 231. This, of course, is the main pillar of the Coherence Theory of Truth. Bradley adds in a note: 'In my view. . . the "and" is a developed and yet degraded form of the immediate unity, and throughout implies that. Make the contents of the felt totality both objective and relational and then abstract from any special character of the relations and any special character of the totality—and you have what is meant by "and".'

[2] *Essays on Truth and Reality*, pp. 176–7; and *Appearance and Reality*, 1st ed. pp. 468–9.

which it started in a higher synthesis between feeling and thought.

Such a view of the given must be conceded to be a surprising result of 'the re-examination of perceptual situations in the light of theoretical considerations' of which the Naive View concerning the dispute regarding the nature of the given speaks. It is, moreover, a view which must be very shocking to common-sense, since it effectively involves the overthrowing of the common-sense view of the ordinary man by its insistence that the whole world of subjects and objects is no more than an abstracted intellectualized view of reality which is only partially true. But this shock to the ordinary man does not weigh very much in Bradley's estimation, for he castigates the common-sense view which we all have before we come to re-examine our knowledge of things, as in its essence a one-sidedness which we must not be afraid to mark as stupid or even, perhaps, to denounce as immoral.[1] Why, he asks, should not the result of the deepest philosophic investigation after all be accepted as the truth and what we ordinarily take to be our sensuous presentment be recognized to be a misinterpretation of reality?[2]

At any rate, when Bradley re-examines his experience, and asks himself what is given, he never finds a 'Many', i.e. a plurality, either of sense-data or of objects, but only a 'One', namely 'immediate experience'. He knows well enough that there are others who profess to find a 'Many', but he figuratively throws up his hands in despair when he says

. . . is it not better to recognize that on this point there is no agreement and little more than a variety of opinions?[3]

It should be noted that he professes to 'find' this 'immediate experience'. This, according to the Naive View, must mean that he is claiming the existence of 'immediate experience' as an empirical fact. But is 'immediate experience' an empirical fact, capable of being discovered by simple inspection?

(III) SOME FINDINGS OF THE PSYCHOLOGISTS

In evaluating the factual basis of the claims of immediate experience,

[1] *Collected Essays* p. 640.
[2] *Principles of Logic*, p. 589.
[3] *Essays on Truth and Reality*, p. 200.

to be what is directly presented in sense perception, the following findings of the empirical psychologists seem particularly relevant.[1]

(1) The dominant trend of psychological investigation has discounted the notion of 'sensory atomism' which used to be characteristic of the older Associationists. According to that view sensation consists of the reception of separate sensations which are unconnected with and independent of any previous conditioning in perceptual orientation, or of the interpretation which might be placed upon these sensations. An imposing list of psychologists in this century have insisted that such an idea, which seems to underlie the views about perception held by classical philosophers such as Locke, Berkeley, Hume and Kant, is not consistent with the facts, which indicate that individual 'sensations' are discriminated out of a sensual continuum rather than received as individual atoms by the perceiver.

(2) The work of European psychologists and of the Gestalt Psychology in particular, has emphasized the fact that interpretation is an important part of sensation and that previous conditioning and expectation influence radically the nature of what is sensed.

(3) The theory that has been called 'the Discursive Inference Theory' which is associated in particular with the great pioneer of the empirical investigation of the perceptual processes H. Helmholtz has now come to be almost universally discredited by psychologists. According to this theory, what happens in perception is that after sensation has brought about the reception by the perceiver of a sense-impression, a process of interpretation is initiated. The mind then becomes 'active', embarking upon a process of interpretation or inference which concludes with a perceptual judgment. It has been pointed out by psychologists that no temporal gap is observable between the sensation and the perceptual judgment, that no mental activity appears to be involved, and that it is impossible, in fact, to distinguish between the 'passively' sensed impression and the mental 'activity' of inference. The Discursive Inference Theory has been displaced, in the works of those who care to maintain the distinction between sensation and interpretation, by the so-called 'Sensory Core Theory'.

[2] See references below p. 168 note 1.

(IV) IMMEDIATE EXPERIENCE AND THE
SENSUAL CONTINUUM

These three points are all recognized and indeed emphasized in the IET: (a) The rejection of sensory atomism was one of the dominant themes in the English 'Absolute Idealist' tradition, which looked to T. H. Green's criticism of Hume as the classic statement of this rejection. Bradley regarded his concept of 'immediate experience' as being built on this foundation. (b) The inter-dependence of sensation and interpretation was strongly emphasized by the insistence that knowledge of any sort was impossible without interpretation. It was this that was intended in the misleading slogan that 'there is no given' in knowledge. And (c) the Discursive Inference Theory was decisively opposed by the view that sensation ought to be regarded not as providing raw materials which are subsequently interpreted in some thought process, but as 'immediate experience', a unity of feeling in which subject and object have not yet been discriminated and which remains as a felt background never superseded even though mediated by thought to provide objects known to a knowing subject.

There is thus a clear empirical basis, confirmed by psychological investigation, for some of the strands which are woven together to form the concept of 'immediate experience'. But this by no means implies that this term denotes something empirically discoverable.

(1) On the contrary, in the accepted meaning of 'empirical' which implies something capable of being perceived or introspected *by a person*, 'immediate experience' is ruled out from the start as an empirical fact since by definition it can exist in its pure state only when the person is not yet conscious of his own existence. It exists before subject and object have been discriminated; thus it cannot be 'discoverable' to the subject in any ordinary sense. This is no mere matter of terminology, but indicates a real difficulty in Bradley's concept of 'immediate experience'. Bradley himself appreciates this difficulty and deals with it as the problem 'How can Immediate Experience Ever Be Known?' in his paper 'On Immediate Experience' in *Essays on Truth and Reality*. He finds this problem insoluble, since knowing it would require that 'immediate experience' become an object to a subject whereas, by definition it transcends the distinction between subject and object.

In a number of passages scattered throughout his works,[1] Bradley expresses his doubts whether an experience of pure 'esthesis' such as 'immediate experience' was meant to be, could ever be found as a stage in our actual experience either as children or as adults. He seems to have supposed that though this 'ultimate fact' became apparent whenever we considered our knowledge of things, it might never occur in its unmediated purity during our conscious lives. Its pure state was a sort of ideal to which our knowledge pointed but which might never be realized in actual fact. Certain approximations to this ideal which form the experiential basis for its recognition were given by Bradley as illustrations. These are the sort of undeveloped intellectual stage to be found in early childhood, or the vague states of semi-consciousness which we have in day dreaming. Bradley regards these as possible though doubtful candidates for the role of 'immediate experience'.

But we may question whether these could even in principle be regarded as possible states of awareness of a non-relational unity. Possibly in an attempt to give the term some concrete application which would enable us to have an idea of the sort of experience that could be regarded as non-relational (i.e. not involving the duality of subject and object), Bradley equates 'immediate experience' with 'feeling'. It is doubtful whether such an equation can be sustained.

(i) Feeling is certainly less 'relational' an experience than the cognition of an object by the subject, since we speak of feelings even when there are no objects which are felt. But even feeling, as ordinarily understood, cannot be regarded as 'a self-contained whole' which is simply 'there'. Can there be a feeling without someone who feels it—a disembodied feeling as it were?[2]

(ii) Bradley speaks of immediate experience as if it were somehow outside time, and beyond the influence of time's passing. But our familiar experience of feelings gives us no inkling of what a feeling of this sort will be like. You cannot catch any particular feeling except as passing into something else.[3]

These and other questions may serve to illustrate the fact that to

---

[1] *Essays on Truth and Reality*, pp. 174–5; *Principles of Logic*, 2nd ed. p. 156, note 5, etc.
[2] See F. Strange, 'Bradley' Doctrine of Knowledge', *Mind* 1911, pp. 459–60, and J. Ward, 'Bradley's Doctrine of Experience', *Mind* 1925, pp. 14–17.
[3] Strange, loc. cit. p. 461.

identify 'immediate experience' with feeling, as Bradley has done, leads to an unfamiliar and impossible distortion of the latter concept. In attempting, rightly, to express the non-fragmentary character of sensation in perception, Bradley has set up 'immediate experience' as an ideal of pure esthesis above and beyond our usual 'relational' experience. In doing so he seems to be creating a mythical phenomenon which is not only not in fact to be found in our actual experience, but which could not be found there even in principle. The concept of 'immediate experience' is unwarranted by anything in our empirical experience.

(2) Bradley's account of 'immediate experience' comes primarily to assert a certain view of the relationship between thought and sensation (or intuition) which he shares with Henri Bergson and others, according to which thinking involves the 'mediating' of a sensual 'immediacy' which is regarded as the basis of mental advance at least in the sense that it comes first in time. But it is to be noted that Bradley's concept of 'immediate experience' also embodies his metaphysical monism, his view, that is, of the world as a unified whole. The 'mediation' of immediate experience is alleged to involve an inevitable fragmentation of this primary unity, which distorts its nature. Hence relational thought is less fundamental or concrete than sensation or intuition (a view also shared by Bergson, though for different reasons), and judging is said to 'cut loose', 'alienate', 'prescind' or 'separate' the contents of thought out of the whole experience.[1]

William James' concept of 'pure experience' has much in common with Bradley's concept of 'immediate experience'. But James declared himself a pluralist, and did not regard 'experience' as evincing a 'non-relational' whole. For this he was criticized by Bradley.

There seems to be a clear indication therefore that the concept of 'immediate experience' involves not only the description or discovery of a fact but embodies also the expression of a particular metaphysical view i.e. metaphysical monism.

(3) Moreover the non-fragmentary character of sensation which is so important a part of Bradley's concept of 'immediate experience' is brought out equally well by James Ward's theory of the 'presen-

---

[1] For a detailed criticism of Bradley's concept of judgment see G. F. Stout, 'Mr. Bradley's Theory of Judgment', *Proceedings of the Aristotelian Society*, 1902–3, pp. 8–25.

tational continuum' mentioned before, according to which we have at any moment of our lives a certain whole of presentations, a 'field of consciousness', psychologically one and continuous. A new sensation is really a partial modification of this pre-existing and persisting presentational whole. The non-fragmentary character of sensation is also embodied in C. D. Broad's theory of 'sense-fields' and 'sense histories' and in similar views held by other philosophers.

In the same way the ubiquitous character of mental activity and interpretation as forming the background and the basis of sensation is expressed not only in Bradley's concept of 'judgment' which complements his theory of 'immediate experience', but also in Ward's theory of 'attention', and in the work of such thinkers as Brentano, Meinong, G. F. Stout and William James.

Hence the empirical facts of the non-fragmentariness of sensation and the pervasive influence of interpretation by no means add up in any simple or straightforward manner to form the concept of 'immediate experience'. This concept then, is not to be regarded as something discoverable upon inspection. Its formation has involved the surreptitious introduction of all sorts of *a priori*, metaphysical and non-empirical assumptions.

Chapter 6

PROBLEM OR PSEUDO-PROBLEM

---

(1) DIFFERENT CONCEPTS OF DIRECT PERCEPTION

In the last three chapters we have been trying to show the mistakes
of the Naive View of the dispute with regard to the nature of the
given, in suggesting that the theorist is in each case drawing attention to something which may be empirically discovered within our
experience. The so-called 'discovery' of 'immediate experience',
'sense-data' or even 'objects', turns out to involve all sorts of other
factors and can by no means be regarded as a simple recourse to the
facts.

In the present chapter I wish to show that the Naive View of the
dispute is mistaken in another and even more crucial respect. Even
if it *were* the case, as it is not, that each of the theorists was simply
calling attention to some factual element in perception which he
regarded as basic, in order to ascertain whether they were indeed
arguing with each other, we should have to be sure that they meant
the same thing in claiming that something was given. If they mean
different things, then there need be no real argument. But do the
theorists mean the same thing? Can we really make sense of the
claim that 'It is not the sense-datum but the object (or immediate
experience) that is given'?

Let us firstly examine the question with respect to the issue
between the SDT and the OT. We have already seen that the
claim concerning the givenness of sense-data is connected with the
expression 'direct' or 'immediate' perception. Moore, it will be
recalled, regarded it as part of the very meaning of the assertion
that a person is perceiving in the ordinary sense that he 'directly
perceives' something, namely, according to him, a 'sense-datum'.
Ayer pointed out that 'direct perception' was here a technical term
concerning which there was no uniform usage amongst philosophers. But whether Moore or Ayer is right, in order for there to be
a genuine argument between the SDT and OT, we must be in a

position to apply this conception of 'direct perception' in the OT as well, for otherwise it would be open to us to retort that indeed 'objects' may be given in some other sense, but it is not the case that they are given as the objects of 'direct perception'. In this latter sense, we should say, only 'sense-data' are given.

Though there have been, and still are, many forms in which the OT has been expressed, the basic contention of this theory is so simple (apparently at any rate) that it can be formulated in a way that would be acceptable to all its proponents. Briefly, this is the contention that in sense-perception we are in direct perceptual contact with material objects themselves and are immediately conscious of their existence. But when we try to rephrase this in terms of the technical sense of 'direct perception' spoken of by SDT theorists, grave difficulties arise.

We may try to say simply that the OT maintains that the experiencing of a sensible appearance (i.e. what has erroneously been taken to be a distinct entity, the 'sense-datum') is in fact identical with the perceiving of the object. I think all OT supporters might agree to this formulation too, but this is only because the nature of the identity referred to is undefined. The moment we try to define this more precisely, we discover different versions of the OT. One version of the OT would interpret the identity claimed in terms of the technical sense of the expression 'direct perception' as it appears in the SDT. According to this version what is 'directly perceived' is identical with certain features of the physical object. In the case of tactual and visual perception, for example, the sensible appearance is literally *part of the surface* of the physical object which we are perceiving.

This version of the OT has indeed been maintained. But it has wrongly been supposed to be the only interpretation open to holders of the OT. For this reason, exponents of the SDT[1] have been able to regard all forms of the OT (whether Direct Realism, the Theory of Multiple Location, the Theory of Compound Objects, or the Theory of Appearing) as agreeing that what is directly perceived is a 'sense-datum', but disagreeing with the SDT only in identifying this 'sense-datum' with some feature of the physical object. Such SDT exponents have then been easily able to show that this contention was implausible in view of the arguments

[1] e.g. H. H. Price in *Perception* (London, Methuen, 1932).

from differing appearances, illusions, and so on. All these differing appearances would have to be identifiable with some real feature of the physical object, or else we should have to offer some explanation why some appearances are so identifiable whereas others are not.

It is undeniable that certain OT supporters have seemingly espoused this version and set themselves the problem of explaining why some appearances were identical with features of the objects, whereas others were not. But most exponents of the OT have fought shy of this version and preferred rather more subtle ways of interpreting the identity claimed between the sensible appearance and the object. Some, while agreeing that to experience a sensible appearance is in fact to perceive an object, have held that the sensible appearance is not simply 'directly perceived'. Thus John Laird allows himself to use the term 'sense-data' to refer to the sensible appearances of an object, but insists that these are not merely data but also *meaningful* data. They are as much signs as facts, and as signs, the experiencing of them is *eo ipso* the direct perception of physical objects.[1] In perception a sensory complex confronts the mind directly. This complex is a sign-fact which has the kind of meaning that is elaborated into the common-sense notion of a physical thing. Illusory appearances, changing appearances, and so on, are explained by the fact that sign-facts may easily be misread. Though the material world is broadly what it is perceived to be, there is much error and enormous risk of error in our perception. Such errors can generally be overcome by closer attention or allowed for by careful reflection.[2]

These first beginnings of the notion that perception is a form of judgment are developed and accentuated in the version of the OT maintained, in particular, by some of the philosophers who have subscribed to the Theory of Appearing (e.g. G. Dawes-Hicks). These philosophers would also agree that the experiencing of a sensible appearance *is* the perception of the object. But this is so, according to them, because sensible appearances are merely the ways in which the object is apprehended.[3] Thus, what is called the 'direct perceiving' of a sense-datum is really the perceiving of an object in a particular way. And the fact that objects present them-

[1] J. Laird, *A Study in Realism*, (Cambridge, University Press, 1920), pp. 19–25.
[2] ibid., p. 36.
[3] G. Dawes-Hicks, *Critical Realism* (London Macmillan, 1938), p. 29.

selves to percipients in different ways is due to the circumstance that

'... the crudest act of sense-apprehension is still an act of discriminating and comparing, an act involving, therefore, the characteristic that, in a highly developed form, is fundamental in an act of judging.'[1]

Again, the fact that perceiving involves discrimination and comparison gives rise to the constant possibility of error. Any material object whatsoever consists of a vast number of elements and features, and those features of it which are discriminated, and of which there is, therefore, awareness, will at best be a fraction of the totality of features which the object itself possesses. What is at any time discriminated obviously depends on all sorts of circumstances, and so there need be nothing surprising in the fact that the shape or size or colour of an object will seem different to two observers who view it from different vantage points.[2]

Thus, the formula that the experiencing of the sensible appearance is in fact the direct perceiving of the object, which is fundamental to the OT, may be interpreted in *at least* three ways:[3] (1) that the sensible appearance is in fact identical with some of its physical features; (2) that the sensible appearance signifies the object, and the recognition of this signification is already contained in the very experiencing of the sensible appearance; (3) that the sensible appearance is just a way in which the object presents itself to an observer. The order in which these three versions of the OT has been stated reflects the fact that versions (2) and (3) represent a progressive realization that perception is a form of judgment.

But it is clear that only version (1) can at all be capable of being interpreted in a fashion which will allow us to make use of the technical term 'direct perception' in the sense in which this term

[1] ibid. p.24.

[2] ibid., pp. 70-6.

[3] D. M. Armstrong's theory, outlined in Chapter 4, may be interpreted to provide yet another version alongside the three here distinguished. But this would have no bearing on the conclusions drawn since, in spite of the fact that 'direct perception' is defined by Armstrong to exclude the making of 'inferences', it is obviously a very different confrontation of the object than is meant by SDT exponents when they speak of the 'direct perception' of sense-data. It is much more akin to what H. H. Price calls 'taking for granted' than what he calls 'direct perception'.

has been used by exponents of the SDT. This term implies a mode of awareness which is free from inference or any other such process as abstraction, intuitive induction, or the passage from sign to significate. But in version (2), objects are apprehended only by the passage from sign to significate, and it is this that is implied in Laird's calling sensible appearances 'sign-facts'. The experiencing of a sensible appearance is not 'direct perception' followed by an interpretation; it is an active process, something like judgment, which *reads* sign-facts. Again, in version (3), where perception is quite explicitly said to be a form of judgment, there can be no possibility of any such form of awareness as 'direct perception'.

So it seems clear that holders of versions (2) and (3) of the OT, and in fact of any version of the OT other than version (1), are in no position to claim that objects are given in the way in which 'sense-data have been alleged to be. I suppose that what all such theorists can be interpreted as doing when they claim (if they *do* make this claim) that 'it is objects and not sense-data which are given in sense perception', is to be expressing a rejection of the use of such hypothetical entities as 'sense-data' in describing the phenomena of changing appearances, illusions, after-images, hallucinations, and so on. But is such a rejection legitimately to be phrased as the assertion that objects are given?

Thus only in version (1) of the OT can there be a legitimate possibility of claiming that objects are given, for here the physical feature of the object which is directly perceived is supposed to be 'directly perceived' in exactly the same way that 'sense-data have been held to be.

However, we need only remind ourselves of the classic exchange of opinions between Samuel Alexander and G. F. Stout, summarized in Chapter 4, to realize that if such exponents of the OT use the technical term 'direct perception' at all, they must decide whether it is the sensible appearance which is 'directly perceived' or the object as such. If the former then we are faced with the reappearance of the gap between the sensing of the appearance and the awareness of the object as such which we have seen to be inevitable in every form of Epistemological Dualism. And in any case the 'direct perception' of the sensible appearance alone would certainly not justify the claim that 'it is not sense-data but objects that are given'. If, however, the term 'direct perception' is applied to the awareness of the object as such, as is attempted in Alexander's claim that this awareness is given in a process of 'intuition', then again we must decide whether to retain the notion of the 'direct perception' of *sensible appearances* or to give it up. If this notion is retained, then we are faced, like Alexander, with the uncomfortable problem of explaining the relationship within perception between the 'direct perception' of sensible appearances (i.e. real features or parts of the object) and the 'direct perception'/'intuition' of the object as such. If the notion of 'direct perception' of sensible appearances is given up, then the idea of the object itself being somehow 'intuited' without any judgment or interpretation which could explain the phenomena of differing appearances, illusions, etc., becomes implausible.

Now it is only in the case of such exponents of versions (1) of the OT who permit themselves to speak of the 'intuition' of the object as such that we can find any justification for the claim that 'it is objects and not sense-data that are given'. Such exponents have certainly been only a very small minority amongst those who support the OT. Hence, certainly the majority of exponents have not really been using the expression 'the given' in the same sense as it is used by most exponents of the SDT.

But further consideration casts doubt upon whether even this small minority of exponents of the OT can really have been using the expression 'the given' in such a way as to be genuinely consistent with SDT theorists' use of the expression 'direct perception'. For the perception of objects is notoriously corrigible, whereas the incorrigible character of the sensing of 'sense-data' has been one of the most important features with which the notion of 'direct perception' has been invested. We may recall that this feature was the fundamental characteristic upon which Price's exposition of the 'sense-datum' as the given was based.

But even where the awareness of the object as such is called 'intuition', as by Alexander, it has to be admitted that 'intuition' is not an incorrigible process. It is true that Alexander maintains that 'intuition' is infallible *in principle*, but since, as he agrees, our 'intuitions' can only come to us through our senses and our senses may deceive us, in practice our 'intuition' must be fallible as well. It is, therefore, at any rate in practice, quite different in this respect from 'direct perception'. Hence, there seems no basis even in the case of this small minority of exponents of the OT who do speak of the 'intuition' of objects, for the claim that 'it is objects that are given rather than sense-data'. We may reply to them that objects may indeed, if they are right, be revealed in a process of intuitive awareness, but they are still not given in the way that 'sense-data' are given. It is only the latter that can be 'directly perceived' for only they can be incorrigibly and certainly be perceived.

(II) OSTENSIBLE PHYSICAL OBJECTS AS THE GIVEN

This conclusion that we have reached is similar to the one arrived at by R. Firth as a result of his discussion of the claim that 'it is objects and not sense-data that are given in sense perception'. Firth reaches his conclusion primarily as the result of his contention that the Percept Theory which he defends[1] shows that not objects but only 'ostensible physical objects' are given. Hence he argues:

(1) If the claim is taken to mean that physical objects are 'directly presented' in sense perception, then this is simply a mistake which arises from a confusion between 'ostensible physical objects' and physical objects themselves. The Percept Theory shows only that 'ostensible physical objects', which are what is revealed by direct inspection of a single state of perceptual consciousness, are directly presented. But a physical object is something that transcends any one of the states which might be called a perception of it, and certain basic properties of physical objects such as durability are inaccessible to the direct inspection of a single perception.

(2) If the claim is interpreted to mean that what the ordinary man means when he says that the table is round is the same as what the philosopher means when he says that the 'ostensible physical object' is round, then again it is untrue. Even the ordinary man can distinguish on reflection between the 'ostensible physical object' and the physical object as such, as is evidenced by his ability to recognize an illusion.

(3) Of course, the claim that physical objects are given may mean that 'ostensible physical objects' are not 'ostensibly ostensible'. Strictly we cannot say that we are presented with '*ostensible* physical objects' because their ostensibility is not one of their presented characteristics. On the other hand it would be misleading to say,

[2] See above Chapter 4 (VIII).

because of this, that we are presented with physical objects, because truths about physical objects are not determinable by a single state of perception. This constitutes a terminological difficulty which may give rise to pseudo-problems.[1] And it may be in order to prevent such pseudo-problems that the assertion is made that physical objects are given, i.e. they are not ostensibly ostensible.

But, says Firth, if we confine ourselves to the epistemological view, it is quite permissible to say that we are presented with 'ostensible physical objects'. And from this point of view physical objects cannot be said to be given, whereas, according to the SDT, sense-data can.

What therefore emerges from Firth's discussion seems to be the conclusion that the only correct interpretation that can be given to the claim that 'objects are given and not sense-data' is that 'ostensible physical objects are given and not sense-data'.

But even if we allow for the legitimacy of a concept such as that of an 'ostensible physical object' (which we have already questioned)[2] it can still not be the case that Firth is right in supposing that sense-data and 'ostensible physical objects' could be given in the same sense. This is clearly demonstrated by H. H. Price's remarks in speaking of the quasi-intuitive nature of the awareness of objects. The notion of 'ostensible physical objects' (as Firth admits) is borrowed from Price who draws attention to the fact that from the first it is the complete material thing that we 'accept' or that 'ostends itself' to us.[3] Firth complains that it is a mystery to him how Price could admit this and still remain a supporter of the SDT. But Price makes it clear that the reason for rejecting the claim to intuition in our awareness of the object is due to the fact that we may be mistaken. The intuition of objects is not incorrigible.

Price's argument is plain enough and cannot be rejected, as Firth would reject it, as the introduction of irrevelent epistemological considerations. What it makes apparent is the fact that for the proponent of the SDT, the concept of the given includes as a defining quality the demand that its apprehension be certain and incorrigible. If this defining quality is to be used in demarcating the concept of 'ostensible physical objects', then the latter turn out

[1] *Mind* 1950, p. 47.
[1] See p. 73 above.
[3] H. H. Price *Perception*, pp. 151–2.

to be virtually identical with 'sense-data'. But if the quality of incorrigibility is not to be contained in the notion of givenness, then it is again clear that 'ostensible physical objects' cannot be given in the same sense in which sense-data have been claimed to be given.

Hence, it seems clear that supporters of the OT can never be meaning quite the same thing as supporters of the SDT when they use the expression 'the given'.

(III) DIFFERENT MEANINGS

The above conclusion gives rise to the thought that perhaps there is no problem at all regarding the nature of the given in sense-perception. And this may be regarded as confirmed by a closer examination which reveals that each theory is talking of 'the given' in quite a different sense.

It would be ridiculous to attempt to compile a list of everything that could possibly be meant by philosophers when they use the expression 'the given' with respect to sense-perception. However, there seem to be a few clearly distinguishable things which they could be intending to say, and which are relevant to our argument.

(1) The expression could be used to refer to that which comes temporarily first in perception. In this sense, 'the given' could indicate either that which we *in fact* perceive first in any case of perception, or else that which later examination shows to have been what we must have perceived first in perception. The latter possibility fits in very well with the Naive View of the dispute regarding the given, for it might be said that if later examination shows that we must have perceived something first in any case of perception, then in future we may be able to perceive this something first consciously since our eyes have been 'opened' to this fact.[1]

This sense of 'givenness' might be called the 'temporal sense'· In fairness to the IET it should have to be said that when we talk of 'that which we in fact perceive first in any case of perception', we do not necessarily mean that there is a 'we' to experience or a 'that'

---

[1] J. Lowenberg has distinguished between 'pre-analytic' and 'post-analytic' data. But it is not clear that he would have agreed that the latter could subsequently be actually perceived as given.

which is experienced. We mean simply that perception begins chronologically with a certain 'givenness'.

(2) The expression 'the given' could also be used to mean that the perception of which is indubitable, which could not possibly be mistakenly perceived. What is given within perception in this sense, which we may call the 'noetic sense', would be that part of what is perceived in any case of perception about which there could be no mistake. We might mis-describe it, but we could not mis-perceive it. The 'noetic sense' of givenness in fact suggests that describing what we see is quite different from perceiving it.

(3) Another meaning which the expression 'the given' could be used to convey is that of being logically or 'analytically' primary. In this sense what is given in sense-perception need not at any time have occurred first; nor does later inspection have to show that it occurred *first in time* (i.e. in the 'temporal sense'). All that is meant in saying of something that it is given in sense-perception in this sense, which we may call the 'post-analytical sense', is that the occurrence of sense-perception implies that this something must have happened, and that nothing else in the perception could have taken place unless the givenness of the given had been a factor.

(4) The expression could also be used to mean that something is 'directly present', in the sense that the perception of it does not involve an inference or any other sort of intellectual process such as abstraction, intuitive induction, or the passage from sign to significate. This is to say more than that what is given provides a premise or ground for any subsequent inference, or intellectual process, for in this latter sense there can be many things given which need not be 'directly perceived', e.g. the data of the historian. To be 'directly perceived' and hence given in the present sense, which we may call the 'non-inferential sense', what is presented in sense-perception must not itself be the result of any previous inference or intellectual process. (5) We may distinguish, finally, a usage of the expression 'the given' according to which only that which is completely revealed at the instant of perception can be regarded as given. We may call this the 'instantaneous sense' of the expression 'the given'.

We have, therefore, briefly, distinguished 'givenness' in the following five senses:

(1) Temporal givenness,

(2) Noetical givenness,
(3) Post-analytical givenness,
(4) Non-inferential givenness,
(5) Instantaneous givenness.

It may be argued that some of these forms of givenness really imply each other, e.g. (2), (4), and (5). But whether this is so or not requires proof and is not capable of being simply assumed from the outset.

(IV) CROSS PURPOSES

Though the above list of possible meanings that could be given to the expression 'the given' is not necessarily exhaustive, it is quite sufficient to enable us to demonstrate that the three theories regarding the nature of 'the given' are at cross-purposes and cannot be said to be arguing with each other about the nature of the given in sense-perception in the simple manner suggested by the Naive View.

The fundamental points which the SDT has wished to assert in claiming that sense-data are given, are that these are non-inferentially (4), noetically (2), instantaneously (5), and post-analytically given (3). Particular stress seems to have been laid on the non-inferential, noetical, and instantaneous aspects. But his position does not necessarily commit the upholder of the SDT to the view that it is the sense-datum which comes temporarily first in perception (temporal givenness), even though there have in fact been supporters of the SDT who have held this view as well. In earlier expositions this was in fact the usual view. But nowadays most supporters of the SDT would agree that the awareness of physical objects might be chronologically contemporaneous with the sensing of the 'sense-datum'. If we were therefore to try to offer a rough definition of 'the given' as understood by the SDT, this might run as follows: 'The given in any situation where perception takes place is that which is wholly revealed to the observer at the instant of perception in such a way as to be directly and non-inferentially present and incapable of being mis-perceived.'

It will now be easy to confirm that the OT means something quite different when it talks of objects as being 'the given'. Objects are by no means indubitably perceived; we are perfectly capable of being mistaken in our perception of them. Nor are they wholly revealed to us at the instant of perception. Nor can it be said that supporters of the OT are necessarily committed to the view that objects are post-analytically given (3). A supporter of the OT might agree that objects are what are perceived first in time, usually, at any rate, and are, therefore, temporally given (1). But this is not the main thing he is trying to assert when he says that objects are 'the given' in sense-perception. What he is positively trying to assert becomes, indeed, a little problematic. He *may* be trying to assert that objects are non-inferentially given (4). This is certainly what some supporters of the OT (e.g. Alexander and D. M. Armstrong) seem to be trying to stress. But others (notably Laird and Dawes-Hicks) are certainly not committed to this view. The claim that objects are given seems primarily intended to *deny* the claim that sense-data are given. Hence it is difficult to offer any rough definition of the sense in which the OT is using the expression 'the given'. The following may serve as a try: 'The given in any case of perception is that which is first perceived by the observer in such a way as to be directly or non-inferentially present.'

On the other hand, when the IET speaks of 'the given', it is clear that what is stressed is the temporal and logical priority of 'immediate experience' in any cognitive situation. Supporters of the IET might agree that, in a manner of speaking, 'immediate experience' was incapable of being mistaken; and they would certainly agree that it was non-inferentially or directly present, since it is part of their doctrine that all judgment consists of discrimination. Thus we may say that for the IET the given may roughly be defined as: 'that which is non-inferentially present, temporarily first and logically primary in any situation where perception takes place.'

Thus the one thing which all three theories may be said to mean in common when they talk of something being given is that this something is non-inferentially present. It is possible that they also all intend to say that this something is logically or post-analytically given as well, but this is not so certain. For the rest they all lay down different specifications before they will agree to say that something is given.

I can imagine someone at this stage protesting as follows: 'Surely all this analysis only goes to show the direct opposite of what you wish to demonstrate? You wanted to demonstrate that there was no argument as to the nature of the given. Yet your own analysis has shown that the three theories are arguing about what it is that is non-inferentially present in any situation where perception takes place. Moreover this is exactly the sort of dispute which what you called the Naive View suggests, and which you alleged was a misrepresentation of what was actually happening in this argument as to the nature of the given.'

I should like the reader to ask himself two questions at this point: (a) are the three theories mutually incompatible? and (b) are they in each case the same considerations which lead the respective theorists to assert what they do about the character of the given?

(a) I think that if the reader ponders upon this question for a moment he will see that there is in principle no reason why there should not be many things given in sense-perception. Why should there not be *several* things that are all non-inferentially or directly present? Though the supporter of the SDT may be ever so insistent in his assertion that sense-data are what is given, is there anything which really compels him to deny that objects and 'immediate-experience' may be non-inferentially present as well? Surely not. And it is interesting to recall that where certain well-known SDT-ists (such as Broad, Price, Stout, and Ewing) have been hesitant about calling the remainder of the situation in which perceptual awareness takes place a process of inference in any ordinary sense (because there seem to be no discoverable steps in the inference, it seems to be instantaneous, etc.) they incline to say, as Price says quite explicitly, that we know of objects by 'perceptual acquaintance', that we all naturally 'take' the sense-datum to be an object, that we all 'instinctively believe' that what we see is an object, or that the object is 'immediately known' by thought. What prevents them from saying outright that objects are given *as well as* sense-data? Are they not in effect coming near to saying that objects are non-inferentially present in perception?

Another indication that there is nothing which compels us to say that there is only one thing that is given, is the fact that there are some Absolute Idealists, who naturally would tend in the direction of the IET, who none-the-less give a qualified approval to the SDT. There would, therefore, seem to be no contradiction involved, in principle at any rate, in maintaining that both 'immediate experience' and 'sense-data' are directly presented.

Again the reader may object as follows: 'Doesn't the fact that there is no particular reason for the respective theorists to deny each other's claims and yet they do so, tend to show that the Naive View of their dispute is correct? There is no reason why the SDT supporter should say that only sense-data are given, that is, non-inferentially present in perception, except that he *sees* it so. Nor is there any reason why the OT theorists should maintain that only objects are given except that he sees it so. And the same applies to the exponent of the IET.'

But I should reply that on the contrary the fact that all theories are in principle compatible while the theorists nonetheless insist on pressing the claims of their own theory and deny all the rest, shows that when they speak of 'the given' they do *not* mean merely to indicate that which is non-inferentially present in any case of sense-perception. For if one considers the terms 'non-inferentially' or 'directly' present, one can readily see, as in fact some of our previous discussions have already indicated, that this term is by no means exact and unambiguous. It is a technical term concerning the usage of which there is no agreement among philosophers. How are we then to be able to decide, simply by inspection, whether something is or is not 'non-inferentially present'?

(b) This brings us to our second question. In stating the Naive View with regard to the dispute about the given in sense-perception, I have continually spoken of the theoretical considerations which might serve to open the eyes of philosophers to what it is that is really given in perception. But are these considerations in fact the same considerations which give rise to each of the three theories? Examination reveals that the considerations which bring respective theorists to their views regarding the given are in each case different.

The theoretical considerations which allegedly draw the proponent of the SDT to the realization that the given in sense-perception is a 'sense-datum' are the existence of such phenomena as changing appearances, illusions, hallucinations, etc. But the considerations which lead proponents of the IET to the insight that it is 'immediate experience' which is given are, by Bradley's own admission, the 'dissatisfaction' and 'uneasiness' which the intellect feels with regard to the adequacy of ordinary objects of common-sense to give expression to the full perceptual experience at any moment. As for the OT, it is not at all clear that there are any positive considerations which lead its proponents to say that what are given are 'objects'; their motive seems to be mainly negative, namely, to deny certain implications of the SDT.

Thus the considerations which bring respective theorists to the re-examination of their perceptual experience, which is alleged by the Naive View to take place, are different in each case. If we examine the three theories of the given solely from the point of view of the considerations which have prompted their formulation, we shall be able to confirm that each theory must give quite a different meaning to the technical expression 'non-inferentially present'.[1]

(v) THE NON-INFERENTIALLY PRESENT

In view of the considerations which have prompted the formulation of the SDT, it is no accident that its supporters stress the fact that the given in perception must be what we have called 'noetically given'. Since their concern is to analyse sense-perception in such a way as to explain the phenomena of changing appearances, illusions, and hallucinations, the tendency is quite naturally to look for something in perception which is incapable of being doubted, concerning which there could be no mistakes, and which would serve as the basis of all the illusions and mistakes which do occur. These theorists are assuming that the phenomena of changing appearances, illusions, etc., insofar as they give rise to real perceptual error, do so solely because of mistaken inferences. Since they are not ready to regard perception as just an act of judgment, they are looking for a residue, over and above the interpretation which they admit to be involved in any case of perception, which is both non-inferentially present and incapable of being misperceived. If it were capable of being misperceived then it would seem that this must be on account of an erroneous interpretation which is involved. Since, therefore, this theorist is looking for a given which is both non-inferentially present as well as incapable of being misperceived, he believes he must disqualify objects, for though

[1] Note that the word 'inference' is used here initially in a very vague and undefined manner. It does not designate any particular intellectual process nor even a process that is necessarily connected with thinking. It may even include bodily dispositions or reflexes which are produced when the observer perceives something presented. Its use here is meant to be neutral with respect to the issue between the Causal Theory, Phenomenalism, etc.

these may seem to be non-inferentially present, they are not incapable of being misperceived. Again he refuses to consider the claim of 'immediate experience' because this does not seem to help him to explain the possibility of changing appearances, illusions, and so on. Moreover just because he is looking for an element in perception which is both indubitable and non-inferentially present, he regards inference as something which proceeds from the indubitable to that which is corrigible. So that now he even refuses to recognize that objects can be non-inferentially present at all, since objects are not incorrigibly perceived, and are, on the contrary, very liable to be misperceived.[1]

Thus it comes about that when proponents of the SDT feel qualms about saying that objects are arrived at by 'inference', in the strict and narrow sense, they are nevertheless reluctant to say that objects are given. They persist in maintaining that objects must somehow be arrived at by a sort of vague 'inference', such as a 'quasi-belief', a bodily adjustment to the sensing of sense-data, etc. They will never go to the length of reinstating objects as being 'non-inferentially present', for the perception of objects is corrigible, whereas incorrigibility is for them a necessary factor, part of the very meaning of the phrase 'non-inferential presence'. Thus they maintain that objects can never be given, and as such it is natural for them to adopt the view that our general conception of physical objects and the belief in the existence of a physical object corresponding to any particular sense-datum is always subject to *justification*, whereas the belief in the existence of a present 'sense-datum', which the SDT has introduced as the indubitable non-inferential element which will serve to analyse sense-perception, is never subject to any call for justification

In similar fashion, the proponent of the IET, because he is trying to supplement the 'unsatisfactoriness' of objects and to give a 'complete' account of the *whole* of what is perceived at any moment of perception, turns to the perceptual situation at its temporal origin, since he feels that it is where perception is not yet fully developed that he is likely to deal with it in its entirety. At the point where cognition is just beginning, the IET-ist finds only organic sensations which he associates with 'feeling'. And since in this

[1] The line of reasoning outlined in this paragraph is mirrored to some extent in H. H. Price's *Perception*, pp. 150–6.

feeling there is as yet no discrimination (since, as a matter of fact, cognition has not yet properly begun), the theorist supposes that this 'feeling' must be an undiscriminated or 'felt whole', a 'blur', within which, with the natural growth of cognition, there will emerge discriminations and relations. It is this, then, that the IET will agree to recognize as 'given', because this is a non-inferential presence which encompasses the *whole* of the cognitive situation, since, strictly, it exists where the cognitive situation has not yet developed. Both sense-data and objects, therefore, even if they were non-inferentially present in sense-perception would not meet the purposes of the IET. And since his conception of 'a whole of feeling' that is first, both temporally and logically, induces him to think of cognition as the successive discrimination of details within this whole of feeling, the IET-ist will now even be inclined to argue that neither sense-data nor objects *can* be non-inferentially present, since they are objects of thought and their presence is thus the result of discrimination within the primitive whole of feeling which he calls 'immediate experience'.

The purpose of the proponent of the OT, we shall assume, is mainly negative. On the one hand he is unwilling to accept the initial assumptions of the SDT that (a) misperception must always be the result of faulty interpretation since perception as such cannot be mistaken, and yet that (b) acts of perception are not merely acts of interpretation or judgment. On the other hand, he probably sees no reason for the IET's 'dissatisfaction' with the objects of common-sense, and no reason to go back, logically or temporally to a pre-cognitive state of feeling. So that the OT-ist finds himself with no special inclination to interpret 'inference' as necessarily involving the passage from incorrigible data to corrigible perceptual beliefs, or as necessarily involving the passage from a unity of feeling to a 'many' of thought. And thus he has no reason to disqualify objects for the title of being 'non-inferentially present', since objects do not seem to be reached by an intellectual process involving the passage from premises to conclusion, sign to significate, etc. Awareness of them, as has generally been admitted (even by Price), is 'quasi-intuitive'. And the fact that we may make mistakes in perceiving them does not mean that they are not non-inferentially present, for incorrigibility is not regarded by the OT as a necessary feature of non-inferential presence.

So that it seems clear that each theory does indeed mean something different when it uses the expression 'the given'. And the fact that all the theories appear to agree that one of the factors included in something's being given is its non-inferential or direct presence turns out to be of no significance. This is so because, as we have seen, if we try to relate each theory with the 'theoretical considerations' which have led to its formulation, we find that in each case a different criterion is being used in order to establish whether 'inference' is or is not present.

The three theories, then, are at cross-purposes. Each arises as an attempt to answer a different challenge. And if the expression 'the given' means something different in each case, then I claim to have established my assertion that there is no problem as to the nature of 'the given' in sense-perception. There is no one central concept, 'the given', about whose meaning everyone is agreed but concerning the nature of which there is a dispute among three rival theories. There are only three theories, at cross-purposes with one another, each making use, for needs of its own, of the expression 'the given', and thus naturally misleading everyone into supposing that we have here three attempts by philosophers at a more accurate reformulation of the facts of perception revealed to direct inspection.

(VI) THAT THERE IS A PROBLEM

Let me now try to explain why I think that it must nevertheless be said that there *is* a problem regarding the nature of the given in sense-perception.

I readily admit that if all three theories are using the expression 'the given' in a somewhat different sense, there cannot be a problem of finding out what the given is. In other words, if 'the given' means something different in each case, one cannot speak of a single concept, 'the given', and various reports as to its nature. I therefore conclude that the Naive View as to the nature of the dispute, which certainly implies that there is a problem in precisely this way (i.e. a single concept 'the given' and rival reports as to its nature) is in error. In this respect there certainly is no problem as to the nature of the given.

But we must consider, if what we have been saying is the whole truth about the matter, why it should be the case that the exponents of the different theories regard themselves as being involved in an argument. It is undeniable that Bradley pits his theory of 'immediate experience' against both the SDT and the OT.[1] And it is as plain as daylight that defenders of the SDT and the OT consider themselves to be very much at loggerheads. What is more, not only is it the case that the theorists themselves think they are arguing with each other, but it can also not be denied that, in spite of everything we have said, there does seem to be some genuine point at issue between them. This is why the Naive View as to the nature of their dispute, erroneous and misleading though it may be, seems so very plausible and seductive. Say what one likes, it is difficult to avoid the impression that the different views about the given are somehow genuine alternatives to each other. If so, there must be some substance to the argument between them. What then is the point at issue?

Our analysis has revealed that all three theories would agree that 'non-inferential presence' is one of the factors that is involved in determining whether something is or is not given in any case of perception. We saw, however, that each theory was using a different criterion for establishing what was inferential, and what was not inferential. This criterion in fact seemed to depend on the other factors that each theory would regard as being necessarily involved in determining whether something was given or not.

This state of affairs is very suggestive. It may be that if we are to make any sense of the fact that the different theories of the given appear to be at issue, we should be able to do so by showing that the dispute as to the nature of the given in sense-perception takes place within a context in which the different concepts of what inference is assume a special significance.

It is not at all difficult to see that each of the theories of the given is laying stress on one aspect of what is involved in the perceiving of things at the expense and perhaps to the detriment of the other aspects. It will now be our concern to try to establish that this emphasis is due, in each case, to the influence of certain broad concepts, models, and analogies, which provide a background to each of the respective claims regarding the given.

---

[1] See above Chapter 2 (II)

Chapter 7

MAKING OR FINDING
THE FACTS

———————

(I) THE NATURE OF THOUGHT:
CORRESPONDENCE AND COHERENCE

An initial suggestion as to some of the broader implications involved in the dispute regarding the nature of the given in sense-perception is provided by a brief glance at another of the contexts in which an argument regarding the question of 'the given' occurs. This is the controversy between the Correspondence and Coherence theories of truth. Examination will show that this controversy is connected with the question of the relationship between 'Knowledge' or 'Thought' and 'Reality', i.e. with the problem of 'the nature of thought'.

It is very interesting to note that the argument between these theories of truth which, after being one of the primary areas of interest to epistemologists in the first quarter of this century, came to be regarded subsequently by many philosphers as a blind alley,[1] has been revived once more by leading contemporary philosophers.[2] I shall have a little to say here about this argument in its modern form, but I am interested more in the older form of the dispute, for it was there that the issue between the Correspondence and Coherence theories of truth was formulated as the question whether or not there are any 'given facts'. Even this earlier phase of the dispute, which was carried on so acrimoniously, turned out to be extremely complicated and tortuous, on occasion, and so I cannot undertake to say any more than a few words here about the matter. The whole topic is in any case not directly connected with the argument of this book, and I refer to it only to gain certain corroborative

---

[1] Such as F. P. Ramsey, *Foundations of Mathematics* (London, Kegan Paul, 1931) pp. 142–3; A. J. Ayer, *Language, Truth and Logic* (London, Gollancz, 1936), etc.
[2] Such as L. J. Austin, F. P. Strawson, G. J. Warnock and others in various papers.

evidence regarding the issues involved when things are said to be 'given'.

(II) THE GIVEN FACTS

That true statements are those which correspond with the facts seems to be one of the most obvious of observations. Yet Coherence Theorists have argued that this formula is very obscure and plainly inadequate as a summary of what is involved in arriving at a true judgment. Even historical judgments, which are supposed to be one of the clearest examples of truth depending on correspondence with the facts of the past, turn out to depend for their truth on coherence with the body of our historical and social knowledge. Thus in the statement that 'Caesar crossed the Rubicon', our test of its historical accuracy will depend upon its connection with vast numbers of further judgments that we are compelled to make when we investigate the sources. And the same applies to even the simplest judgments of perception. Take the case of 'this is a dog', offered as a true judgment which happens to be true. There is no 'solid chunk of fact' which acts as the test of its truth. To recognize what we see as a dog is a considerable intellectual achievement involving much discrimination. Only by seeing how the statement fits in with all the other statements which are ascertainable regarding the situation can we be sure that it is a true statement.

There are, therefore, no 'given facts' in judgments of perception, or anywhere else, according to H. H. Joachim[1], and his view is echoed in Strawson's claim[2] that facts are 'pseudo-objects' and that Austin's kind of talk about them[3] involves a fundamental mistake. Strawson argues that facts, as opposed to particular things, cannot be dated or located; to speak of them would be merely a short hand way of expressing what might otherwise require a long chain of assertive sentences. We must be careful not to 'objectify' them and turn them into eternal objects, somehow timelessly present. Strawson suggests that those who speak of given facts in such a way as to make truth depend on 'the correspondence between statement

---

[1] H. H. Joachim, *The Nature of Truth*, (Oxford, Clarendon Press, 1906); see also P. Blanshard, *The Nature of Thought* (London, Allen & Unwin, 1939) Vol. 2.

[2] F. P. Strawson, 'Truth', *Analysis* 1949; 'Truth', *Proc. Arist. Soc.* XXIV 1950; 'Truth: A Reconsideration of Austin's Views', *Philosophical Quarterly*, 1965.

[3] L. J. Austin, 'Truth', *Proc. Arist. Soc.* XXIV 1950; 'Unfair to Facts', 1954. Both included in *Philosophical Papers* (Oxford, Clarendon Press, 1961).

and fact' have been misled by thinking of a statement as *describing* that which makes it true in the way in which a descriptive predicate may be used to describe, or a referring expression to refer to, a thing. The statement 'the monarch is deceased' is not related to anything (facts, states of affairs, etc.) in the way in which the expression 'the monarch' is related to the monarch.

R. M. Chisholm has pointed out[1] that Strawson's case against facts depends upon his ability to show precisely how talk about facts is merely an abbreviation for statements about things, and he doubts whether Strawson, Brentano or anyone else has ever been able to construct an adequate way of talking about the things in the world which does not involve reference to such things as 'facts' or 'states of affairs'. Certainly Austin has noted that to suppose that a fact is a 'pseudo-entity' is to treat a wholesome English expression as though it were a philosopher's invented expression. As Chisholm says, the situation is analogous to that of the phenomenalist, who has to show how a wholesome expression such as 'an object' can really be only an abbreviated way of talking about 'appearances'.

Now it is not clear at all that Strawson would wish to throw in his lot with the Coherence Theory of truth. But his rejection of 'given facts' is certainly reminiscent of the earlier arguments of the Coherence Theorists, and the argument between Austin and Strawson could well be summarized as the argument whether there are or are not 'given facts'. A revealing insight into the sort of motives which lead to the assertion or denial of the 'givenness' of facts is afforded by the discussion of the question whether knowing affects what is known.

(III) DOES KNOWING MAKE A DIFFERENCE TO WHAT IS KNOWN?

One of the assumptions that Coherence Theorists alleged to be involved in the Correspondence Theory is that 'experiencing makes no difference to the facts'. The truth or falsity of this assumption was discussed in an absorbingly interesting exchange of notes and articles between H. H. Joachim, Bertrand Russell and G. E. Moore in 1906 and 1907.[2] The same issue has been re-opened in contem-

[1] R. M. Chisholm, 'J. L. Austin's Philosophical Papers' *Mind* LXXIII 1964.
[2] *Mind* volumes XV and XVI.

porary discussion by A. Donagan's defence of the Cook-Wilsonian
Realist position that 'what is known exists independently of being
known' against the criticisms of R. G. Collingwood. But whereas the
recent discussion has concentrated on the logical analysis of a particular argument used by Collingwood, the dispute at the beginning
of the Century was more revealing since it laid bare some of the
metaphysical issues which were involved.

According to Joachim[1] the Moore-Russell position with regard to
truth rested entirely on the dogmatic assumption that 'experiencing
makes no difference to the facts', and his chief arguments against
this assumption were firstly, that no relations are purely external,
and secondly, that if it were correct the fact that anything ever is
experienced would be a 'miraculous coincidence'. Actually both
arguments were interlocking, but it is worthwhile to consider them
separately for the moment. Let us consider the second point first:

(1) If the facts are independent of experiencing, then in the
perception of a thing which is green, 'greenness' is independent of
our experiencing it. It is 'an ultimate entity which has its being
absolutely in itself'. How it can depart from its 'sacred aloofness'
and be apprehended, and how its 'immaculate *perseitas*' is still
preserved, are, claims Joachim, questions to which apparently the
only answer is the dogmatic reiteration of the supposed fact 'it is
so'.[2] Joachim's objection seems to be that if the facts are independent
of experience, they cannot be experienced, and nothing at all can be
known. This is just a particular example of a general argument of
the form 'if A is independent of B, A cannot be related to B', and
this latter argument formulates the doctrine of 'internal relations'.
(2) Joachim, Russell and Moore all agree that their controversy
is bound up with the question of 'internal relations'. Moore urges
that if no relations are external then the facts are dependent on the
experience of particular individuals, to whom they are 'internally
related' at the time of their perception, quite as much as they
depend upon experiencing in general. But would this not make all
communication impossible?[3] Joachim appreciates the force of this,
and replies that in loose and popular language facts may be said to be

[1] *The Nature of Truth*, p. 39.
[2] ibid., p. 42.
[3] 'Mr Joachim's "The Nature of Truth"', *Mind* XVI, 1907, pp. 229-35.

externally related with any particular *individual's* experiencing of
them. When we extract the assertion 'A is B' from the situation in
which it is asserted and apply it 'correctly' to another situation, we
have only a coincidence of co-existing elements which we have
selected out of the entirety of things and grouped together. These
bundles of co-existents are 'one' or a 'whole' by courtesy only, or,
at most, insofar as they are associated in our thoughts.

It is obvious that Joachim's conception of internal relations relies
on his notion of 'a genuine whole', i.e. he maintains that a plurality
of absolutely independent simple elements cannot constitute a
'genuine unity'. If the relation really unites and constitutes one
thing in place of two, he argues, the relata thus united cannot be
absolutely independent, but must be inter-dependent features of a
whole. If on the other hand, the relation really is 'external', with
the two there is now conjoined a *third* thing, the relation. But the
two are no more genuinely one than the contents of a waste-paper
basket.[1] In calling them 'interdependent', Joachim means to imply,
therefore, that the two factors are not really two at all, but merely
distinguishable as two by being 'cut out' of a single unity. Thus in
any complex which forms a genuine unity, only the whole complex
is real, and the constituents are not.

When the issue between them is reduced to this, all the dispu-
tants become very pessimistic about the possibility of coming to an
agreement. Joachim says that in the hands of Russell and Moore,
the assumption that 'experiencing makes no difference to the
facts' gets established by a kind of ontological proof. Russell finds
this unsatisfactory, but in the end admits that arguments for and
against will only appear cogent to those who already admit the
conclusions which the argument sets out to prove. This state of
affairs seems to render the progress of philosophy almost hopeless.
Indeed, at first sight, it does seem very discouraging that philosophical arguments should be reduced to the attempt to communi-
cate rival insights such as, for example, whether the world is or is
not a 'genuine unity'. Moore at first thinks this unduly pessimistic,
and offers three carefully-phrased propositions which he asks
Joachim to say outright whether he accepts or denies. But Joachim
objects to the implication that he must either accept these propo-

[1] 'A Reply to Mr Moore', *Mind* XVI, 1907, p. 412.

sitions as absolutely true or reject them as absolutely false. Meta-physics, he insists, does not allow of simple 'yes' or 'no' answers. By denying Moore's three propositions, with reservations, Joachim leaves the dispute in an indecisive situation.

(IV) FINDING OR MAKING?

It is interesting to observe how integral a part of the argument between the Correspondence and Coherence theories are the analogies that are involved in deciding whether knowing is after all more like finding or like making. Thus even the most extreme Coherence theorists admit the existence of the relation between judgment and reality to which the Correspondence theory draws attention.[1] 'Truth, to be true, must be true of something, and this something itself is not truth. This obvious view I endorse.'[2] What turns out to be at stake is whether the notion of 'correspondence' adequately characterizes the significance of this relation. The Idealists and Coherence Theorists stress the fact that judgments do not simply *copy* reality, but also *represent* it. The more they actually possess of truth, the more they can take the place of the real, as containing in themselves more of its nature. Thus the relation of judgment to reality does not hold between a particular mental event, or a proposition, or a statement, and a real fact, but between a one-sided aspect of reality and reality as a whole. According to the Coherence Theorists this relation cannot correctly be described as 'correspondence'. Instead it is likened, by one of its more recent exponents[3] to the relationship which obtains between a seed and a flower, or between a sapling and a tree; in other words, between something whose purpose is partially fulfilled and something whose purpose is completely fulfilled. Thought *is* its object realized imperfectly, and a system of thought is true just so far as it succeeds in embodying that end which thought in its very essence is seeking to embody. To call this 'correspondence' is misleading, for the word suggests a view as to the relation between thought and reality which Coherence Theorists are concerned to deny.

[1] A. C. Ewing points this out in his *Idealism* (London, Methuen, 1933) p. 200.
[2] F. H. Bradley, *Essays on Truth and Reality*, (Oxford, Clarendon Press, 1914) p. 235.
[3] P. Blanshard, *The Nature of Thought* (London: Allen & Unwin, 1939) Vol. 2. p. 273.

So it becomes more apparent that the issue between Coherence and Correspondence theorists is basically an issue between two rival views as to the relation between thought and reality. According to the Coherence Theory, to think is to seek understanding, and to seek understanding is to achieve systematic vision, and so to apprehend what is now unknown to us as to relate it necessarily to what we know already. We think to solve problems; and our method of solving problems is to build a bridge of intelligible relations from the 'continent' of our knowledge to the 'island' we wish to include in it. When we have achieved this systematic vision in our knowledge then our thought must be true of reality.[1] We must get rid of such misleading analogies as 'copy and original', 'stimulus and organism', 'lantern and screen'—all of which are suggested by the term 'correspondence'—because these assume that the facts and our experiencing of them are related externally, whereas thought and reality are really internally related. To think of the thing is to get that thing itself to some degree within the mind; thought is related to reality as the partial fulfilment is to the complete fulfilment of a purpose. Thought has two ends, one immanent the other transcendent. On the one hand it seeks fulfilment in a special kind of satisfaction, the satisfaction of systematic vision; on the other hand it seeks fulfilment in its object. These ends are really one: reflection always assumes that the satisfaction of its own immanent end is not only satisfying, but revealing. That these two processes are really one is, according to Blanshard, the metaphysical base on which the belief in Coherence is founded. Reality is a system, completely ordered and fully intelligible, with which thought in its advance is more and more identifying itself.

'Truth is the approximation of thought to reality. It is thought on its own way home. Its measure is the distance thought has travelled under the guidance of its inner compass, toward the intelligible system which unites its ultimate object with its ultimate end. Hence at any given time the degree of truth in our experience as a whole is the degree of system it has achieved. The degree of truth of a particular proposition is to be judged in the first instance by its coherence with experience as a whole, ultimately with its coherence with that further whole, all-comprehensive

[1] ibid., p. 261.

and fully articulated, in which thought, can come to rest'.[1]

Reflection confirms that all this is merely a newer version of what Bradley must have meant when he maintained that relational thought consisted of discrimination within our 'immediate experience', and that the first discrimination which emerged was that between the self and its objects, the basis of the common-sense view of the world. Thought, by nature relational, sought to reattain relationally that unity out of which it sprung. Thought was a system of truths in their relations to one another. The truth of any particular judgment depended upon its coherence within the system, but the extent to which this system as a whole satisfied depended on its not con-flicting or jarring with the felt background out of which it had arisen. The aim of thought was to give expression, ever more systematically, to the whole of this felt background of 'immediate experience'. But to gain complete satisfaction it would have to reinclude those felt aspects of 'immediate experience' which, as thought, it had deliberately left out. So that the complete satis-faction of thought could only be attained when thought passed beyond itself and re-united with 'immediate experience' in the achievement of the 'Absolute Experience'.

It seems clear when one studies this aspect of the Coherence Theory, that the fundamental issue between those who hold up the relation of 'correspondence' as being the essential of truth, and those who, while admitting the existence of some such relation, insist that truth's essential feature is the 'coherence' of any particular true statement with the whole body of our systematic knowledge, is one concerned with the relation between thought and reality. The Correspondence theorists are implicitly committed to the 'copy and original' analogy, whereas the Coherence theorists support 'the sapling and tree' analogy (though perhaps Bradley himself would have preferred a different model).

It is to be noted, too, that the Coherence Theory becomes much more comprehensible when the idea of 'immediate experience', or something of the sort is used to complement it. We thus have an indication that the IET may be connected with the sort of view concerning the nature of thought expounded at length by Blanshard in his work.

[1]ibid. p. 264.

Making or Finding the Facts

(v) ayer's view

This interim observation will already enable us to say a few words about an historic over-simplification concerning the issues between the Correspondence and Coherence Theories of truth. I have already mentioned the fact that for a period during this century, the whole question of the different theories of truth was regarded by many as a misleading pseudo-issue. An irenic explanation of what the whole argument was about was offered, in this connection, by A. J. Ayer.

Ayer's view was stated at length in his famous book *Language, Truth, and Logic* (Chapter 5), and neatly summed up in an article on the 'The Criterion of Truth',[1] which was intended as a reply to the interesting difference of opinion between Moritz Schlick and a group of 'Logical Positivists' known as 'Physicalists'. Schlick had insisted, in opposition to the Physicalists, that the truth of a system of synthetic propositions did not consist merely in the freedom of the system from self-contradiction, but rather in its agreement with reality.

After quoting with approval F. P. Ramsey's statement that 'there is really no separate problem of truth but merely a linguistic muddle',[2] and interpreting this to mean that since 'truth' and 'falsehood' are not genuine concepts, there can be no logical problem concerning the nature of truth, Ayer went on to suggest that the theories of truth should be regarded as misleading attempts to answer the genuine empirical question 'How are propositions actually validated?' Schlick was to be interpreted as saying, correctly, that people accepted a synthetic proposition as true only if it asserted that certain sensations would occur in a given set of circumstances, and these sensations did occur. But this did not mean that propositions recording direct observations were certain or unalterable. The statement 'I am in pain' was not valid on account of its form alone.

Ayer's suggestion that theories of truth are merely confused attempts to say how propositions are actually validated seems to be extremely inadequate. I think Ayer had not tried sufficiently to understand Schlick's insistence that he was a 'genuine empiricist'.

[1] *Analysis* vol. 3 (1935–6), pp. 28–32.
[2] *Foundations of Mathematics*, pp. 142–3.

What this meant, I think, is that Schlick wished to affirm the view that cognition is more like 'finding' than like 'making', that there is a 'given' in knowledge. The argument between Schlick and the Physicalists is merely a version of the argument between the Correspondence and Coherence theories of truth. Though Schlick would probably have rejected the charge that he was adopting a 'metephysical' position with respect to the problem of 'the nature of thought', it remains true that Schlick would have found the analogy of 'copy and original' more congenial to his outlook than any analogy that is associated with the Coherence Theory.

In fact Schlick's claim shows quite clearly how closely the issue between the Correspondence and Coherence Theories of truth is connected with the problem of 'the nature of thought'. That this issue of 'the nature of thought' is also involved in the question of the nature of the given in sense-perception seems also to be indicated. Both areas of dissension involve the throwing of different emphases on certain undisputed facts about knowledge, and these emphases are connected with rival theories as to 'the nature of thought'. In attempting, therefore, to clarify the issues in the dispute as to the nature of the given in sense-perception, and evaluating the appeal to the given in this area, we shall perhaps incidentally be throwing light on the argument between the Correspondence and Coherence Theories of truth.

Chapter 8

THOUGHT AND COGNITION

(I) DIFFERENT VIEWS OF COGNITION

We have seen that although each theory of the given claims as a distinguishing characteristic of what is given that it must be non-inferentially present, each theory has a different way of deciding whether something is or is not non-inferentially present. In other words, each theory means something different when it talks about 'inference', and these different conceptions of inference are connected with the interests which brought each theory into existence.

If we press the implications in the case of each of the theories of the given just a little further, we shall be able to extract a fairly clear picture of the way, in each case, in which thought is regarded as participating in perception. These three pictures may be called, respectively: (1) The Interpreter View, (2) The Constructor View, and (3) The Spectator View.

(II) THE INTERPRETER VIEW

In the SDT, the knowledge that we have about objects is held to be mediated knowledge, whereas the awareness of sense-data is regarded as yielded by immediate cognition. The expressions 'mediate' and 'immediate' signify only that there has or has not been some thought process involved. Thus in achieving our knowledge of what happens in the world of objects, thinking plays an indispensible part in converting the 'raw' data of our immediate awareness into a knowledge of objects. How has this process of thinking taken place?

The simplest way of regarding the matter would be that the thinking (or 'inference') by which the mind converted its acquaintance of sense-data into knowledge concerning the world of objects, is a literal thought process which takes time and some small effort. This is the Discursive Inference Theory[1]. What happens according

[1] R. Firth, 'Sense-Data and the Percept Theory', *Mind* 1949 and 1950.

to this view, is that the mind first becomes aware of some datum or data, then sets to work thinking, and offers an interpretation which is formulated in a statement asserting what it is that is known. But this theory has weaknesses which have led to its almost universal abandonment by present day philosophers. It seems to contradict the plain fact that no time elapses between the awareness of a datum and our perceptual consciousness of the object to which it belongs. We are neither conscious of any thought process, nor is there any effort involved. Helmholtz insisted that thought process must nevertheless be present, and that perhaps one is not conscious of inferring only because it is done so quickly. But this defence has not seemed very plausible to most of the supporters of the SDT. H. H. Price has summarized[1] some of the approaches developed by philosophers as alternatives to the Discursive Inference Theory:

Some have said that our perceptual knowledge of physical objects is not, in fact, reached by any thought process at all, but simply by some intuition which, however, may be *defended* by discursive inference. But others are suspicious of this, arguing that it would be most likely that a defence of the conclusions would simply be a reconstruction of the actual inference process which led to them. Another approach known as the Causal Theory maintains that past inferences based on causal arguments have established the inductive generalization that whenever a given sense-datum exists, a corresponding object exists too. We now apply this generalization mechanically to all similar sense-data which come along. Sense-data have now become signs of objects. According to this account, knowledge of physical objects could be justified by reference to the original inductive generalization which is presupposed.

However, other supporters of the SDT, particularly C. D. Broad, have doubted whether it is possible to justify our knowledge of objects in this way, and concluded that we over-intellectualize the facts when we say that the sense-datum gives rise to a 'belief' that we are perceiving a physical object. At the purely perceptual level we have only bodily *feelings*, which accompany the automatic adjustment of our sense organs in a certain way, incipient movements of the body, etc. To 'believe' in physical objects, at the perceptual level, really means to act as it would be reasonable to

[1] *Perception*, Ch. 4, pp. 66–9; Ch. 6, pp. 156 ff.

act *if* one believed in physical objects. The different 'quasi-beliefs' which are generally involved in all perceptual cases may be formulated in abstract terms in certain propositions that can be said to define the concept 'physical object'. However, such propositions are not justifiable or provable; they are 'postulates', innate principles of interpretation which we apply to sense-data.[1] This is what Price calls the Bodily Adjustment Theory. He also talks of an Emotion Theory very similar to the Bodily Adjustment Theory which describes the perceptual consciousness of objects as a certain 'emotion' or 'volitional attitude' produced by a sense-datum. For various reasons, which we have no need to reproduce, Price regards both the Bodily Adjustment Theory and the Emotion Theory as unsatisfactory, and offers his own view, according to which the perceptual consciousness of objects is not 'knowledge' (for it may be mistaken) nor 'belief' (for this involves inference, evidence, and is accompanied by an element of doubt) nor even 'quasi-belief'. It is described as 'an absence of disbelief', or 'being under the impression that', 'taking for granted', or 'perceptual acceptance'. This is 'prejudicial'—it simply provides the perceiver with a theme or subject matter to think about.

But the ostensible object which is 'perceptually accepted' is not a particular like a sense-datum; it is a *set of propositions*. Hence 'perceptual acceptance' is an intellectual accompaniment to the direct awareness of a sense-datum, and the set of propositions which are 'taken for granted' include concepts, the concepts of 'material thinghood', which are not exemplified in sense-data and could not have been abstracted from them. Both these concepts and the power of 'taking for granted' are innate, and our knowledge of physical objects is based on a series of such 'perceptual acquaintances'. This series constitutes the justification of this knowledge, for what is involved is a progressive confirmation of the original 'perceptual acceptance' which leads finally to 'perceptual assurance'. This cannot strictly be identified with 'knowledge', since it is not absolutely certain; there is always a possibility that it may be mistaken. But it is quite sufficient for all the purposes of science and of daily life.

We may learn from Price's summary that whereas, in the simple Discursive Inference Theory the perception of objects was regarded

---

[1] *Mind and Its Place in Nature*, pp. 151 ff.

as the production of perceptual beliefs by the mind acting upon the raw material of sensation, there is a gradual realization that this alleged process of interpretation is mythical. It is thus progressively invested with more and more cognitive characteristics, until, in Price, this second aspect assumes the proportions of a semi-cognitive process (perceptual acceptance), always occurring at the same time as the sensing of the sense-datum, which, however, unlike the latter, does not yield indubitable data, but only 'perceptual assurance', and this, only after a whole series of checks. In Price's version, this second process is not at all dependent upon the sensing of the sense-datum in the way in which 'discursive inference' was conceived to be. But it seems that however many cognitive characteristics we may wish to reinvest in 'perceptual acceptance', supporters of the SDT would never be prepared to admit that it could be a genuine cognitive process. The perception of physical objects may be mistaken. And this is sufficient, according to these thinkers, to demonstrate the fact that perceptual consciousness must always be inferior, in its cognitive value, to the sensing of sense-data.[1]

It is, therefore, perhaps not unfair to regard the more sophisticated versions of subsequent philosophers as, in a sense, merely watered-down versions of the Discursive Inference Theory. At any rate, it is the latter theory that offers the basic picture of the role of thought in perception which the SDT seems to hint at. One suspects that supporters of the SDT would like to adopt this view but are mindful of the inherent weaknesses of the position. It is significant that even in Price's account, the terminology of 'perceptual acceptance', i.e. 'taking for granted', 'specifying the unspecified', etc., is taken from the vocabulary of intellectual activities and inference. We may, therefore, reasonably maintain that the SDT naturally suggests a specific view of the role of thought in perception even though this view has not always in fact been endorsed by expositors of the SDT. This view of the role of thought may be summarized in the following way: the perceptual awareness of objects is brought about by a process of thought which begins chronologically and/or logically from sense-data, and ends by providing us with perceptual knowledge of the physical world.

Thought is thus a process which supervenes between the sensing of sense-data, which is the *real* perceptual element, and the per-

[1] This point has been discussed in Chapter 4 above.

ceptual knowledge of physical objects. The latter is not provided directly by a *perceptual* process, but results only after real perception has been mediated by thought. Thus it may be said that the SDT, basically, and in its unsophisticated versions, explicitly, regards thought as playing a constructive role in the formation of our perceptual knowledge of the world of physical objects. Taking up a position midway between the OT and the IET (as we shall see in a moment), the SDT suggests that the mind is partly active and partly passive in the cognition of the physical objects of the ordinary world. It is passive in as much as it is presented with given sensory data which form the raw material of ordinary perception; it is active in as much as it somehow operates, in thought, on these sensory data, 'binds together' the different data, and 'builds up' or constructs a picture of the world of physical objects. Since the sensory data upon which thought is held to operate are, in a sense, *indications* of the world of physical objects, we may call this view of the role which thought plays in perception 'The Interpreter View'. The picture is that of a person deciphering code symbols and piecing together a full account of what there is to be known.

(III) THE CONSTRUCTOR VIEW

It is similarly quite easy to characterize the view of the role of thought in perception which is suggested by the IET. Thinking, according to this theory, is judgment, which is variously described as the 'alienation' of a content from our 'immediate experience', its loosening from its background of existence in the given, the separation of a 'what' from a 'that'. All thinking involves the 'cutting up' of an original whole of 'feeling'. Our common-sense world is what thought discriminates, at a certain level, within this 'felt whole', and it is unsatisfying because it is only a relational representation of the 'felt whole' which leaves out the experiential and emotional factors, and is thus only partially true to the original.

Thus, within a 'finite centre' of 'immediate experience', thought arises, and this thought brings a progressive discrimination which extracts contents from the felt whole. Perception is a primitive level of thought. Perceptual knowledge of the physical world is nothing more than an abstracted version of experience which is only partially true. Thought is, therefore, something constructive in our perceptual and intellectual lives. It creates its contents as part of an eternal striving to grasp the unified experience out of which it arose, by an ever-wider and more coherent system of relations. From another point of view, thinking is also a *destructive* process, in which more and more is alienated from its experiential basis.

Thus, as conceived by the IET, thinking is vastly different from mere 'inference' when the latter is considered only as the drawing of conclusions from premises according to the laws of logic. This sort of 'inference' is rejected by Bradley as 'low grade thinking'. As conceived in the IET, thought is completely active in the construction of the common-sense world which we perceptually know. The analogy of the spider spinning its web readily suggests itself. It is enlightening, but misleading in at least two respects: (a) the spider has no raw material other than that which he draws out of his own body; but thought although it does not, according to the IET, operate on *particular* sensory materials, does have raw material. 'Feeling' as such may be described as the 'raw material' out of which thought crystallizes; (b) it is the spider which does the spinning, but there is no person or thing which 'spins the web' of perceptual knowledge except thought itself, which is, however, more properly comparable to the spinning process than to the spider. The mind is not that which does the spinning since it is itself one of the things which is 'spun' out of 'immediate experience' by the spinning process of thought.

However, as both the spider web and perceptual knowledge may be said to be constructed in circumstances where no raw materials are immediately apparent, the analogy of the spider spinning its web is a useful way of describing the role which thought plays in the genesis of our perceptual knowledge of objects according to the IET.

(IV) THE SPECTATOR VIEW[1]

If we assume the OT to be bent primarily on denying the implications of the SDT or the IET, then when objects are said to be 'non-inferentially present' what is meant is merely that no process

---

[1] This term occurs in a similar context in J. Dewey *Experience and Nature* (London: Allen & Unwin, 1929).

of inference is discernible in the acquisition of perceptual awareness of objects. It may well be that when the mind is thinking, it is greatly preoccupied with drawing inferences, in deducing or inducing conclusions from premises, in interpreting signs, and so on. But at the perceptual level, the proponents of the OT are convinced that they find no inference of this sort. Hence thought is regarded as playing no part at all in the genesis of the perceptual knowledge of physical objects. We may, of course, sometimes learn about some of the characteristics of physical objects through all sorts of intellectual processes and inferences; but in simple perception, when we see or touch or hear something these characteristics are non-inferentially given.

The mind is thus conceived to be completely passive in perception. The so-called perceptual 'act' is more like the recording of a scene by a photographic plate than anything else. We 'open' our senses, and in flows the perceptual knowledge of the ordinary world, which the mind proceeds to record, classify, and interpret. But no thinking at all is involved in the actual genesis of perceptual knowledge. There is therefore plenty of justification for calling this view of the role of thought in perception 'the Spectator View'. The spectator of a play takes no part in it but merely observes, takes note, and evaluates what he observes. And the mind too, in this view, is a mere spectator, a sort of photographic plate.

To sum up, then, we have three different conceptions of the role played by thought in the attainment of perceptual knowledge concerning the world and its objects. On the one end we have the view that the mind is completely active in perception, somehow constructing the objects which it perceives. At the other extreme we have the view that the mind is merely passive in perceptual knowledge, no thinking being involved in perceiving the world and its objects; the mind is a spectator and merely records what it observes. Lying between these two extremes, we find the view that the mind is partly active and partly passive: passive to the extent that it is sensually presented with sense-data, and active in so far as it 'arrives at' its information about physical objects through interpreting the sense-data with which it is presented. These are views which each theory of the given respectively suggests.

(V) CONCEPTS OF THE MIND

Each of these conceptions of the role which thinking plays in perception naturally conjures up a distinct view as to the nature of the mind.

(a) That the SDT is connected with a particular conception of the nature of the mind is nowadays widely recognized, as a result of the influence of L. Wittgenstein and his followers. Ryle, in particular, has made much of the extent to which the SDT goes hand-in-hand with what he calls 'the myth' of 'the ghost in the machine'.

If thinking, according to the SDT (at any rate in its most unsophisticated versions), plays an essential role in perception in constructing our picture of the world of objects on the basis of the interpretation of the sense-data with which we are presented, we tend naturally to think of the mind as an inner personage imprisoned in the body and dependent for its knowledge of the external world on data which are channelled to it through the body's limited avenues of perception. These data out of which the mind has to build up all its knowledge of the real world outside, are fragmentary, and act, at most, as signs or indications of the external reality. It is not surprising, therefore, that sceptical doubts arise concerning large tracts of our common-sense knowledge. 'How do we know of the existence of other minds?', 'How do we know that the real world is anything like we imagine it to be?'. These and similar questions easily suggest themselves when we picture the mind as an inner spirit contained in our bodies and dependent on them for what it can know of the real world. Ryle has suggested the following analogy:

'There is immured in a windowless cell, a prisoner who has lived there in solitary confinement since birth. All that comes to him from the outside world is flickers of light thrown upon his cell walls and tappings heard through the stones; yet from these observed flashes and tappings he becomes, or seems to become, apprised of unobserved football matches, flower-gardens and eclipses of the sun.'[1]

The mind thus performs miraculous feats of construction, working with very scanty materials which are given to it. Only that which is directly given by the senses is free from all possibility of error and

[1] G. Ryle, *Concept of Mind* (London, Hutchinson, 1949) p. 223.

indubitably certain. This is the conception of the mind which goes with the role assigned to thought in perception that is suggested by the SDT.

(b) When, however, the mind is conceived to be wholly active in perception, as in the view which is associated with the IET, quite a different picture arises of the mind and its place in nature. For this theory, perceptual knowledge of the world of objects is the result of a process of crystallization within the felt totality from which all cognition starts. At a certain stage thought emerges, and the unity of 'immediate experience' is broken up into awareness of ourselves and of the objects of our cognition. Hence since the 'self' or 'subject' are the products of discrimination within our 'immediate experience', it is clear that the mind is not to be regarded as any substance which thinks. Mind is not a static entity at all, but a *process*, the process of thinking which is something disembodied and abstract and requires no thinker. This is the Hegelian view to which many of the supporters of the IET subscribe to a greater or lesser extent, though there are many different variations on this basic theme.

Though F. H. Bradley seldom uses the word 'mind', preferring the word 'spirit', his view is not essentially different from that of Hegel. All reality is spirit in some degree of purity, and the Absolute is pure spirit. But pure spirit is not 'thought', for thought is merely as aspect of reality which arises, at a certain stage, out of a finite centre of immediate experience. The 'finite centre' itself may be regarded, says Bradley, as a 'soul', but then this is an ideal construction, legitimate only within limits, according to which a 'finite centre' is regarded as 'an object existing in time with a before and after of itself'.[1]

Again, if we like, we may regard the objective process called 'thought' as 'mind', but we must then remember that mind is, in that case, merely a process of crystallization which breaks up our immediate experience and tries to reunify it by creating an ever more inclusive and coherent system. Final reunification is possible only when thought (the 'mind') disappears through the reconciliation of thought and 'immediate experience' in a higher reality called the Absolute Experience.

B. Bosanquet differs somewhat from Bradley in this respect, and

[1] *Essays on Truth and Reality*, p. 414.

explicitly identifies thought with the mind. But for him too 'mind' is merely a process, a tendency towards the development of greater wholeness, which is characteristic of all experience. The Absolute is 'a perfect union of mind and nature'. Thus, though Bosanquet prefers to talk of mind rather than of thought, he rejects the ordinary conception of mind as an entity.

'The doctrine of mind as an immaterial being, other than, and, so to speak, behind or below the uniting consciousness or experience, seems to be unintelligibly formed on the analogy of a material thing.'

Superstition regards finite minds 'as substances, crystal nuclei, fallen or celestial angels, or both at once'. But the mind, on the contrary, must be interpreted positively in its own right by what it is or does; it is not a thing, nor yet a mere power or attribute of a thing (e.g. of a body or of a brain), nor even 'life'. It is a 'whole' of a special kind, with a structure and concreteness of its own.[1] Thus the role of thought in perception which is implied by the IET suggests the notion that the mind is not an entity but a cosmic process.

(c) In the OT the role of thought in perception is minimal. Its part in perception is that of a spectator. But since the mind merely records what it sees and since its contents at any time consist of nothing beyond all the objects with which it is acquainted and their relations, there is a tendency to deny the independence of the mind. If all the mind does in cognition is to record, then the only way it shows its existence is in the 'action' of knowing. But the mind, then, need be nothing more than a name for a 'continuum of acts of knowing'. This is Alexander's view: 'mind' is not something over and above any particular act of knowing, but on the contrary, this act of knowing is, in a sense, its very substance. The tendency is obviously in the direction of abolishing altogether the mind's existence as something separate, apart from the body. In fact many of the supporters of the OT have adopted a Behaviourist or near-Behaviourist conception of mind. Alexander himself sympathizes with Behaviourists who regard mind merely as a special sort of bodily process, but feels that the Behaviourists cannot do justice to the feelings of 'self' which are involved in every act of awareness.

[1] B. Bosanquet, *The Principle of Individuality and Value* (London: Macmillan, 1912) pp. 218, 372.

Thus he offers his well-known theory according to which every cognition consists of an act of awareness which is 'enjoyed' and the object of this awareness which is 'contemplated'. The mind is a continuum of acts of enjoyment. It is not a thing by itself, but, though distinct from its object, not independent of the body to which it belongs. On the other hand it is not identical with the bodily processes which carry it—it *emerges* from them. For the human observer the mind can never be anything more than the 'enjoyed' part of an act of awareness; but for some higher being some 'angelic spectator', mind would be an object of contemplation.[1]

Thus in minimizing the role of thought in perception, the function of thought is in general lessened in importance, and the possibility is opened for thought to become the merest bodily reaction, albeit of a very peculiar and special sort. The OT, with its attendant spectator view of the nature of cognition, is sometimes tempted to allow the mind no individual and independent existence at all, or vacillates between regarding it as a special sort of emergent quality or reducing it merely to a mode of behaviour.

(VI) THE RELATION OF THESE TO THE APPEAL TO THE GIVEN

Thus in pursuing suggestions which are associated with each theory of the given we have discovered that the issue between them is associated with three different views of the role of thought in cognition and of the concept of the mind. When we have reached this stage, it becomes apparent that we have reached the boundaries of the issue that we agreed to call 'the nature of thought', for the argument as to whether cognition is to be regarded as analogous to finding, on the analogy of 'copy and original', or rather to be like making, with its associated model, suggested by Blanshard, of 'seed and sapling', is hardly distinguishable from the issue regarding the true concept of the mind and the function of thought in perception.

When, however, we say that these theories of the given suggest these different views regarding the role of thought and the concept of mind, we by no means mean that everyone who wishes to maintain a particular view of the given must also maintain the corre-

[1] 'The Basis of Realism', *Proceedings of the British Academy*, Vol. 6. 1913–14.

sponding views about thought in perception and about the mind. The views regarding these different matters are certainly not connected to each other by any logical *necessity*. In saying that they suggest one another, we do indeed mean that there is some sort of logical connection between them. But this connection falls far short of logical necessity or entailment. It is not merely that they are compossible, i.e. that they do not contradict each other; they somehow *belong* together.[1]

This can be explained a little more fully if I may be permitted to make use of the concept 'world-view'. A 'world-view' is a distinct angle from which the basic facts about the world may be regarded. It has sometimes been taken to be synonymous with a metaphysical system, but I shall have some reservations to offer concerning this later on.[2] For the present it is sufficient to say that when I claim that one view suggests the other, I mean that they both form part of a single world-view. Since a world-view is a distinct and clearly recognizable way of looking at things, it may be said that when one view suggests the other, the acceptance of one would naturally provide an argument, though not necessarily a conclusive argument, for accepting the other. Thus a view may be acceptable because it fits in more naturally with another view which a philosopher holds, even though it woud be quite consistent for the philosopher concerned to reject this first view and take up another. Since views suggest each other, in the way in which we have explained, it is often the case that the acceptance of a certain view by a philosopher may be a part cause for his holding another view which is suggested by it.

It is in this fashion that the theories of the given seem to me to suggest these broader and more metaphysical issues regarding the philosophy of mind, and the place of mind in nature. And though I have no doubt that there are many philosophers who would assert a particular view of the given while denying the broader associations which seem to me to be suggested by this view, it is possible to find some philosophers, whom I choose to regard as specially representative, who have held respective views of the given and at

---

[1] In explaining the nature of the connection I assert between the theories of the given and the respective views regarding the role of thought and the concept of mind I am indebted to a suggestion communicated to me by A. C. Ewing.

[2] See later Chapter 12 (v).

the same time also held the corresponding views regarding the role of thought in cognition and the concept of mind.

Unfortunately since the logical relation holding between two views, one of which 'suggests' the other, may be extremely tenuous, the point which I wish to establish, namely that the argument concerning the nature of the given in sense-perception carries with it a distinct metaphysical repercussions, is not capable of proof in the strict sense and does not admit of conclusive demonstrations. The only way I can convince the reader of this thesis is by relying upon the plausibility of the connections which I claim to have discovered between the respective theories of the given and the corresponding views with regard to thought and the mind.

Are we then saying that the argument as to the nature of the given in sense-perception really turns out to be an argument about the role and the nature of the mind?

No. This is not the case. The argument as to the nature of the given is certainly *connected with* these different views regarding thought and the mind, but it is not *reducible* to the argument between these views. It is not necessary, nor in the least bit obvious that the argument between these views should take the form of a dispute concerning the given in sense-perception. Most of the exponents of these classic positions in the philosophy of mind do not seem to have even thought of formulating a view concerning the nature of the given in sense-perception. And certainly when the debate rages around the topic of the concept of mind and thought, an appeal to the given would seem to be out of place.

The discussions as to the nature of thought and regarding the concept of mind are particularly complicated ones, and seem as interminable and indecisive as most philosophical arguments. None of the parties appears to go very far in convincing the others that their views are wrong. And yet the fact that we have shown that these issues are somehow connected with the dispute as to the nature of the given in sense-perception is surely significant. While we may not be able to say very much about the nature of thought and the concept of mind, it is to be hoped that the connection between these issues and the question of the given will cast some light upon the significance of the appeal to the given.

Chapter 9

THE REAL ISSUE

(1) THREE HINTS

We shall attempt, in this chapter, to offer an interpretation of the argument about the nature of the given, and, in consequence, an evaluation of the appeal to the given.

We have already seen that the Naive View which suggested that the argument about the nature of the given was an empirical one, must be rejected. On the other hand, even though the different theories did not seem to be meaning the same thing when they make use of the expression 'the given', they did leave the impression that there is some real issue between them. In casting around for leads as to the nature of this real point of issue, we have so far found only an indication that different views regarding the role of thought in perception and the 'nature of thought' might be involved.

But though the realization that each theory of the given is vaguely connected with and suggests a conception of the role of thought in perception is illuminating and suggestive, it does not suffice to explain what it is that the rival theories of the given are really arguing about. In fact, pointing out such a connection between the theories of the given and the corresponding views about thought and the mind, may at first seem to have made our task more difficult, for now, instead of our one original problem of explaining why the theories of the given seem to be at issue, we find ourselves saddled with a second problem, namely, that of accounting in some way for this connection.

It may be the case however that the solution of the second of these problems will also be found to yield a solution to the first. If we can account for the connection between each theory of the given and the corresponding views as to the role and nature of thought with which each is connected, we may well come to understand why it is that there has seemed to be a real argument concerning the nature of the given in sense-perception.

A second look at the different theories of the nature of the given, bearing in mind this connection with the respective views as to the role and nature of thought, will perhaps suggest some explanation about the true issue at stake. It so happens that each theory of the given, upon further investigation, yields a hint regarding the true nature of the argument. We shall therefore re-examine these theories, one by one, follow up the hint that each provides, and see whether we can build up from these hints a full account of the real issue at stake between the different theories of the given.

(II) RYLE'S SUGGESTION

Let us take the SDT first. This was formulated in an attempt to analyse the facts of sense-perception in order to explain the pheno-mena of illusion, changing appearances, and so on. It is not the only possible analysis, nor even the most satisfactory one. But supporters of the SDT are stubborn in their insistence that acts of perception are divisible into a nucleus of perception proper ('sensing') together with an element of interpretation, whose presence alone renders the perceptual judgment corrigible. The assumption behind this is the conviction that perception proper *must* be an infallible process yielding incontrovertible data. Arising out of this we have the suggestion that the SDT-ists have been enamoured with the mistaken ideal of mathematical certainty.

Gilbert Ryle pursues this line in his section on the SDT in *Concept of Mind*. He suggests that in desiderating a mistake-proof brand of observation, the sensing of sense-data, epistemo-logists have been assuming that whatever is known has been learnt either by inferences from premises or, in the case of ultimate premises by some sort of non-inferential confrontation called 'immediate awareness', 'acquaintance', etc. This dichotomy 'either by inference or by intuition' has its origin in the deference of epistemologists since Descartes to Euclidian Geometry, the truths of which are either theorems or axioms.

This suggestion is helpful. It states, in effect, that the quest for a given on the part of the SDT is a search for something like axioms in Geometry which are themselves certain and on which all thought is to be based; the quest is then due to the attempt to picture the acquisition of knowledge using a geometrical model. This is certainly consistent with our own observation that the SDT is connected with the Interpreter View of thought. The appeal to the given is thus a quest for certainty, which is the result of an attempt to conceive cognition as a process of mathematical inference.

Ryle thinks this attempt fundamentally mistaken, and tries to refute it by a simple confrontation with the facts. The assumption of similarity between the ways in which we acquire knowledge and the procedures for finding out truths in geometry is false; for

'. . . there are lots of different ways of ascertaining things which are neither blank acquiescent gazings, nor yet inferrings. Consider the replies we should expect to get to the following "How-do-you-know?" questions: "How do you know there are twelve chairs in the room?" "By counting them." "How do you know that 9 times 17 makes 153?" "By multiplying them and then checking the answer by subtracting 17 from 10 times 17." "How do you know the spelling of 'fuschsia'?" "By consulting the dictionary". . . In none of these situations should we press to be told the steps of inferences, or the counterparts of any axioms; nor should we grumble at the adoption of these different techniques of discovery, but only, in cases of doubt, at the carelessness of their execution. Nor do we require that tennis should be played as if it were, at bottom, a variety of Halma.'[1]

But does this confrontation really refute the assumption that knowledge is attained 'either by inference or intuition'? Presumably Ryle wishes to impress us with the fact that such cognitive processes as counting, multiplying, looking at a dictionary and so on are neither inferences nor intuitions. But there remains the possibility that each of them is a complex process containing *both* inference *and* intuition. It might be the case, for example, that counting consists (roughly) of intuiting a series of sense-data and inferring from the *a priori* rules of arithmetic that when one datum is followed by another, and then another, etc., we have the formula $1 + 1 \ldots = 12$. Or alternatively, perhaps we intuit a sense-datum, then another, and infer from the rules of arithmetic that 1 plus 1 equals 2; 2 plus 1 equals 3, and so on. Similarly multiplying, consulting a dictionary, etc., may break down on analysis into so many intuitings and so many inferrings.

[1] *Concept of Mind* (London: Hutchinson, 1949) pp. 239–40.

This confrontation, then, certainly does not *of itself* refute the dogma that all knowledge reaches us 'either by inference or intuition'. I suspect that Ryle was thinking here of something which he tried to establish elsewhere in his book,[1] namely, that we are mistaken in thinking that the actual processes of thought correspond to the steps in the verbal statement in which the results of such thought processes are set out. Thus 'inferences', 'assumings', etc., are not distinct mental processes; and the dogma that knowledge is reached 'either by inference or intuition' is wrong because it assumes that thought and cognitive processes are composed of so many smaller processes of 'inferrings' and 'intuitings', in much the same way as a brick wall is composed of bricks. But since, according to Ryle, inferrings and intuitings are not distinct mental 'processes' at all, it seems to follow that counting, multiplying, etc., cannot be complex mental processes built up out of them.

This latter suggestion is very penetrating; but is it wholly true? Are 'inferrings' not processes of thought at all, and does thinking not proceed at all by way of ground and consequent? Ryle has certainly not *demonstrated* this; he has merely suggested the possibility that thinking might be different from the verbal formulae in which its results are summarized. And if he is correct in supposing that the view that maintains a parallel between the thinking process and the verbal formulae which summarize its results is the one which is assumed by supporters of the SDT, it is a question of Ryle's word against theirs.

But Ryle has helped us in pointing out that the SDT is connected with the assumption that empirical knowledge is based either on inference or intuition, and that this assumption arises (a) from trying to construe thought as a geometrical process, and (b) from assuming that the thought process corresponds to the form of the verbal statement in which it is expressed. This is, in effect, the familiar truth that, Descartes' quest for certainty is an attempt to arrange all knowledge on the lines of mathematical knowledge, and all thought in the order of geometrical inference.

But will this suggestion help us to find the point at issue in the dispute as to the nature of the given? It is certainly the sort of explanation towards which we have been feeling our way. We know that the dispute cannot be an empirical one; we know that

[1] ibid., p. 303.

the nature of thought is somehow involved. Ryle's suggestion explains the connection in the case of the SDT. According to this, the mischief starts when epistemologists attempt to consider thinking and knowing as mathematically expressible processes. Thus on the one hand a view of the nature of thought emerges, and on the other hand, we look around for an infallible species of observation which will act as the premise of all our knowing. The conception of the mind as a 'ghost in the machine', a substance imprisoned in the body, arises partly because of this preoccupation, and also independently for other reasons and misunderstandings, and helps to sustain this misconception of thought and cognition.

But unfortunately Ryle's explanation seems to have no bearing on either the IET or the OT. The IET does not seem to be seeking after certainty; nor does it seem to be connected with the attempt to represent empirical knowledge after the model of geometry. Nor does the OT appear to be committed to the assumption that all our empirical knowledge comes to us either by inference or intuition.

So Ryle's suggestion is helpful in the case of the SDT, but will not help us to understand the other theories of the given or the argument between them. And we may therefore suspect that Ryle's suggestion is only part of the truth regarding the SDT. The truth which it contains, an important one, is that the SDT is connected with a search for certainty and this search explains the particular view of thought and the mind which this theory suggests. But Ryle has overstressed the extent to which the SDT is influenced by the example of geometrical reasoning. It is certainly very doubtful whether all or most supporters of the SDT have regarded empirical knowledge as being divisible into axioms and theorems. And this may well lead us to conclude that Ryle has not fully appreciated the significance of this quest for certainty. What this quest is, we shall discuss in a moment. But, if I am right, the truth of the matter is that this search is something quite different and distinct from the influence of geometrical reasoning. It is indeed the quest for certainty which has led philosophers to suppose that sense-data were given; but that some proponents of the SDT, misled by the influence of mathematics, have gone on to suppose that empirical knowledge is divisible into something like theorems and axioms is a *subsequent* step, and not the one which has led them primarily to postulate sense-data as the given.

(III) ANOTHER SUGGESTION

Another suggestion presents itself when we look again at the OT. Proponents of the OT, we have been assuming, have only wished to deny the SDT or the notion that there is any ground for dissatisfaction with our normal ways of describing things as objects. But, like supporters of the SDT, they have often felt themselves to be directly concerned with such phenomena as changing appearances, illusions, etc. These phenomena, according to Ryle's account, would seem not to constitute a problem to which the SDT is a solution but rather a pretext for the SDT to give expression to the quest for certainty. However, if we do *not* accept this view, and prefer to take the preoccupation with the phenomena of perception seriously, the following might then be said:

All three theories of the given are connected with the insight that the perceiving of an object, in such a way as to know that it is this particular object, is not an instantaneous process. At any instant that which is revealed to perception is only a part or a single characteristic of the object. For example, we never see all six sides of an opaque cube at once; yet we nevertheless, through perception, come to be aware of the whole object and its enduring characteristics. The question is raised, how do we pass from the perception of part of the object to the perception of the object as a whole, seeing that the whole object is not revealed immediately in the instant?

The well-known phenomena of changing appearances, illusions, and hallucinations tend to make us think that the single characteristic of the object which is instantaneously revealed to us is not liable of itself to be misperceived, and it is only in passing from this revelation to the cognition of the object as this particular thing, here and now, that we are liable to err. So we start thinking of the time which may elapse between the instantaneous awareness of the single aspect, and the conscious assurance that it is the object we are perceiving, as being one in which we infer the characteristics of the object from our instantaneous awareness of a single characteristic. Thus there arises the concept that the awareness of the single characteristic is quite independent of the consciousness of the object, and the phenomena of double vision, etc. as well as other factors which support the theory of epistemological dualism, now incline us to say that what we instantaneously perceive is not really a part of the physical object at all but only something else, namely a sense-datum, from the acquaintance with which we infer our knowledge of the physical object.

This concept 'the sense-datum' proves a useful tool in accounting for many cases of perceptual illusion. However, the question naturally arises, 'How do we justify this inference in which we become aware of physical objects?' Also we are now inclined to think of direct perception as being mediated by thought in the sense that it is through the intervention of thought that we acquire perceptual knowledge of physical objects, and with this is suggested the concept of the mind as a spiritual entity imprisoned in the body. Thus there arises, from these considerations, the SDT, together with all accompanying views concerning thought and the mind.

Second thoughts remind us that there is surely no real doubt as to the existence of these physical objects, and that we are usually instantaneously aware of them in sense-perception as well. So that it is far-fetched to say that we 'infer' or 'deduce' the existence of the object. We somehow know or believe it to be there, we 'take it for granted' or 'perceptually accept' it. The question is only whether afterwards we can justify this belief. We are still reluctant to give up the idea that sense-data are independent of physical objects, because this has proved such a useful tool in explaining perceptual phenomena. Also, we may, consequently, still be enamoured with the idea that the awareness of the object as such is somehow dependent on our prior awareness of single characteristics of the object, the latter forming the 'evidence' for the former. Hence the call for justification.

But gradually we can rid ourself of these prejudices too, and we then insist that the particular characteristics of which we are instantaneously aware literally belong to the object, and are not independent of it. We try other methods for accounting for the phenomena of perception, and we no longer are convinced that there need be any temporal gap between the awareness of the particular characteristic of which we are instantaneously aware, and the consciousness of the presence of the particular physical object. There may have been a temporal gap before we learnt about the constitution of this particular object, but once we have learnt it, we are able, in perceiving any characteristic which belongs to it, to recognize immediately that it is this particular object of which we are aware. We have learnt to *see* its meaning (this is Laird's position). The object as such, we now say, is intuited. And it is this object which we assert to be given, denying thereby the view that we reach it by inference. The particular characteristic as a mere part is what later reflection discriminates. We can, then, for theoretical purposes, distinguish the apprehension of the particular characteristic and consider its relation to the apprehension of the object as a whole. But at the time of actual perception, there is no thought process which intervenes between the apprehension of the particular characteristic and the apprehension of the whole. Thought is a different activity, which does not normally enter into perception at all, for, in perception the mind is simply a spectator of the objects which are presented to it. Here we have the characteristic features of the OT.

The IET starts, it may further be suggested, by accepting the assumption of our first position that the relation between the particular characteristic and the consciousness of the object as a whole is one of ground and consequent. But it avoids the question of justifying this inference by going on to say that the apprehension of the particular characteristic too is something which involves inference. All thought and cognition is inference or discrimination which (since it must start somewhere) is held to start from a unity of 'feeling'. It is this feeling which is 'the given'.

Thus the three theories of the given are all misleadingly drawing attention to the fact that the apprehension of the object is somehow different from the instantaneous apprehension of one of its particular characteristics.

This account is reminiscent of a well-known contemporary technique. It also fits in quite well with Ryle's suggestion that the culprit is the attempt to construe empirical cognition as a geometrical process. It embodies a certain amount of obvious truth. But I submit that this is only a part of the truth, and cannot possibly be the whole truth about the matter:

(1) This suggestion does not tell us anything at all about the connection between each theory of the given and the corresponding theories of the role of thought in perception and the nature of the mind. It asserts rather than explains this connection.

(2) Though this suggestion rings true in connection with the dispute between the SDT and the OT, particularly insofar as this concerns issues of changing appearances, illusions, etc., it involves down-right distortion of the IET: (a) Bradley (as we have seen above) and Joachim[1] clearly reject the suggestion that the relation between 'immediate experience' and the mediacy which transcends it is one of ground and consequent. 'Judgment' is not 'inference' in the sense in which either of the OT or the SDT understand this term; (b) the suggestion alleges that the motive for postulating the existence of 'immediate experience' was the attempt to solve (however indirectly) the 'problem' of changing appearances, etc., whereas Bradley makes it absolutely clear that we are forced to the idea of 'immediate experience' because of our dissatisfaction with the adequacy of describing the world in terms of objects in expressing all the felt side of our perceptual experience.

(3) Nor is it possible to attempt to restrict the explanation to just the SDT and OT and to say that these two are, at any rate, misleading ways of drawing attention to the difference between the awareness of a particular characteristic, and the consciousness of the object as such, whereas the IET is an entirely unrelated affair, which is concerned with something different. Though this is true enough, inasmuch as it reflects the fact that the SDT and OT are more directly concerned with the problems of perception than the IET, it nevertheless obscures the fact that there is a dispute between all three theories.

I, therefore, conclude that this suggestion, too, is unsatisfactory, and will not help us to understand what the argument between the different theories as to the nature of the given is really about.

(iv) THE CLUE FROM BRADLEY

When we turn to the IET, to find some hint about the real issue between the theories of the given, our attention is drawn by Bradley's profession of the reason which led him to the idea of 'immediate experience'.

In his 1909 paper on 'Our knowledge of Immediate Experience',[2] Bradley explains that the idea of 'immediate experience' arises

---

[1] *Immediate Experience and Mediation* 1919, pp. 9 ff.
[2] Reprinted in *Essays on Truth and Reality*.

because the ordinary objects of common-sense failed to satisfy us. They fail to give expression to the whole of our experience at any moment; there is always a fringe of feeling and emotion which forms a felt background to all our cognitive situations, and which somehow gets left out of our ordinary descriptions of the world in terms of objects. We realize the whole of our experience does not break up, without remainder, into a subject, on the one hand, and its objects, on the other. This gives us a feeling of uneasiness, and it is this 'blind uneasiness' which insists on satisfaction, and acts as the judge of all the relational systematic content which transcends the 'immediate experience'. The intellect is driven on by this uneasiness to the idea of an 'object' which is complete, and which contains the missing elements. The idea of such an 'object' gives us theoretical satisfaction; but the full experiential satisfaction of all our desires attending the expression of all our experience at any moment, is achieved only in the Absolute Experience. Thus what at length results from our dissatisfaction with our normal ways of describing experience in terms of objects is the attainment of the Absolute, and the first step towards this is the formulation of the idea of 'immediate experience'.

Surely there is something remarkable here. On the one hand it is the intellect, or thought, which disturbs the smooth and unbroken unity of 'immediate experience', giving rise to relational content, and on the other hand, it is the same intellect which somehow realizes its own inadequacy and rises to the thought of 'immediate experience', the reunion with which would mean the doom of its own separate existence as thought and its function with 'immediate experience' in the Absolute Experience.

We are surely justified in wondering whether this 'dissatisfaction' which we feel with the objects of common-sense is genuinely an *intellectual* dissatisfaction. The same contempt towards our theoretical understanding of reality, which omits all the fringes of emotion and feeling which somehow contribute most towards making our lives worth living, is found not only in Bradley, but in an impressive list of philosophers, ancient and modern. It is a view shared by the great mystics, and binds together such diverse thinkers as Plato, Parmenides, Spinoza, Hegel, Bergson, and William James. Can it be said to be an *intellectual* dissatisfaction which drives all these thinkers beyond our common-sense world?

It might be more accurate to say that it is a *speculative* or *metaphysical* dissatisfaction which is involved. And it is significant that James Ward has said that in spite of himself Bradley gives the impression that it is the idea of the higher unity, i.e. Absolute Experience, which gives rise to the idea of the lower unity, i.e. 'immediate experience' rather than vice-versa. He says:

'Altogether Bradley's expositions of "immediate experience", whether psychological or metaphysical seem but very precarious ventures, the reasons for which are not at once obvious. Yet behind these he must have had what seemed to him good reasons, or he could hardly have clung so pertinaciously to his "view", as he calls it. And looking back we shall find, reading between the lines, that his prime reason was not any indubitable fact found in "immediate experience", but a speculative conviction, "inherited from others", and notably from Hegel: "that there is but one Reality and its being is experience" ("Appearance and Reality", p. 455 fin.). This was his veritable starting point.'[1]

The secret of the concept of 'immediate experience', then, is that is is derived from Bradley's search for the Absolute. Our dissatisfaction with the ordinary common-sense view of the world is due to the fact that it seems dry-as-dust, and inadequate to our hopes and aspirations. It is not 'spiritual'; it lacks the coherence which would make of the universe a unity. In fact, as many a critic has observed, Bradley's scepticism in epistemology, is a mask for his mysticism. At all events Bradley's 'given' is that which is connected with his search for metaphysical satisfaction.

It is perfectly clear how Bradley's theory of the given is connected with his view that thought actively constructs its own perceptual objects. If 'immediate experience', by hypothesis, is to overcome the division of subject and object, and this division is regarded as essential to thought, then it is plain that it is only the emergence of thought out of 'immediate experience' which brings with it the objects which we claim to perceive.

But it is not yet apparent how, if at all, Bradley's explanation of his motives can help us to understand the connection between the other theories of the given and their corresponding views of the role of thought in perception. Nor do we seem to be any closer to

[1] *Mind* 1929, pp. 78-9.

understanding why there should be the appearance of a dispute between the different theories of the given.

The SDT reflects the search for certainty. The IET reflects the search for the Absolute. Is there any connection between them?

(v) THE QUEST FOR CERTAINTY

Let us examine this 'quest for certainty' more closely. We have met it in the SDT as the insistence that if empirical knowledge is to be well founded, perception must be infallible and its data incontrovertible. Consequently it is argued that since ordinary perceptual acts are liable to error, they must consist of a nucleus of genuine perception which is infallible together with a peripheral element of interpretation.

But the main ground upon which it is held that the validity of empirical knowledge necessitates that perception should be infallible, has, since the sixteenth century, been some variation or other of Descartes' celebrated argument from the ever-present possibility of error and illusion. According to this, we have no guarantee of the truth of any empirical preposition because of the possibility of our being in error. We may even be dreaming. Thus those who are concerned to ensure the validity of perceptual knowledge claim that perception proper (that is 'direct perception' or 'sensing') *is* infallible and yields incontrovertible data. In this way Descartes' scepticism reveals to us the existence of a datum whose presence is incorrigibly revealed. I may doubt whether it is indeed a table that I am seeing, but it cannot be doubted that I am 'directly seeing' something, namely, a 'sense-datum'.

But the conclusion that because it is possible that I may actually be suffering a hallucination, or be otherwise in error, when I claim to be seeing a table, I am therefore not justified in being sure that I am seeing a table, has been subjected to grave criticism. It has been repeatedly argued by contemporary philosophers that the possibility of perceptual error implies the possibility that I may be perceptually correct. It makes sense to claim that there are times when our senses deceive us only if we admit that it is possible that there are times when they do not. Therefore, the extreme scepticism which would conclude that all perception is illusory, would be to deprive the concept of 'illusion' of any real meaning.[1] Now a more

---

[1] For an example of this type of argument see G. Ryle, *Concept of Mind*, p. 95.

moderate sceptic may urge not that all perceptions are bound to be illusory, but only that we can never really know that any are not. To him we can reply that unless we know that some appearances are trustworthy we could never discover that others were deceptive. So when the sceptic urges 'it may be a hallucination', we could reply 'it may not be a hallucination'. Thus the possibility that in all our perceptions some demon is mischievously causing us to perceive hallucinations, necessitates it being logically possible for us to perceive things which are not hallucinations. And since it is presumably more reasonable to suppose that there is no such mischievous demon than to suppose that there is one, the onus of proof seems to lie on the sceptic.

It is felt, however, that the mere possibility that our perception is not delusive does not justify our being *sure* that is it not delusive. But then this is to make sureness depend on its being logically impossible for a thing to be otherwise, and this is not what we normally require in our experience.[1] In normal life if an empirical assertion were questioned we should set ourselves a series of empirical confirmatory tests (e.g. How does it sound when struck? Does it look like a table from the bottom?, etc.) and if the results of these tests are positive, we should feel justified in being absolutely sure that what we perceive is a table. But the sceptic regards it as sufficient to raise the mere possibility that we may be wrong. He may suggest, for example, that we are dreaming. Again this is no ordinary doubt. In ordinary life we should know well enough how to convince our friends that we were not dreaming. But the sceptic will urge that we are never absolutely sure; it is still *possible* that we may be dreaming. It is always in principle possible to think up an eventuality against which we have made no confirmatory empirical test.

So no empirical certainty will ever satisfy this sort of scepticism. All that the sceptic requires is that errors should be possible. He will then question our standards of proof not on the grounds that they work badly, but on the grounds that they are logically defective or at any rate logically questionable. Many contemporary philosophers have, therefore, pointed out that the certainty which the sceptic seeks is a logical certainty of the sort to be found in mathematics, where we find *a priori* statements which are necessarily true

[1] A. J. Ayer, *The Problem of Knowledge* (London: Pelican, 1956) p. 39.

and where there is no possibility of falsehood. It is from this that the accusation arises that Descartes and other philosophers have been attempting to construe all knowledge after the model of mathematics. We have no need to consider this interpretation of Descartes here. It may be over simplified, but it undoubtedly has an element of truth. It was indeed the geometrical certainty to which they were accustomed which Descartes and other Cartesian philosophers would have wished to find in philosophy. But was it merely this that they sought?

A common answer nowadays is that it was. But it seems to be most uncharitable to suppose that this can be the whole truth about the matter. If Descartes, for example, wished that empirical assertions should be subject to the same criteria as assertions in geometry, then he was making a most unreasonable demand. I may be sure beyond all reasonable doubt that I am in fact looking at a table, but I can never be sure beyond all *possible* doubt. To know something to be true and which could not possibly be false is to know something which is necessarily true. But it is obvious that assertions about what is in fact the case are not necessary truths, for the facts might always have been different.[1] The standard of logical necessity is therefore not applicable to assertions which formulate the results of our perception. Some philosophers might wish, like Leibniz,[2] to put all true statements of fact on a level near those of formal logic or pure mathematics, and introduce some notion of factual necessity. Indeed the problems of individuating things in the world are normally taken to necessitate that there should be some form or other of factual necessity. But whatever this factual necessity might be like, it is clear that it would yet fall short of the standard of logical necessity, where there was no possibility of error or falsehood.

If empirical statements, asserting, for example, what it is that we perceive, fall short of logical necessity, it would nevertheless be quite misleading to regard them as merely probable, for this suggests that the standard is applicable but, unfortunately, unattainable. It is therefore quite correct to say that we can be as certain about matters which we have learnt through perception as we are concerning the necessary truths. And this is so not merely

[1] ibid. p.41.
[2] See specially his *Correspondence with Arnauld.*

APPEAL TO THE GIVEN

because the certainty that we have about empirical statements is different from the certainty that we have about necessary statements. On the contrary, the certainty in both cases would seem to be the same.

A priori statements which are logically necessary are not *ipso facto* immune from doubt. It is possible to make mistakes in mathematics or in logic. There is no special set of necessary statements of which it can be said that these are beyond doubt. There can be doubt so long as there is the possibility of error, and every statement whatsoever can be stated in error. It does not follow that if a statement is necessarily true, it is necessarily known to be true.[1]

Now it may be the case that philosophers in the sixteenth century would not have accepted this distinction between the knowledge of a statement, whether certainly known or not, and its truth, which might be factual or necessary. It may be the case that they thought that necessary truths could be certainly known.[2] Yet it remains true that if their demand that we be sure about our perceptual assertions involved the claim that these be necessarily true, then the above reply would be crushing. But I cannot believe that Descartes or anyone else simply made this obvious mistake without having something else in mind. So what can be the reason for this insistence that empirical propositions can be guaranteed only if there is no possibility of their being in error? How can we explain this otherwise unreasonable demand?

The intellectual history of the period is interesting in this regard, but does not fully explain the motives of Descartes and his contemporaries.[3] It was the revival of interest in the ancient Greek sceptics in the sixteenth and seventeenth centuries which both reflected and contributed towards the development of the attitude that we now call 'the scientific outlook'. It would seem that at first thinkers were interested in overturning the dogmatism of the Middle Ages. But then they quickly turned their sceptical weapons against the

---

[1] See Ayer, ibid., pp. 41–3. For a similar discussion of the 'quest for certainty' see N. Malcolm, *Knowledge and Certainty* (Englewood Cliff, Prentice-Hall, 1963).

[2] Descartes, by the way, certainly did not think this. See his *Meditations on First Philosophy*, Meditation I, where he considers the possibility that a malignant demon is deceiving him even in the case of *a priori* truths.

[3] See H. G. Van Leeuwen, *The Problem of Certainty in English Thought* 1630–90 (The Hague, 1963).

possibility of developing a new science. And in fact scepticism was used to defend the religious convictions of the past in the face of the new science. They insisted that human reason could lead nowhere, and only revelation could impart knowledge.

In contrast to this destructive tendency, another sceptical movement with which Descartes seems to have had closer connections, attempted to couple a complete epistemological scepticism with an advocacy of pure empirical scientific research as the only profitable type of enquiry because nothing could be truly known about the nature of reality itself. This view was espoused in particular by Descartes' contemporary Pierre Gassendi, who sought a *via media* between scepticism and dogmatism. Descartes himself seems to have been searching for a criterion of certain truth which would enable him to overturn the sceptical attacks on the new science. But he was still influenced by the earlier views which sought to discount human reason and make true knowledge depend on God's revelation. Thus he and the other Cartesians succeeded in combining at one and the same time a rejection of the dogmatism of the medievals, an optimism concerning at any rate some aspects of the new science, and an insistence that the very possibility of true knowledge depended upon God's existence and illumination. His was a form of modified dogmatism, which is distinguishable from the attitude which later became characteristic of the Royal Society in England and of what is now known as 'British Empiricism', which eschewed the search for certain knowledge and sought instead a limited certitude provided by the standards of ordinary life, which could yield conclusions acceptable to any 'reasonable man'. The quest for certainty in the sixteenth and seventeenth centuries, then, took different forms, and different thinkers had different motives.

But if we follow the clue from Bradley, about which we have spoken in the previous section, further light may be thrown upon certain aspects of this quest. It may be suggested that the insistence on the uncertainty of our ordinary empirical knowledge of objects may at least sometimes be prompted by the same 'dissatisfaction' and 'blind uneasiness' of which Bradley has spoken. In short, the tendency to dismiss what is empirically observable as mere appearance, illusion, or possibly hallucination, stems very often from a dissatisfaction with the empirical world. This dissatisfaction is metaphysical or ontological, and tries to imply that the world of objects is not itself the ultimate reality. Descartes' application of the method of universal doubt, one recalls, was supposed to lead him to the conclusion that only the existence of his own self was intuitively certain, that God certainly existed, and that God's goodness guaranteed the veracity of our empirical observation. His quest for certainty may then be interpreted as starting from a metaphysical dissatisfaction with what we ordinarily take for granted,[1] and a search for some metaphysically adequate reality more basic than the world of objects. It may well be that Descartes' mathematical interests are in part responsible for the fact that this search for metaphysical satisfaction takes the form of a search for what is certain and indubitable. There is certainly no doubt that it is the mathematical ideal that has led Descartes and some of his successors to make the mistakes which critics profess to find in their thought. But if we are right in following up this suggestion, the quest for certainty is not to be interpreted as being primarily the result of an obsession with geometrical methods, but the search for a Reality behind Appearance, something which is more 'satisfying' to our speculative demands.

Since the argument from the ever-present possibility of perceptual illusion and hallucination is one of the central pillars upon which the SDT rests, this enables us to see the SDT in the same light. Metaphysically interpreted, the SDT expresses a rejection of the ordinary world of common-sense. And since this is true, as we have seen, of the IET as well, we are able to conclude that in both the SDT and IET, the appeal to the given is part of a rejection of the common-sense world in an attempt to find some reality which is metaphysically more adequate. This suggestion, when carefully considered, throws considerable light on the whole dispute concerning the nature of the given in sense-perception.

(VI) DISCREDITING THE COMMON-SENSE WORLD

The appeal to the given is part of an attempt to discredit the claim to ultimate metaphysical reality of the common-sense world. This

---

[1] Perhaps this dissatisfaction stemmed also from contemporary science. This was after all the age of the spread of the new atomic theory, with its distinction between Primary and Secondary Qualities.

is the suggestion which emerges as an explanation of the appearance of a real dispute between the three views as to the nature of the given.

We have seen that 'non-inferential presence' was the one characteristic which all the theories agreed that the given had to possess, but there was no agreement as to what they meant when they spoke of 'non-inferential presence'.

I do not wish to withdraw this conclusion. Indeed, considered as an argument about the empirical facts, the circumstance that there is no agreed meaning to the expression 'the given' shows that there is no genuine argument at all. So the Naive View of the argument must be mistaken, because according to this view the argument is an empirical one which arises when the philosophers closely re-examine their perceptual consciousness and come to *see* that either sense-data or objects or 'immediate experience' are what are really presented in sense-perception.

But what gives to the dispute its semblance of a genuine quarrel, is that fact that, in *addition* to whatever else the theorists are trying to point out when they say that sense-data, objects, or 'immediate experience' are given, they *also* mean that these are the sole representatives, at the perceptual level, of Reality—ultimate metaphysical Reality. Thus when they say that something is given, they mean that this constitutes our *contact with reality*. This is a metaphysical statement, based on the metaphysical distinction between Appearance and Reality.

Thus the philosopher asks his question, 'What is it that is really given in any particular cognitive situation?' because of a meta-physical or speculative interest, not out of mere disinterested curiosity. Something 'catches his eye' about our perception of any object; but what catches his eye is not necessarily the gap, true or false, between the apprehension of the particular characteristic of an object and the consciousness of the object as a whole. Nor is it the phenomena of changing appearances, illusions, and hallucina-tions which he necessarily has in mind, though these may indeed stimulate his attention. Neither of these would of themselves normally be sufficient to lead him to deny that physical objects were given and assert that something else is given. These 'catch his eye', when they do, because of a flash of insight in which he realizes that the 'world of things' is somehow not as important or solid as we normally take it to be. He is interested in rejecting the claim to ultimate reality of our ordinary common-sense way of looking at things. When it is asserted that not objects but only sense-data or 'immediate experience' are given, the ordinary common-sense world is made to seem somehow more insubstantial than we all commonly suppose. On the other hand, when the proponent of the OT replies with his accustomed vehemence (since he is, after all, defending common-sense) that, on the contrary, what he and every-one else, when in their right senses, find as given is a 'world of things', our ordinary common-sense world of objects seems more starkly revealed in all its well-known and familiar features. In each case, the philosopher's assertion that something is given makes us see the ordinary world differently, in a different light. The argument as to the nature of the given in sense-perception seems to consist mainly of these different emphases.

In the case of both the SDT and the IET, some particular aspect of what happens when we perceive is being stressed to the detriment of all other aspects, in an attempt to single this out as the sole solid foundation on which our perceptual cognition rests and imply that the common-sense world of physical objects is not, as it seems, the real world, but only an appearance or shadow of Reality.

This is clear enough in the case of the IET. Here an attempt is made to discredit the world of physical objects by stressing overtly the importance of the organic feelings which accompany sense-perception. Since in 'feelings' consciousness of the distinction between subject and object disappears, it is concluded that this distinction, which parcels up reality into so many objects for a particular subject, arises as a result of and together with intellectual discrimination or thought. And since the division of reality into objects does not do 'justice' to the felt side of our experience the world of objects is regarded as a mere appearance and not the ulti-mate reality itself.

But in the case of the SDT, it is not immediately apparent that any attempt is being made to discredit the world of objects, and this may even be heatedly disputed. Such an attempt is obvious enough in the case of a few of the classical exponents of the theory of Representa-tive Ideas (the forerunner of the modern SDT). Berkeley, for example, uses the theory to fight what he calls 'materialism', and establish his view that all the impressions we receive in perception are 'ideas' set up in our minds by the will of God. The 'world of objects' is thus an erroneous interpretation of these ideas which assumes the existence of a material substance that transmits to the observer the impressions he receives in sense-perception. This, according to Berkeley is atheism, and he complains that

'It is a very extraordinary instance of the force of prejudice, and very much to be lamented, that the mind of man retains so great a fondness, against all the evidence of reason, for a stupid thoughtless *somewhat*, by the interposition whereof it would, as it were, screen itself from the providence of God, and remove Him further off from the affairs of the world.'[1]

Thus in Berkeley the emphasis on changing appearances and illusions is certainly part of an attempt to discredit the world of physical objects. He wishes to demonstrate divine providence in the world, and the common-sense view with its material objects blocks the way and screens divine providence from our gaze.

But Berkeley is by no means a typical exponent of the SDT. And such modern supporters of the SDT as Russell and Broad have quite certainly had no theological axe to grind when they put forward their views.

I do not wish to assert that these philosophers have been trying to offer any positive conception of what ultimate reality must be like when they propounded the SDT. But I am nonetheless convinced that even Russell and Broad have been partly desirous of discrediting the claim to reality of the common-sense world of objects. I think both have been influenced by (and expressed) the view that modern science, and in particular physics, has shown that the real world is far different from what we suppose it to be in common-sense, and contains no such stable and enduring objects as the ordinary man supposes. It is this scientific prejudice which serves as the background to their detailed analyses of the differences between what the object sensuously 'appears' to be, and the qualities which it is supposed really to possess. And their conviction that it is sense-data which are sensuously presented is thus partly but covertly motivated by their belief that the world of common-sense objects is not the ultimately real world.

According to this suggestion, then, both the SDT and the IET are trying to discredit the common-sense world, whereas the OT

[1] *Treatise Concerning the Principles of Human Knowledge*, Section 73.

is trying to defend it. This would certainly explain why the three theories appear to be arguing.

(VII) THE ROLE OF THOUGHT

Additional force is led to this hypothesis by its usefulness in explaining why each theory of the given should be connected with corresponding views as to the role of thought in sense-perception.

We have already noted that it is the SDT and IET that stress the part played by thought in perception, while the OT denies thought any part whatsoever. This stress on the part played by thought corresponds with the rejection of the claim to reality of the world of objects. It is associated with the idea that the world of objects which perception seems to reveal, emerges only as the result of some process of intellectual construction on the part of human observers. In other words, the implication is that in our perception of objects we are not, as we suppose, face to face with ultimate Reality but rather with a mere interpretation, which is only an Appearance of Reality.

Thus the rejection of the adequacy of the common-sense world is expressed both by the singling out of some particular aspect as the given, and also by the emphasis on the part played by thought in achieving our conceptions of objects. The two go hand in hand. So that it is not surprising that the OT, which defends the world of objects, sometimes feels constrained to deny emphatically that thought plays any role at all in sense-perception.

The fact, therefore, that this hypothesis explains so well why each theory of the given should be connected with corresponding opinions as to the role of thought in perception, seems to me a strong argument in its favour.

But finally there is one consideration which points very strongly in the direction which I am suggesting. This is the fact that what I have called the Naive View as to the nature of the dispute concerning the given, the view, namely, that the dispute is a sort of empirical one, is so very plausible. This, in my opinion, is no accident. It arises from the intertwining of the empirical and metaphysical issues which are involved. But this is a long story which requires separate treatment. We shall return to this point in the final chapter of this work.

Chapter 10

EPISTEMOLOGY AND THE
SCIENTIFIC STUDY OF PERCEPTION

---

(1) THREE APPROACHES TO THE PHILOSOPHY OF PERCEPTION

Three main approaches to the topic of perception within epistemology are discernible in the writings of contemporary philosophers. They reflect different appraisals of the nature of epistemology and of the goal that the philosopher should set before himself in dealing with this subject:

(a) There are some who believe that the philosopher must take cognisance of the investigations of Psychology and Physiology and offer a comprehensive theory which will enable the findings of all the specialists who deal with the topic of perception to be related and harmonized.

(b) There are many who affirm epistemology to be an analytic discipline, forming part of the philosopher's task of the 'analysis' of concepts, language, or common-sense. According to them the epistemologist must analyse the key concepts that are involved in perception (e.g. sensation, observation, etc.) in order to clarify them and relate them to the more general concepts (e.g. belief, knowledge, etc.) that are central in epistemology.

Either of these approaches may be combined or dissociated from a third approach, which is the approach of those who believe that

(c) the epistemologist must deal with the topic of perceptions in such a way as to connect this with the 'justification' of our claim to knowledge. This is the traditional conception of the epistemologist's task, according to which the epistemologist must allay the doubts attaching to our ordinary beliefs by constructing a theory of knowledge which will provide a detailed account of how we can arrive at knowledge of things through sense-perception.

This third approach to epistemology connects the topic of perception in the most apparent manner with the quest for certainty, and much of our previous discussion will have obvious bearing on the conception of the epistemologist's task. But before taking any further the implications of our suggestion regarding the nature of this quest for certainty and its association with the claim to ultimate metaphysical reality of the common-sense world, it will be as well to consider briefly the first two approaches to the topic of perception. This I shall do in this chapter and the next. I shall attempt to show that neither of these approaches offers any real direction to the epistemologist, but can at most provide him with additional goals or methods of procedure. The traditional task of the epistemologist of allaying sceptical doubts must continue to be his primary concern.

(II) NEUROLOGY AND PERCEPTION

A distinguished group of English Neurologists has devoted particular attention to the topic of perception in such a way as to make use of and throw light upon the philosophical discussions of this topic. One of the common complaints of these writers has been that philosophers have lost touch with the latest scientific advances in the field of perception, and in particular have confined themselves to just a small group of examples of illusions and hallucinations without taking account of all the detailed empirical investigations into illusion and hallucination that have been produced within the last half century.

Thus J. R. Smythies,[1] after criticizing the existence of two separate studies of perception, that of modern Neurology and that of epistemology, between which there is little liaison, attempts to construct the outline of a comprehensive neurological theory of perception which will cause the philosophical puzzles about perception to 'wither away'. Such a comprehensive scientific theory will explain just how our raw sensory experience is related to the physiological process of perception. Philosophers have neglected this side of the question and have tended to regard the problem of perception as a *logical* problem about the logical status of our knowledge of the external world. But the methods used in investigating this problem have usually consisted of a careful analysis of the philosopher's own normal perception in an attempt to discover what exactly is occurring in perceptual situations, as well as of purely linguistic or

[1] J. R. Smythies *An Analysis of Perception* (London: Kegan Paul, 1956).

logical analysis of statements that could be made in various perceptual situations. Smythies argues that these methods are inadequate to give us a comprehensive and valid theory of perception. Linguistic analysis of ordinary language is insufficient for the analysis of perception; important phenomena that are necessary to our understanding of perception are inaccessible to normal perception and can only be revealed by using special methods, or by studying perception in unusual or pathological states of the nervous system; no one is entitled to talk about hallucinations who has not made a close study of the extensive psychopathological literature concerning these phenomena.

Thus while alleging that few contemporary philosophers appear to consider that physiology or neurology could contribute to the solution of the fundamental problems of perception and mind-brain relation, Smythies insists that the evidence from physics, physiology and neurology—which according to him, have clearly demonstrated the causal nature of the processes of perception which are a necessary condition for any perception to occur—must be taken into consideration in giving a satisfactory account of perception. And the consideration of this evidence leads Smythies, in company with the other writers among this group of philosophizing Neurologists,[1] to adopt the 'Representative Theory of Perception', otherwise known as 'The Causal Theory' in accordance with which we are said to be directly in contact only with certain sensual stimuli and our knowledge of objects is really an indirect awareness of them as the causes of our stimuli.

This is in fact the theory widely maintained by scientists and philosophers ever since the sixteenth century, the philosophical difficulties of which have been exposed fairly extensively in the discussions of the views of such philosophers as Locke, Berkeley, Hume and Kant. Smythies, as well as Eccles, Brain and others, expound this same theory with considerably more subtlety and finesse, in such a way as to attempt to overcome the philosophical objections that have been raised. Smythies, using the example of television as a model, suggests that the complex pattern one sees on looking at a flashing light in a stroboscope are similar to those which appear on a T.V. screen when the light is being televised and that the 'private' visual field of sense-data, which we all possess, should therefore be regarded as constructed by a mechanism in our brain

[1] See the works of R. Eccles and Lord Brain.

or retina, just as the picture on the T.V.-set is constructed by the electron beam travelling regularly over the screen. Our pure egos can directly observe only the T.V. picture consisting of sense-data which represent the external world which causes them. The existence of the external world is a hypothesis which offers the best explanation. In constructing this Causal Theory Smythies, however, attempts to avoid the pitfall of saying that physical objects are unobservable things-in-themselves. He distinguishes between direct and indirect observation and argues that directly observing an event or object is synonymous with sensing a sense-datum, and indirectly observing an event or object is synonymous with perceiving a material object. Hence, objects are observable indirectly. By sensing sense-data we observe material things and so gain knowledge about the physical world.

It has been shown[1] that even so sophisticated theories as those of Smythies and Brain do not succeed in avoiding the fundamental criticisms that have been offered of the Causal Theory, even though they do offer interesting explanations of puzzling physiological facts. What is significant for our present discussion in the work of such theorists is the insistence that any treatment of perception that intends to be ultimately satisfactory must be a comprehensive one which will relate the philosophical aspects to the scientific data concerning perception established by psychology, neurophysiology and physics. This view is shared even by certain philosophers, such as R. J. Hirst, who reject the Representative Theory.

(III) THE DOUBLE-ASPECT THEORY

Hirst starts with a sympathy for the Representative Theory which he proceeds to modify and dilute until it becomes in some respects indistinguishable from Naive Realism.[2] But he retains the conviction that the philosophical problems of perception arise mainly because of the clash between common-sense notions and the factual evidence concerning the occurrence of illusions and hallucinations, and the role played by complex causal and psychological processes in perceiving. For this reason he believes that the problems cannot

---

[1] See R. J. Hirst *Problems of Perception* (London: Allen & Unwin, 1959).

[2] See the relevant chapters of his *Problems of Perception* for these various points. Compare also a later and more condensed form of the theory in G. M. Wyburn, R. W. Pickford and R. J. Hirst, *Human Senses and Perception* (Edinburgh: Oliver & Boyd, 1964).

be adequately dealt with by linguistic or conceptual analysis, but require examination of this evidence and the construction of a comprehensive theory to interpret it.

His comprehensive theory retains the common-sense assumption of publicity, in accordance with which a person is one entity in and interacting with a world of public entities and events, and perceiving his relation between a person and public entities and events by which he discovers their existence and characteristics. Hirst rejects, however, the common-sense assumption that perceiving is a simple direct confrontation of the person by the object of his perception. This is rendered impossible by the causal processes involved in perception. The assumption of confrontation also fails to take account of the relativity of perception. Hirst's hypothesis is based on the recognition that perceiving is variable in quality and accuracy.

Perceiving involves mental activity and so presents two aspects: (a) an outer aspect, i.e. what X's perceiving an object is to an independent observer, namely a causal process describable in physical and physiological terms, and (b) an inner aspect, available only to the percipient which is his 'consciousness of an external object'. This consciousness is not yet 'perceptual consciousness', for the latter is the term properly reserved for the whole activity presenting both aspects. According to Hirst these two aspects are identical in the general sense that they are the one relation or situation of perceiving viewed in different ways, the one by external observation and the other by the percipient's personal experience. From a third or correlator's point of view this identity is discoverable in the fact that a given content of perception is closely linked with a certain brain activity which is its necessary condition. But there is also a disparity between the outer and inner aspects of perception, for while the content is the whole inner aspect the brain activity is only part of the outer one. This leads to a distinction between 'perceptual consciousness' and 'perceiving', the former, a theoretical notion, indicating something conceived from a third point of view which a correlator adopts in trying to take into account the various facts and aspects of perception, the latter indicating the whole process of perception successfully completed.

According to Hirst the relation between 'perceiving' and 'perceptual consciousness' consists of the fact that while both are whole activities of a person whose inner aspects are indistinguishable from each other, they differ in outer aspects since 'perceptual consciousness' consists of certain brain and nervous activities while 'perceiving' consists in addition of the whole causal chain from the external object that normally causes it. While 'perceptual consciousness' and 'perceiving' normally go together, the former is possible without the latter. 'Perceptual consciousness' is but part of 'perceiving' and is caused by the earlier stages of the perceptual process. This causation is a theoretical position reached from the correlator's view-point. 'Perceptual consciousness' in its inner aspect is an act/object mode of awareness. But from the correlator's point of view it is a mode of experience of the person, in which no distinction of act and object can be made. From this point of view 'perceptual consciousness' is adverbial, and one should not attempt to supply private objects for it. 'Perceptual consciousness' may vary considerably in type or level, being sometimes close to a postulated sentience and at other times considerably modified and far from it.

Hirst thus recognizes 'perceptual consciousness' as a sort of 'representative' caused by the perceiving of a public object, but he believes that his account of it overcomes the weaknesses traditionally associated with the Causal Theory. The essential innovation in his account of 'perceptual consciousness' as a 'representative', consists in his insistence that this must be regarded from two points of view, namely the percipient's, from which it is an act/object awareness, and the point of view of the physiologist (and philosophic correlator) from which it must be regraded as 'adverbial'. What is obscure about this is his statement that 'inner aspects' of perception and 'perceptual consciousness' are identical and that the outer aspect of perception is a whole causal process from object to brain; on the other hand, the outer aspect of 'perceptual consciousness' is the last stage of this causal process so that 'perceptual consciousness' is part of perceiving. It is very difficult to grasp how Hirst can maintain that the same perceptual experience can be identified with (as being the last inner aspect of) both the whole transmission process and the last stage thereof. The notion of different viewpoints does not seem adequate to explain this.

It has been urged[1] that Hirst's version of the Representative Theory, with the substitution of 'contents of perceptual consciousness' in place of 'Ideas' or 'sense-data' really does not render it more defensible since Hirst speaks about the former much as the older

---

[1] O. W. K. Mundle, 'Common Sense Versus Mr Hirst's Theory of Perception'. *Proceedings of the Aristotelian Society*, vol. LX (1959–60) pp. 66–7.

Causal Theorists spoke about the latter. Hirst distinguishes awareness of *contents* from perception of *things* and speaks of the contents of 'perceptual consciousness' as containing 'various objects with parts and properties'. Thus the contents of 'perceptual consciousness' are reified to form a distinct object. This, Hirst insists, is the percipient's viewpoint only. But the correlator must also recognize that for the percipient the contents of 'perceptual consciousness' comprise distinct objects and parts. Hence may we not press the question: 'What is it which is visibly red and round when I look at a tomato?' Both common-sense and sense-Datum Theorists provide precise, though different, answers to this question. Hirst's appeal to the 'adverbial analysis' and his distinction between the viewpoints of the percipient and the physiologist and correlator seem to be an attempt to dodge a precise answer to the question.

Hirst has attempted to reply to these criticisms.[1] To the criticism that he is dodging a precise answer to the question 'What is visibly red and round when I look at a tomato?', he replies, in effect, that the question is ambiguous since it depends upon one's viewpoint. If asked from the percipient's viewpoint the answer would be that the tomato *qua* distinguishable within the content of 'perceptual consciousness' is what is red and round. If asked from the viewpoint of the correlator then the answer would be that what is red and round is the tomato itself, in the sense that the 'perceptual consciousness' it causes would be described by the percipient as awareness of a red round tomato. But this reply seems to confirm the fact that Hirst allows of the reification of 'the contents of perceptual consciousness' in such a way as to distinguish between a seeming-object (what the percipient seems to see) and an object in itself, which the percipient observes by being in contact with the seeming-object. Hence Hirst is not justified in saying that by his recognition that perceptual experiences might be both act/object and adverbial from different points of view, he avoids the reification of ideas or sense-data which was characteristic of the older theories. Hirst's position seems to be that he is not really reifying the contents of perceptual experience since he is not supposing that they are real entities *in fact*, i.e. from the correlator's point of view. But since from the percipient's point of view the reification seems real enough, the question that is raised is the age-old problem of the relation between the percipient's

[1] ibid., p. vi.

'private' seeming-world and the 'public' actual world viewed by the correlator. Hirst in some passages quite clearly seems to be supposing the superiority of the correlator's point of view: perceptual consciousness merely *seems* to be of an act/object nature to the percipient, though it is *in fact*, i.e. to the correlator, an adverbial activity. But he fails to explain adequately why the correlator's point of view should be regarded as superior, and not merely that of just another percipient. Moreover this does not seem to square with Hirst's treatment of the Representative Theory as 'the best hypothesis' and his saying that the existence of physical objects is an hypothesis.

Hence Hirst's account of 'perceptual consciousness' remains obscure and his theory does not seem to succeed in avoiding the weaknesses of the Representative Theory by simply distinguishing the percipient's viewpoint from that of the correlator. Hirst's Double-Aspect theory largely serves the purpose of enabling him to introduce the scientific findings of the neuro-physiologists into the discussion, for the observer who observes from the outside, as it were, and looks down into the mind of the percipient, is at the same time the neuro-physiologist, conscious of the brain processes involved and their causal dependence on the presence of the object. Thus while the percipient himself naturally regards his 'perceptual consciousness' as an act/object mode of awareness, and an external observer sees only the presence or absence of the object as the initial link in a causal chain describable in physical and physiological terms, the correlator realizes that the 'perceptual consciousness' of the percipient is adverbial and identifiable with the last link in the causal chain described by the external observer. Whereas the epistemological problem of the relationship between our beliefs and the things in the external world has traditionally been put from the percipient's own personal point of view, and has therefore been framed in terms of the relationship between the contents of his act/object mode of awareness and the real things of the world, Hirst seeks to overcome this limitation and present the problem from the correlator's point of view. From this standpoint the empirical details about the nature of the causal chain become relevant, and in fact provide the basis of the answer to the epistemological problem.

But it may be objected that the epistemological problem, as conceived from the percipient's own point of view, was a philosophical or logical problem regarding the relationship between our knowledge of the object and the perceptual experiences upon which this knowledge is based. The external observer may deal with the percipient's acquisition of knowledge from an empirical and causal point of view. But his *causal* explanation of how the belief got into the percipient's mind throws no light on the *logical* problem with which the percipient is himself concerned. From the percipient's point of view, the information about the causes of his belief may be brushed aside as irrelevant, for the external observer who provides this information is merely another percipient faced with exactly the same logical and philosophical problem as himself. The epistemological problem which seeks to establish the logical relationship between the perceptual knowledge and its experiential basis is thus logically prior to any causal explanation offered from an 'external observer's' point of view. Does Hirst really make the logical and the causal explanations of perception relevant by introducing a correlator who 'identifies' the two? Surely the correlator can at most merely *see* the epistemological problem as it presents itself from the percipient's point of view *at the same time* as he takes note of the causal explanation offered by the physicist and neuro-physiologist from the external point of view. His vantage point by no means provides him with a way of identifying the epistemological problem with the causal problem. He can himself phrase the epistemological problem not from his priveleged position as correlator but only by virtue of his being a human percipient like anyone else. And from his point of view as plain percipient, causal explanations remain as irrelevant as ever.

Hence it remains doubtful whether Hirst has succeeded in his attempt to provide a comprehensive theory of perception which will unite the discussions of the philosophers with the findings of the scientists.

(IV) PSYCHOLOGY AND PERCEPTION

However, Hirst's call for a comprehensive theory which will take note of the discoveries provided by the scientific studies of the topic of perception is by no means confined to the relevance of the causal chain involved in the acquisition of perceptual beliefs, different links of which are the subject of Physics, the Physiology of the organs of sense and Neuro-Physiology. His thesis extends also to the relevance of the psychological investigations of perception, a consideration of which he and many others have regarded as indispensable for the construction of an adequate philosophical theory. Since Psychology has developed as a separate discipline only within the last century, the call for a comprehensive theory which will unite philosophical and psychological discussions concerning perception seems to be on much firmer ground. Though the psychological and philosophical elements were virtually indistinguishable in discussions of the topic until a century ago, the growth of experimental and empirical psychology has brought about a divorce between the treatment of this topic by psychologists and its treatment by philosophers. There are some who lament this divorce both for the sake of philosophy and for the sake of psychology.

For the sake of philosophy it is argued that by neglecting to follow up the psychological discoveries[1] regarding the importance in perception of such factors as motivation, background, the use of cues (e.g. shadows, perspective etc.), object constancy, and the effects of learning, interest and past experience on perceiving, philosophers have deprived themselves of important conclusions which might have weaned them away from some of the older epistemological theories which seem to be *prima facie* based on sensory atomism and Associationism. Thus the theory of 'ideas' which, since the beginnings of modern philosophy has been the primary vehicle for the discussion of epistemological problems, and which was explicitly connected with these ancient psychological notions, still casts its shadow over most versions of the Sense-Datum Theory. Philosophers such as R. Firth, P. Blanshard and R. J. Hirst have each made use of the newer psychological conclusions in order to reject different aspects of the Sense-Datum Theory. In Firth[2] the psychological data are used in order to reject the possibility of dividing acts of perceptual consciousness into two distinct parts, sensuous and non-sensuous, and to support his 'Precept Theory' which maintains that perception is a single state of mind. Blanshard[3] makes use of this same material, and dwells particularly on the quasi-interpretative factors in perception, in order to reinstate a version of the view that per-

---

[1] These discoveries are described in the standard introductory textbooks on Psychology, e.g. E. R. Hilgard, *Introduction to Psychology* (New York, Harcourt Brace, 1962, 3rd ed.); D. Krech and Crutchfield, *Elements of Psychology* (New York, Knopf, 1958) etc. The works of E. G. Boring, *Sensation and Perception in the History of Experimental Psychology* (New York, 1942) and especially F. H. Allport, *Theories of Perception and the Concept of Structure* (London Chapman and Hall, 1955) provide much detailed information.

[2] 'Sense-Data and the Percept Theory', *Mind* 1949 and 1950.

[3] *The Nature of Thought*, Vol. I, (London, Allen & Unwin, 1939).

ception is a form of rudimentary judgment. Hirst[1] uses the psychological data in order to reject the Sense-Datum Theory and in order to develop the details of his notion of 'perceptual consciousness'.

All these philosophers, as well as others, have sought to remedy the isolation between psychological and philosophical treatments of perception by letting the facts influence the formation of philosophical theories. Many other philosophers have, however, rejected the relevance of these psychological discoveries to philosophical theories. Their position is that philosophical theories of perception have been formed to deal with philosophical problems and not with the factual questions which are the subject of empirical psychology. Hence the facts ought to be able to be described equally well in terms of any epistemological theory. Thus A. J. Ayer wrote[2] that whereas the decision between the Sense-Datum Theory and its rivals was merely one concerning the adoption of rival philosophical terminologies, the question whether the 'Gestalt' or Atomic Theory more adequately describes the nature of our visual fields must be decided by an examination of the empirical evidence. Whatever decision we reach concerning the latter question will be capable of being phrased in terms of the Sense-Datum Terminology. Indeed some of the leading exponents of the Sense-Datum Theory such as C. D. Broad[3] and H. H. Price[4] have been well aware of the psychological findings concerning perception and have in fact referred to them explicitly in formulating their versions of the Sense-Datum Theory. These philosophers while willing to concede that the empirical findings of psychology can only be ignored by philosophers at their own peril, would in all likelihood deny the possibility, let alone the desirability, of combining the psychology and philosophy of perception so as to form a single comprehensive subject.

A decision as to the merits of the respective positions of those who champion the relevance of psychology for philosophical discussions of perception and those who deny its relevance would seem to depend largely on the question whether the aims of the epistemologist

[1] See note 2 p. 162 above.

[2] A. J. Ayer, *Foundations of Empirical Knowledge*, (London, Macmillan, 1940), pp.113–16. Ayer's, *The Problem of Knowledge*, (London, Penguin Books, 1956) p. 8, reflects the same view.

[3] C. D. Broad, *Scientific Thought*, (London, Kegan Paul, 1923) and *The Mind and Its Place in Nature*, (London, Kegan Paul, 1925).

[4] H. H. Price, *Perception*, (London, Methuen, 1932).

and the psychologist are sufficiently clearly specifiable so as to be shown to be quite different from each other. This is certainly the case if we accept the view of those who assign to the epistemologist his traditional task of allaying sceptical doubts by 'justifying' our ordnary claims to knowledge. This aim is obviously quite different and distinguishable from the psychologist's aim of describing the facts of perception and forming theories which will enable us to explain how empirical factors such as background, attention, etc., affect our perception. There is no reason in principle, then, why the two subjects, epistemology and psychology, should have anything to do with one another since the first, when so conceived, deals with the *logical* or *a priori* problems raised by perception while the latter deals with the empirical facts.

Even if epistemology is regarded merely as the conceptual analysis of cognitive concepts and dissociated from the traditional task of 'justifying' cognitive claims, it will be possible to maintain the irrelevance of psychological findings to the solution of metaphysical problems so long as we can find some clear aim or special purpose for the sort of 'analysis' in which the epistemologist is supposed to be engaged. The most obvious aim which might suggest itself for the task of conceptual analysis which the epistemologist is bidden to undertake is that of providing conceptual clarity.

This fits in very well with the complaint of those who have argued that its isolation from philosophy has allowed psychologists to get away with a great deal of conceptual confusion and lack of clarity in the formation of some of its most important conceptions. Thus D. W. Hamlyn[1] has examined some of the views of psychologists concerning perception and demonstrated the lack of conceptual clarity and the confusion engendered by the attempt to answer two different questions at once or by thinking that one has proved an empirical law when one has only provided a definition or an analytic truth. It is therefore arguable that even if it be the case that the findings of psychologists are irrelevant for the solution of the problems of perception with which philosophers have been concerned, there remains room for a close connection between psychology and philosophy inasmuch as the latter can provide the former with the necessary tools to enable it to conduct its empirical investigations more fruitfully. Hamlyn complains that psychologists do not start with con-

[1] D. W. Hamlyn, *The Psychology of Perception*, (London, Routledge, 1956).

ceptual clarification so that their theories are at best merely rounda-
bout ways of attaining it.[1]

But this view of the philosopher providing the necessary conceptual clarity so as to enable the psychologist to record the facts intelli-
gently is neither true to the history of epistemology nor very realistic
in its conception of the circumstances under which scientific investigations of the facts are conducted. The former point is obvious
enough. If it were merely the task of philosophical discussions to
produce the necessary conceptual clarity for the benefit of the
empirical investigations of the psychologist, a great deal of what
philosophers have hitherto said about perception would be rendered
useless since the clarification of perceptual concepts and the theory of
knowledge in general have usually been connected with the traditional
task of the epistemologist, namely, the dispelling of doubts regarding
our ordinary claims to knowledge and the construction of a theory
which will show how our cognitive claims could be 'justified'.

With regard to the second matter it should be noted that clarification of concepts requires some point; it is not an end in itself. If the
psychologist requires clarification with regard to his basic concepts,
such clarification must be directed to the empirical fruitfulness which
is the aim of the psychologist in his use of these concepts. Now what
concept will prove fruitful in describing and explaining the facts and
what concept will not, is something concerning which the psychologist is far better qualified to judge than the philosopher. In the
same way as it would be misguided to suggest that the physicist
should delay his empirical investigations until the philosopher will
clarify such concepts as 'force' and 'energy', so it would be misguided
to suggest that psychologists delay their empirical investigations
until the philosophers have clarified such concepts as 'sensation',
'belief', 'motivation', etc. If a certain facility in the critical evaluation
of his basic concepts may be a useful prerequisite for the scientist,
this does not mean that science and philosophical analysis must
necessarily be combined.

Hence the 'philosophy of psychology' considered as the conceptual analysis of psychological concepts may be a useful topic for the
psychologist; but it is certainly not a necessary part of psychology.
It can be an important adjunct to the philosopher himself. But
whether this is so or not depends upon what we conceive to be the

[1] ibid. pp. 6, 108 and 115.

philosopher's task in evaluating the concepts which are formed by psychologists in the course of their empirical investigations.

(V) THE COMPLEMENTARITY THESIS

As opposed to the notion that the philosophy of perception has to take account of the theories of the psychologist and physiologist, it may be argued on general grounds that the epistemologist need take no heed of scientific studies of perception, since the latter are to be regarded as alternative or complementary descriptions of the same facts using different categories and with different ends in view.

The notion that different theories may be merely alternative and complementary descriptions derives from Niels Bohr, the celebrated physicist, and is associated with what has come to be called the 'Copenhagen Interpretation' of the Quantum Theory.[1] Bohr's idea of complementarity originated in an attempt to derive a consistent and exhaustive picture of the behaviour of microscopic systems. Physicists have for some time found themselves in the extraordinary situation that with regard to the explanation of light, they are torn between two incompatible views: (1) that light consists of waves, (2) that light consists of particles. Conception (1) accounts for some of the known facts about light, but contradicts (2). Conception (2) accounts for other facts about light, but contradicts (1). It has been hitherto impossible to offer an explanation of light which will unify both conceptions and it is in fact maintained that such a unification is impossible in principle. If the latter is the case this would make the question quite different from previous cases in the history of science where two rival theories presented themselves and one of them was ousted by the subsequent development of science. Bohr argued that the situation with regard to the explanation of light was not merely indicative of an unsatisfactory intermediate stage in the history of science, but necessitated the adoption of an entirely new ideal of scientific explanation. We 'must be prepared . . . to accept the fact that a complete elucidation of one and the same object may require diverse points of view which defy a unique description'. This ideal of explanation was associated with a positivist view of scientific

---

[1] Bohr's views concerning complementarity have been widely expounded and discussed by physicists. Convenient expositions by Bohr are to be found in his contribution to the *The Philosophy of Albert Einstein* in 'The Library of Living Philosophers' (Evanston and Chicago, North Western University, 1938); in *Dialectica* 7/8 (1948) pp. 312 ff. and in the *Physical Review* Vol. 48 (1936).

theories in accordance with which such theories do not attempt to describe the hidden 'mechanisms' of the universe, but merely to offer the logical framework for a systematization of the observable facts which will allow of the possibility of fruitful prediction.

The idea of complementarity introduced into physics in this way by Bohr, was also applied to domains outside physics. In fact its physical origins are merely the occasion of a new ideal of explanation which is logically applicable to many other fields. As has been said, 'Microphysics provides at most an *illustration* and not a *model* of complementarity.' The logical notions involved in the conception of complementarity have been summarized as follows:[1]

Two (or more) descriptions may be called logically complementary when

(a) They purport to have a common reference
(b) Each is in principle exhaustive, (in the sense that none of the entities or events comprising the common reference need be left unaccounted for), yet
(c) They make different assertions, because
(d) The logical preconditions of definitions and/or of use (i.e. context) of concepts or relationships in each are mutually exclusive, so that significant aspects referred to in one are necessarily omitted from the other.

Many examples of complementary descriptions have been offered, the best of these probably being that of the geometrical projection of a three dimensional figure on a two dimensional surface. Any projection is exhaustive, in the sense that it includes all the points of the figure projected, yet necessarily omits an aspect (the ordering of the points in the third dimension) which is validly shown by a second projection perpendicular to it. In one projection a given point may be to the left of another point, in another projection it may be to the right of that point. The question of *standpoint* must be considered before any contradiction can be alleged. It is only the standpoints from which the terms of the description are defined that are mutually exclusive. Thus projection forms a good example of two complementary descriptions from different standpoints.

[1] D. M. Mackay, *Proceedings of the Aristotelian Society*, sup. vol. xxxii, (1958). See also Mackay's articles in *Synthese* 9, pp. 182–98 (1954), in the *Proc. of the Aristotelian Society*, sup. vol. xxvi (1952), in *The Listener* of 9th and 16th May 1957 and in *Mind* vol. LXVI (1957).

Another example of complementarity, in which the descriptions differ not only in standpoint but also in logical level, is the case of descriptions of signs and of what they signify, for example, between a physicist's and telegraphist's description of a morse signal. Both have a common reference in the happenings to which each listened. But it is not only psychologically inevitable that a man who attends fully to the physical structure of sounds cannot simultaneously set himself to read them, but even logically inevitable that in choosing one level of concept for his exhaustive description, he must set aside the others. The telegraphist's message is not a mere *translation* of the physicist's record; talking about signs is not the same thing as talking about things signified.

The application of the notion of complementarity to the relationship between the theories of perceptions offered, for example, by neurologists, and the theories of perception offered by epistemologists would involve the claim that each set of theories makes use of different categories in projecting the facts of perception, as it were, from a different standpoint.[1] The Neurologist is interested in providing an account of all the processes in the nervous system that mediate perception. Hence his stress is on the causal processes which form the necessary condition for any perception to occur. But the epistemologist is not interested in the causal chain (physical object—light—retina—optic nerve—central nervous system) which he regards merely as the *mechanism* of perception. His interest is in the question of the *justification* of perpetual assertions, and this call for justification is connected, as we have seen earlier, with the doubts raised by the philosophical sceptic. The two problems, that of the epistemologist, and that of the neurologist, are entirely different and have no bearing necessarily on each other. The theories offered by each of these separate disciplines conform with the definition of complementary description since (a) they have a common reference, the perceptual process, (b) each is in principle exhaustive, in the sense that nothing in the process of perception need be left unaccounted for from the standpoint of each particular discipline, (c) yet each discipline offers a different assertion, because (d) the logical context of concepts or relationships in each are mutually exclusive,

[1] Other applications of the complementarity thesis have been suggested, e.g. 'A person's subjective account of his own mental activity and the account of the physicist; religious and scientific explanations of different phenomena, etc.

so that significant aspects referred to in one discipline are necessarily omitted from the other.

The application of the complementarity thesis to the relationship between neurological and epistemological theories of perception seems to me exceedingly convincing and confirms the remarks made previously in this chapter. And the application of the notion of complementarity to the relationship between psychological and epistemological accounts of perception seems similarly well grounded. It is of course true that neurologists and psychologists present their facts and theories in terms which are somewhat confused and sometimes much in need of critical philosophical analysis. But as already argued, the clarification of a concept by philosophical analysis cannot be divorced from the purpose for which this particular concept is to be used. Philosophical analysis can assist the psychologist in clarifying the notion of 'visual field' for its more effective use in psychological explanations; but this may have no bearing on the use of such a concept, assuming that it has to be used at all, in epistemological explanations. Neurologists, psychologists and epistemologists may in practice be confused with regard to the relationship between their different disciplines and the use of certain familiar concepts (e.g. sensation, consciousness, etc.) interchangeably in each discipline, but the complementarity thesis offers at any rate an ideal regarding the relationships which ought to exist between the disciplines, and this ideal seems to be supported by the facts themselves.

The complementarity thesis has been widely criticized on the grounds that by accepting the notion of alternative descriptions it facilely shirks the task of co-ordinating our knowledge of the world at depth and of offering a comprehensive explanation of things. It may indeed be the case, it is argued, that two disciplines at present different from each other each conduct their enquiries in isolation from each other and from a different point of view. But this does not mean that there is no possibility of harmonizing the findings of each discipline in a broader unified view which does justice to the discoveries of each. And this broader synoptic view is the goal at which all the disciplines are aiming, even though they lay aside, for the moment, their pursuit of this long term goal in order to concern themselves primarily with their own particular areas.[1]

---

[1] See especially K. Feyerabend, *Proceedings of the Aristotelian Society*, sup. vol. xxxii (1958), R. Harre. *Proc. of Arist. Soc.*, vol. LX (1959–60), etc.

To this it may be replied that there is nothing in the idea of logical complementarity which excludes the possibility of a 'higher' mode of representation which could synthesize two or more complementary accounts. It may at any time be possible, with ingenuity, to combine both accounts in a wider theory. What the complementarity thesis wishes to avoid, however, is the assumption that in providing this wider theory we somehow disqualify the stand-points from which the two complementary descriptions were given. Those standpoints may still be legitimate, and the descriptions given from them may still be the only satisfactory one from that point of view. The complementarity thesis wishes to avoid the prejudice that a wider theory *need* always be sought. Thus it *may* be possible to suggest some standpoint from which the findings of neurologists, psychologists and epistemologists can be combined. But the discovery of such a standpoint would not necessarily disqualify the legitimacy of importance of these separate disciplines; nor would it provide a vantage point from which we could take sides in any issue between the different disciplines or show them to be talking about different things or to be saying just the same things or to be telling just part of the truth. And finally we should need to be convinced that this new standpoint is worth taking up as having any theoretical or practical advantage.

Another criticism of the complementarity thesis relates to its supposed connection with the positivist view of the nature of scientific theories in accordance with which these are only predictive calculuses and not descriptions of the hidden mechanisms of the real world. It is alleged that this positivist view militates against scientific progress, for it is only by adopting the 'realistic' procedure connected with the classical ideal of scientific explanation which regards scientific process as discovery that we can avoid stagnation.[1]

This criticism is rather vague, and may be answered in the following way:

(1) It is true that Bohr and many others of the 'Copenhagen School' did combine the notion of complementarity with a positivist view of scientific theories, but it is not true that such a combination is inevitable. The true 'mechanisms' of the universe may exist at many different levels (wheels within wheels, as it were) each of them dis-

[1] K. Feyerabend, loc. cit.

coverable by inspection from that particular point of view. On the other hand it is true that a more positivistically inclined view of the nature of scientific theory allows for greater play for inventiveness and ingenuity in the formation of new scientific theories, and hence accommodates itself more easily to the view that scientific explanations must not all be sought at one level. Positivism is not a necessary part of the complementarity thesis, but a little positivism may be a useful adjunct.

(2) The criticism that the classical ideal of scientific explanation leads to progress and the complementarity thesis to stagnation is a mere prejudice. The desire to discover is an important motive for scientific enquiry, but it is not the only motive. Simple curiosity also plays its part. And understanding is not equivalent to the ability to describe. Nor is there any reason why we should be so confident of the ultimate unity of all knowledge—that it could all be charted, as it were, on a single map. Different disciplines are not necessarily always dealing with adjacent areas on the map; sometimes they are engaged in providing different maps (e.g. weather maps, political maps and topographical maps) of the same area. And there is no reason, even if ingenuity could provide a map so complicated that all the different data about a given area could be charted at the same time, why such a map should necessarily be more useful or more profound. The complementarity thesis suggests the possibility that knowledge or science might best be regarded as a drawer full of different maps, rather than a single map whose details we are all trying to fill in.

(VI) CONCLUSION

Hence both on the general grounds of the complementarity thesis, which lays down an ideal of explanation in accordance with which different scientific disciplines may co-exist and complement each other without necessarily being ultimately unifiable or harmonizable, as well as on the more specific grounds that the task of the epistemologist is so specific (especially if interpreted in the traditional manner) and different from the aims of the psychologist and neuro-physiologist, that there seems little reason to suppose that their very different theories can coalesce, we may draw the conclusion that the scientific studies of perception need have no bearing on the philosophical treatment of this same topic.

Chapter 11

EPISTEMOLOGY, ANALYTIC PHILOSOPHY AND METAPHYSICS

(I) EPISTEMOLOGY AS ANALYSIS

A large number of contemporary philosophers in English speaking countries are agreed in regarding epistemology as part of analytic philosophy, and the problem of perception, in connection with which the whole question of the given arises, as a particular area amenable to analytic discipline. But while there is some measure of agreement with regard to the methods to be employed, i.e. the analysis of such concepts as 'knowing', 'seeing', 'believing', 'certainty', etc. and even some measure of accommodation between those who would wish to analyse these concepts in terms of ordinary language and usage, and those who would prefer to analyse them by setting up some sort of ideal language or technical terminology which would more adequately exhibit the true relationship between these different concepts, there is little agreement regarding the purpose for which such an analysis should be undertaken. This lack of agreement regarding the purposes for which the analysis of cognitive concepts is to be undertaken, has important bearings upon the question of the given. For this reason we shall investigate one or two of the main approaches that have crystallised with regard to this matter.

(II) AYER'S VIEW

In a recent work[1] Ayer has expounded the view that in asking such questions as 'What is the nature of belief?', 'What is truth?' and so on, philosophers are not simply looking for a definition but are rather seeking to give an analysis of certain concepts. The analysis of cognitive concepts which the epistemologist undertakes may be re-

[1] A. J. Ayer, *The Problem of Knowledge*, (London, Penguin Books, 1956) Chapter 2.

garded as the attempt to reply to the doubts of the philosophical sceptic. This sceptic calls in question not the way in which we apply out standards of proof, but the standards themselves. The philosophical sceptic is not concerned, as a scientist would be, with distinguishing the condition in which the sources of knowledge are likely to fail from those in which they can normally be trusted. The doubt which he raises is whether they can be trusted at any time, whether we are justified in relying upon them at all.

The fact that he regards epistemology as the attempt to reply to the doubts of this philosophic scepticism enables Ayer to find parallels between the different philosophical positions which have been taken up by epistemologists on such different topics as our knowledge of the material world, our knowledge of other minds, etc.[1] In each of these cases the sceptical attack is directed not against factual inference as such, but against some particular forms of it in which we appear to end with statements of a different sort from those with which we began. Thus doubt is thrown on the validity of our belief in the existence of physical objects, the minds of others, the past, etc., by an argument which seeks to show that it depends in each case upon an illegitimate inference. Have we any right to make the transition from sense experiences to physical objects, from the overt behaviour of other people to their inner thoughts and feelings, from the present to the past? Though each of these constitutes a distinct problem, the pattern of the sceptic's argument is the same in every case.

The first step is to insist that we depend entirely on the premises for our knowledge of the conclusion. Thus our claim to know objects is based on our sense experiences; our claim to know other minds is based on the state of other people's bodies and behaviour; the past is known only from present records or memories. In each case our claim to know involves passing beyond our premises. The second step is to argue that the conclusion cannot be deduced from the premises: e.g. however rich our sense experience is we cannot deduce from it the sort of things that ordinary people claim to know about objects. The next step is to argue that our claims to knowledge cannot be regarded as legitimate inductive inferences from our premises: e.g. we cannot pass from premises concerning the contents of our sense experiences to conclusions about physical objects, from pre-

[1] ibid., Section IX.

mises about other people's overt behaviour to conclusions about their minds. The final step is to argue that since the claims to knowledge cannot be inferred either deductively or inductively from the actual experience with which we start, they cannot be justified at all.

In this way the problem which is raised in all these cases by the philosophical sceptic is that of establishing our right to make what appears to be a special sort of advance beyond our data. For those who wish to vindicate our claim to knowledge, the difficulty is to find a way of bridging or abolishing this gap. 'Concern with the theory of knowledge,' says Ayer, 'is very much a matter of taking this difficulty seriously.'[1] According to him the different ways of trying to meet the difficulty mark out different schools of philosophy, or different methods of attacking philosophical questions. There are four main lines of approach, apart from the purely sceptical position, with regard to the claim to knowledge in each of the problematic cases (external world, other minds, the past, etc.), and each of these approaches consists in denying a different step in the sceptics' argument.

(a) Denial of the first step yields Naive Realism or some form of Intuitionism. The philosopher maintains that we are directly or intuitively aware of objects, other minds, the past, etc., themselves and are not restricted to our present experiences.

(b) Those who accept the sceptic's first step but deny the second offer us some form of Reductionism. Physical objects are 'logical constructions' out of the contents of our sense-experiences, statements which appear to be about others' minds are really statements about their behaviour, statements about the past are really reducible to statements about present records.

(c) Those who admit the first two steps in the sceptic's argument but deny the third come up with what Ayer calls 'the Scientific Approach'. They accept the existence of the gap between evidence and conclusion, but hold that it can be bridged by a legitimate process of inductive reasoning. Thus physical objects, though not directly observable in the way in which naive realists suppose, can be known to us indirectly as the causes of our sensation, past events can be known as the causes of our present records and memories, the exis-

[1] ibid., p. 78.

tence of other minds can be known as the cause of their overt behaviour.

(d) Finally, those who accept the sceptic's argument in the first three
steps, and reject Naive Realism, Reductionism and the Scientific
approach as acceptable answers to the sceptic are still free to dispute
the sceptic's conclusion that we are not justified in our claim to
know objects, other minds, the past, etc. There is a gap between our
premises in experience and the claim to knowledge which is our
conclusion, and this gap cannot be bridged by deduction or induction. But this does not condemn our claims to knowledge, for no
justification is really either necessary or possible. One may be called
upon to justify a particular conclusion, and then one can appeal to
the appropriate evidence. But there can be no proof that what we
take to be good evidence really is so. One can doubt whether the
criterion of knowledge is adequate in particular cases, but if one
doubts whether the criterion is applicable at all, or whether any
criterion can be applicable, then one is left without any posibility of
knowing. If there cannot be a proof that what we take to be good
evidence really is so, then it is not sensible to demand one. 'The
sceptic's problems are insoluble because they are fictitious.'[1]

It is at this last stage that one has the uncomfortable feeling that
Ayer has sold the pass. If the philosophical sceptic's problems are
really fictitious then, according to his own previously stated affirma-
tion regarding the theory of knowledge being a matter of taking
seriously the difficulty raised by the philosophical sceptic, we ought
to conclude that the theory of knowledge is not a serious matter at
all. Surely Ayer himself cannot admit of this fourth approach which
he calls 'Descriptive Analysis' as a legitimate answer to the sceptic's
doubts, for according to what he has said, this approach renders the
sceptic's doubt, and consequently any serious concern with epistemology, spurious. It is no good saying that our claims to knowledge
can legitimately be 'analysed' by the Descriptive Analyst who will,
for example, try to show in what conditions we feel confident in
attributing certain experiences to others, evaluate different types of
record, distinguish cases in which our memories or perceptions are
taken to be reliable from those in which they are not, and in general
give an account of the procedures that we actually follow. We have
still to explain what this sort of 'analysis' might be, and how it is

[1] ibid., p. 81.

different, if at all, from the account of the procedures that we actually follow given by the ordinary man, by the psychologist and by the neuro-physiologist.

I consider Ayer's association of the different positions taken up with respect to the various epistemological questions with different stages in the argument of the sceptic to be interesting and instructive. It may well be that this association is not so simple and schematic as Ayer would have us suppose. But the suggestion that the epistemologist is wrestling with sceptic doubts seems to me to be sound both intuitively and as a matter of history. It also fits in very well with the suggestion we have offered with regard to the appeal to the given in the previous chapter, where we saw this to be connected with the quest for certainty, a quest which we have interepreted to be the search for some metaphysical reality. Ayer, as we have seen, does not speak very much about the given. If he explicitly associated himself with the 'Descriptive Analysis' approach we might well interpret him as rejecting the notion of 'the given' completely, as is done by L. J. Austin, G. Ryle, and others. But, as a matter of fact, there is evidence that the firm preferences for the SDT which could be discerned between the lines of his linguistic theory regarding the Sense Datum Theory have been retained, though considerably muted, even in his latest epistemological works.

(III) CHISHOLM'S VIEW

But it is interesting to note that Ayer's remarks regarding philosophical scepticism and its relation to the pattern of epistemological approaches regarding different questions are paralleled by a similar attempt on the part of R. M. Chisholm to delineate certain traditional approaches to epistemological problems in his recent book on the *Theory of Knowledge*. In a chapter entitled 'The Problem of the Criterion',[1] Chisholm considers the problem of 'our knowledge of external things' as just one alongside many other problems such as the question of other minds, etc., in which a certain pattern of typical positions may be taken up. However, Chisholm dissociates these positions from philosophical scepticism and associates them instead with 'the problem of the criterion'. The latter has to do with the

---

[1] R. M. Chisholm, *Theory of Knowledge*, Foundations of Philosophy Series, (Englewood, Prentice-Hall, 1966), pp. 56 ff.

relative stress to be laid on two different questions in the theory of knowledge, namely, 'What is the *extent* of our knowledge?' and 'What are the *criteria* of knowing?' With regard to the claim to knowledge in such traditional fields as the external world, other minds, etc., the typical attitudes in the history of philosophy are 'empiricism', 'common-sensism' (or 'dogmatism') and 'scepticism' (or 'agnosticism'). It is characteristic of 'empiricism' to put forward our 'experience' in one or another of its various senses as the source of our knowledge, and maintain that every valid claim to knowledge will satisfy certain empirical criteria which are related to our experience. The 'dogmatist' or 'commonsense' philosopher, on the other hands, starts by assuming that we do know most, if not all, of those things that ordinary people claim to know. He does not first fix upon a criterion and then measure our claims to knowledge by relating them to this criterion but on the contrary, accepts our established claims to knowledge as primary and discusses the criterion only in terms of working out an adequate scheme which will show what these claims to knowledge presuppose. The 'sceptic' refuses to assume that any claims to knowledge are to be credited prima facie; nor is he prepared to credit any particular criterion as sufficient. He is thus able to conclude that we do not know what, if anything, we know, and we have no way of deciding in any particular case whether or not we know.

Thus whereas Ayer regards the different positions taken up by epistemologists as answers to the sceptic, Chisholm sees these positions, the sceptic position included, as approaches to 'the problem of the criterion'. That the sceptic position has some significance in epistemology, Chisholm is not then denying. But it is not the impulse to philosophical speculation resulting in the theory of knowledge which Ayer claims it to be. The epistemologist is not 'replying' to the sceptic: scepticism is just one possible epistemological position which can be adopted in connection with 'the problem of the criterion'. Chisholm thus reverts to the more traditional approach in which 'the problem of the criterion' is raised in connection with any of the so-called 'sources of knowledge': (1) 'external perception', (2) memory, (3) 'self-awareness' (Reflection,' or 'inner consciousness'), (4) reason. The problem of perception, for example, arises by applying 'the problem of the criterion' to the first of these sources, when we ask 'How are we to decide just *what* it is that is yielded by this properly accredited source of knowledge?' Once we have established that from 'directly evident' premises—premises expressing what is given to us in 'self-awareness'—neither induction nor deduction will yield the conclusion that, for example, 'A cat is on the roof' (in cases where there *is* a cat on the roof which we are now perceiving), there are at least four different ways in which we might react. (1) We may say, with the 'intuitionist' (or 'common-sense' philosopher) that we know external things directly by means of some other type of experience, and not necessarily only through what is given to us in 'self-awareness'. (2) On the other hand we may follow the 'sceptic' in saying that we cannot know that there is a cat on the roof. Those following the middle-of-the-road approach of the 'empiricist', will follow the path either of (3) 'reductionism', or (4) 'critical cognitivism'. The 'reductionist' maintains that 'A cat is on the roof' can be translated or paraphrased into sentences expressing one's self-awareness—more particularly, into sentences about the ways in which one is appeared to. The 'critical cognitivist' will say that our knowledge of external objects such as cats is known 'through' our empirical experience yielded to us by our 'self-awareness'. The ways in which one is appeared to are *signs* or *criteria* of truths about objects which we perceive. The 'critical cognitivist' will say that there are principles of evidence, other than the principles of induction and deduction, which tell us, for example, under what conditions the state called 'thinking that one perceives' will *confer evidence*, or *confer reasonableness*, upon propositions about external things.[1]

Chisholm's theory of perception, as he explicitly says,[2] is a form of 'critical cognitivism', i.e. an 'empiricist' theory which avoids the extremes of 'intuitionism' on the one hand, and 'scepticism' on the other. It arises, then, not in *answer* to the challenge of the sceptic, but constitutes an alternative approach to 'the problem of the criterion' with respect to 'external perception'. It is to be noted, however, that Chisholm's theory bases itself on the notion of 'directly evident' states of 'self-awareness' which, in the case of perception, are the

---

[1] J. L. Austin, on the other hand writes: '... there *could* be no *general* answer to the questions what is evidence for what, what is certain, what is doubtful, what needs or does not need evidence, can or can't be verified. If the Theory of Knowledge consists in finding grounds for such an answer, there is no such thing.' *Sense and Sensibilia*, (Oxford, Clarendon Press, 1960), p. 124.

[2] *Theory of Knowledge*, pp. 68-9.

ways in which we are appeared to. His theory, then, has recourse to the notion of 'the given' as one of its essential foundations. And Chisholm is, therefore, drawn quite openly into offering a defence of the notion of 'the given' which will ward off the criticisms of many contemporary philosophers who have regarded this notion as 'a myth'. Chisholm attempts to revitalize the idea of 'the given' by interpreting it as a way of expressing the notion of an epistemological order to our knowledge.

(IV) THE EPISTEMOLOGICALLY BASIC

Chisholm's restatement of the doctrine of 'the given' may be summarized as follows:

(1) All that the doctrine fundamentally asserts is that our knowledge may be thought of as a 'structure' which rests upon a foundation of absolute certainty.

(2) There is a distinction between 'basic' or 'primitive' knowledge and 'derivative' or 'inferred' knowledge, and the latter is, in some sense, 'based upon' or 'presupposes' the former. This distinction arises because the philosopher finds two sorts of truths which are known, the sort which when he asks himself 'What is the justification for my supposing I know this?' he will answer by referring to something else that he knows, and the sort about which in answer to the same question he is unable to point to anything else which he knows and which would justify his original claim to knowledge.

(3) The 'primitive' truths, are those which describe the ways in which things appear, or which express intimate states of mind, such as what a man believes, what he feels, and so on. There are also some philosophers who include the *a priori* truths of logic and mathematics, within the realm of primitive truths, but others exclude them on the grounds that these are not cognitive truths at all but only something like conventional assumptions or rules of language.

(4) It is not essential to regard derivative knowledge as ever being actually inferred from primitive knowledge. The critics who have based their rejection of 'the given' mainly on the non-existence of such a process of inference have been barking up the wrong tree. When it is said that the belief that there is a table is 'inferred' whereas the assertion of how the table appears is not inferred, all that is

meant is (a) that the assertion about how the table appears refers to immediate experience alone, whereas the belief about the table refers beyond it, and (b) if the observer were to doubt whether it was a table, he would appeal to the way the table appears.[1] The way things appear and the way we feel, think, believe, etc., are the sort of things which serve as the *evidence for* assertions of knowledge which are derivative. The primitive truths themselves are what *confer* the evidence, and they themselves may be regarded as 'pre-evident' (or perhaps 'self evident'). It is not essential to regard these pre-evident truths as being 'known', and so, once more, those critics who have laid great stock on the point that such truths (e.g. 'I feel a pain' or 'it looks red') cannot be said to be certain at all since they cannot properly be said to be *known*, have been on the wrong track. It is sufficient that these primitive truths be what confers the evidence on which our claim to knowledge is based; they need not themselves be 'known'. These pre-evident truths are like the Prime Mover of Aristotelian cosmology which is itself unmoved. 'The given' can confer evidence without itself being evident. If it were possible to construct rules of evidence describing the ways in which 'the given', or pre-evident, confers evidence upon all the other things we know, then the 'structure' of our knowledge will have been demonstrated.

(5) It is to the establishment of these rules of evidence that the efforts of those epistemologists who have spoken of 'the given' have been dedicated, although some of them have been misled into not realizing clearly the task on which they were engaged.[2]

---

[1] R. M. Chisholm, 'Russell on the Foundations of Empirical Knowledge' in *The Philosophy of Bertrand Russell*, Library of Living Philosophers (Evanston and Chicago, North Western University, 1949) pp. 421-30. In his *Theory of Knowledge*, Chisholm has phrased himself somewhat differently: 'the given' is called 'the directly evident', 'derivative knowledge' is called 'the indirectly evident', and the question of 'justification' is dissociated much more clearly from 'challenging' or 'doubting' the truth of any statement, on the one hand, as also from inquiries as to how one came to believe the truth of the statement, or how one would persuade others of the statement's truth, on the other hand. The question of 'justification' is said to be 'Socratic' and therefore not at all of the type that one ordinarily asks. (p. 25.).

[2] This view of the task of the epistemologist is reflected especially in the epistemological writings of Bertrand Russell, in C. I. Lewis *The Ground and Nature of the Right* (New York, Columbia University Press, 1955) and in R. M. Chisholm *Perceiving, A Philosophical Study* (Ithaca, Cornell U. P. 1957). R. Firth writing in the *Philosophical Review* LXXIII (1964) calls this view of epistemology 'the Cartesian tradition'. (pp. 372-3).

From the above statement, all that is meant, when some class of things is said to be 'given', is that this class of things, knowledge of which is pre-evident, serves as the foundation which confers evidence upon the rest of our knowledge, which can be regarded as its superstructure. The notion of 'the given' therefore depends upon the idea of 'epistemological priority', and when something is said to be 'given', what is meant is that this is what is 'epistemologically basic'.

(V) AN ANALYTIC SCIENCE?

Chisholm's restatement and defence of the doctrine of 'the given' seems to me to be unacceptable for a number of important reasons:

(1) The proposed defence dissociates the notion of 'the given' from the sceptical doubts with which it has been traditionally connected. Thus, for example, insofar as Descartes can be regarded as the inaugurator of the interest in epistemology in modern philosophy, we should have to regard his 'methodological doubt' as simply a misleading way of pointing out the epistemological priority of certain truths. Chisholm indeed points out that this 'methodological scepticism' is dubious, for if 'doubt' means the mere suspension of belief then no scepticism would be justified, whereas if it means disbelief it would be completely unreasonable. Like the critics of the doctrine of 'the given' to whom he refers, Chisholm is prepared to reject most of the arguments in support of 'scepticism with regard to the senses' as specious. He feels that the sense in which primitive truths which call attention to 'the given' are to be regarded as epistemologically prior to the derivative truths can be shown without the usual exaggerated emphasis on the notions of 'doubt' and 'scepticism'.

Now Chisholm recognizes that a large number of philosophers have defined the order of cognitive priority in terms of methodological scepticism.[1] If the appeal to the given is really dissociated from 'methodological scepticism' it is not easy to explain why so many

[1] 'Russell on the Foundations of Empirical Knowledge', p. 425; *Theory of Knowledge*, p. 25 n.3. His list includes Russell and E. Husserl, G. Santayana, R. Carnap, H. H. Price. But he asserts that Brentano specifically dissociated epistemological priority from sceptical doubts. He also thinks that Aristotle, Leibniz and Reid dissociated the two things.

of the classical proponents of 'the given' have been misled into supposing the two to be connected. Moreover, although it is true that 'methodological scepticism', when taken at face value, is doubtful, as we ourselves have argued previously,[1] this shows only that the scepticism should *not* be taken at face value. I think the current interpretation of 'methodological scepticism' which shows it to be merely a big mistake is extremely uncharitable to all those philosophers who have used it.

(2) But can the concept of epistemological order really be dissociated from 'the exaggerated emphasis' upon the notions of doubt or scepticism?

Of the two characteristics which Chisholm has indicated as the defining criteria of 'the epistemologically basic', namely that this must be something (a) based on immediate experience and (b) which would be referred to in order to 'justify' our assertion that we know something, the first is obscure and dubious, and the second requires careful consideration. I shall not talk about the notion of 'direct experience', for I have said more than enough about this in previous chapters.[2] But if we consider the sense in which primitive truths are held to 'justify' derivative truths we shall discover that Chisholm refers primarily to the sort of things someone would turn to *if* he were in doubt. If this is meant to be a mere description of what takes place in actual fact when we justify our beliefs in order to remove doubts then this description is partial, selective, and does not tell the whole story. If we were in doubt as to the truth of any particular belief which we had hitherto regarded as unassailable knowledge, we might reassure ourselves by reference to a great many different sorts of things and facts, and would certainly not merely restrict ourselves to referring to the ways in which objects appear, or to our present states of mind. The latter have in fact no priority in the *actual* justification of our beliefs. But if what is meant is not that we actually do justify our beliefs in this way, but that *logically*, if pressed, this is the way, in the last resort, in which we ought to be able to justify our beliefs, then 'justifiable' turns out to be simply a synonym for 'epistemologically derivable'. Logically and epistemologically the

[1] See Chapter 9, (v)
[2] See Chapters 3 and 6. Chisholm has attempted to avoid the notion that the 'epistemologically basic' is based on 'experience' in his more recent writings. See especially 'Evidence as Justification', *Journal of Philosophy* 1961, pp. 746-9.

ways in which things appear, or our present states of mind are, it is being alleged, the bases from which any 'derivative' truth can be 'justified'. But we cannot allow 'justifiable' and 'epistemologically derivable' to be treated as synonyms in this way for (a) it is the latter concept that we are trying to clarify by turning to the fact of justifiability,[1] and (b) if 'epistemologically derivable' means only, as it seems, 'can be logically inferred given the right set of epistemo-logical premises', we are still faced with the problem of explaining how the fact that we can invent a system in which 'derivative' propositions can be inferred logically from 'primitive' truths, can have any bearing on the question of 'justifiability'.

This is the basic difficulty in making sense of the notion of 'epistemological priority'. Either the priority is one in our *actual* process of confirming our beliefs by the evidence, or else it refers to what *ought* to count as the primary sort of evidence. But we actually confirm our beliefs in all sorts of ways, so why should the way things appear and our present states of mind be regarded as the funda-mental sort of evidence to which we ought to turn in the last resort? Let us assume that we can invent a sort of 'epistemological logic' with 'rules of evidence', in such a way that knowledge about the things and happenings in the world can be 'derived' from the evi-dence about the way in which things appear and about our present states of mind. Why *ought* one to use this logic rather than carry on in the way in which we have been carrying on hitherto in ascertain-ing facts about the world? Surely the possibility of being able to invent an 'epistemological logic' of this sort is a question of ingenuity only; presumably by inventing the right intermediate premises it should be possible to show that anything is logically derivable from anything else. But no-one would think it worthwhile to engage in this harmless intellectual pastime unless there were some reason for it. From Lewis' account, as also from Chisholm's approval of Moore's well-known distinction between common-sense proposi-tions which are certain and the analysis of such propositions, it would appear that it might be replied that what is involved in work-ing out an 'epistemological logic' of this sort is the 'logical analysis'

---

[1] Chisholm, in accordance with his latest formulation of the theory (See note 1 p. 186), may well reply that if 'self-justifying' truths are those we would appeal to if we were in doubt, this is only an accident. But this defence would be tantamount to the adoption of possibility (b) which is discussed in the text above.

of perceptual knowledge. But Moore's concept of analysis is notoriously difficult to understand, and it is particularly hard to grasp what can be the purpose of an analysis in the case of beliefs related to perceptual experience, unless this *is* connected with the need to justify. Moore's concept of analysis takes whatever plausibility it has from his commitment to the Sense-Datum Theory. Given that there are such things as sense-data (which Moore regards as so obvious that he cannot understand how anyone could be mistaken about this)[1] and that these sense-data are not identical with actual features of physical objects, the problem of the analysis of perceptual beliefs resolves itself into the problem of relating statements about objects to statements about sense-data. This is analogous to the following problem: given a large expanse (e.g. of paper) which we know to be constructed out of differently shaped units (e.g. small paper triangles) we may try to figure out how the small units can be fitted together in order to form the large expanse. But if we are doubtful about whether the larger expanse ever has been or can be 'constructed' out of, or in terms of, smaller units, and do not know of any definite unit out of which it might have been constructed, then there remains little point in showing that if you specify or hit upon a certain small unit out of which the larger expense *might* have been constructed, you can '*analyse*' how the big expanse can be broken down into these smaller units. Similarly, if we are doubtful about the 'derivability' of perceptual beliefs about objects, and still more doubtful about 'the way things appear' and 'present states of mind' being the basic units from which perceptual beliefs about objects might be derived,[2] then there seems little point in working out an 'epistemology' with 'rules of evidence' in order to show how beliefs about objects can be derived from appearances and stages of mind.

Thus it seems very likely that the use of the expression 'justification' is no accident and betrays the vital connection between the notion of 'the epistemologically basic' and the need to reply to sceptical doubts.

(3) The sort of analyses which explicates the epistemological order

[1] See above Chapter 3 (II).

[2] Which comes first: Chisholm's belief about 'the way things appear' and 'present states of mind' being the given ('epistemologically basic') or his belief that perceptual truths about objects are derivative? If they are merely two sides of the same coin, then how does this gain any currency unless it is based on the notion of 'justifiability'?

of our knowledge seems to be conceived as the discovery of criteria which establish *cognitive* validity (or 'evidence'), in much the same way as Aristotle's analysis explicating the principles of syllogistic reasoning consisted of the discovery of criteria which establish *logical* validity.[1] Conceived this way, epistemology turns into a discipline similar to logic, where 'evidence' takes the place of the notion of 'validity'. But 'evidence' and 'conferring of evidence' are technical concepts which are hard to grasp, and which seem to have been formed by smoothening out the rough ordinary notion of 'evidence' as used in such expressions as 'I know it—it is evident'. It is not clear that the expression 'it is evident' is any more unambiguous than the expression 'it is known', which can perform a variety of different functions in ordinary speech, as has correctly been argued by J. L. Austin and others.[2] The justification for the formation of such technical concepts as 'evidence' and 'conferring evidence' has thus first to be established before epistemology, as conceived by Chisholm, can even begin.

(4) But, finally, turning the doctrine of 'the given' into a way of asserting the fact of epistemological order, or of pointing to epistemological priority, misses some of the distinct metaphysical flavour which we have discovered to be associated with the appeal to the given, at least in some of its forms. Such an interpretation of the appeal to the given fits in only with the SDT, but not with either of the other two chief theories of the given. Chisholm is in fact defending a version of the SDT, and, like C I. Lewis before him, he seems to be disregarding the fact that the exponents of different theories of the given consider themselves to be genuinely at issue with one another.[3]

The fact that there are three different theories concerning the nature of 'the given', which regard themselves as genuinely at issue

---

[1] *Theory of Knowledge*, p. 25.

[2] See J. L. Austin, 'Other Minds' reprinted in *Philosophical Papers* ed. J. O. Urmson and G. J. Warnock (Oxford: Clarendon Press, 1961) pp. 44–84; J. O. Urmson, 'Parenthetical Verbs' in *Essays in Conceptual Analysis*, ed. A. G. N. Flew (London, 1956). Chisholm discusses this view in *Theory of Knowledge*, pp. 15–18.

[3] This criticism is not to be avoided by saying that Chisholm is not attempting to provide a theory about theories of the given. The point is that in assessing the nature of appeals to the given we must take into consideration the fact that there are different theories regarding the nature of the given. And an examination of the issue between these casts doubt on Chisholm's attempt to interpret the SDT in terms of the notion of the 'epistemologically basic'.

with each other, must be considered in evaluating the appeal to 'the given'. But since the argument between these theories does not concern itself with the facts (as maintained in the Naive View) we find ourselves forced to consider the conceptions of thought and the mind with which each theory is associated. And in following up various suggestions as to the possible explanation of the argument about the nature of 'the given', we have seen that a promising explanation is forthcoming if we interpret the 'quest for the certain', so characteristic of the SDT, as being fundamentally connected with the rejection of the claim to ultimate metaphysical reality of the common sense world, which is characteristic of the IET. The argument about the nature of 'the given' is then revealed as in essence a metaphysical argument involving different conceptions of the nature of thought and the relation between cognition and reality.

From this point of view then, there seems reason to support A. J. Ayer's presentation of epistemology as being concerned with the problem of philosophical scepticism, and to reject R. M. Chisholm's presentation of epistemology as an analytical science analogous to formal logic, which is only incidentally, and probably erroneously, associated with scepticism.

(VI) CONCLUDING REMARKS

Our discussions in this chapter and in the preceding chapter therefore seem to point in the direction of the following conclusions:

(1) Of the three approaches to the topic of perception discernible in the works of contemporary epistemologists, namely (a) the 'comprehensive theory' approach which sets the philosopher the task of taking cognizance of the findings of psychologists and physiologists in order to offer a unified theory, (b) the analytic approach which sets the philosopher the task of analysing the concepts or language used in connection with knowledge and perception, (c) the traditional approach which sets the epistemologist the task of allaying the doubts attaching to our ordinary claims to knowledge, approaches (a) and (b) have been found to be wanting and (c) the traditional approach has been found to be most acceptable.

(2) The notion that the philosopher must construct a unified theory, taking account of the findings of psychologists and physiologists, is

to be rejected as involving the unwarranted assumption that this unified theory would somehow provide greater insight into the concept of perception and knowledge. But the claim of the complementarity theorists seems more acceptable regarding the interrelation of these differing treatments of the topic of perception, since the aims of the psychologist, physiologist and epistemologist are so clearly specifiable and different from one another.

(3) The view that the epistemologist should denote himself to the analysis of the fundamental concepts involved in cognition, namely sensation, observation, appearing, believing, knowing, etc., is acceptable as a methodological recommendation. However, the value of such an analysis and the procedure to be followed in conducting it remain obscure unless the analyst sets himself specific aims. Many sorts of conceptual analysis are possible; indeed a certain amount of concept formation and analysis are indispensable to any scientific investigation. The psychologist must formulate and critically analyse basic concepts in order to be able to conduct his empirical investigation into perception fruitfully; so must the physiologist. But unless we assign to epistemology a clear task, e.g. its traditional one, the philosopher's analysis of the concept of perception must be either a purposeless language-game, or else he must conduct a second order analysis of the concepts formed by the psychologist and physiologist in the process of their empirical investigations. But such a second-order analysis is possible only if the concepts formulated by psychologists and physiologists are on the same level so that they can be either contradictory or confirmatory of each other; moreover, the second-order analysis would only be valuable if a unified comprehensive theory provided by the philosopher would somehow bring greater insight or penetration to the psychologist, the physiologist or even to the ordinary man. But this is rejected by the complementarity thesis which we have accepted regarding the relationships between psychology and physiology. Hence, unless the epistemologist has some specific aim, e.g. the traditional one, to his conceptual analysis, epistemology becomes a purposeless language-game.

(4) The traditional view that the epistemologist must aim at removing the doubts concerning our ordinary claims to knowledge by constructing a theory which will provide a detailed account of how we can arrive at certain knowledge through sense-perception and the

other 'sources' of knowledge, is confirmed by our discovery of the factors involved in the appeal to the given which has been a recurrent phenomenon in modern epistemological discussions. But equally our evaluation of the nature of the argument concerning the given has cast doubt upon the philosophical scepticism which has been the traditional source of epistemologisal discussions. This evaluation has shown that philosophical scepticism is a form of metaphysical dissatisfaction with the claims to reality of the common-sense view of the world. We shall argue in the final chapter that this dissatisfaction, justifiable as metaphysics, has unfortunately misled many into a rejection of common-sense. In a sense, the common-sense view is irreplaceable, at any rate as the practical conceptual framework with which we all operate and upon which all our theoretical investigations must be erected as a super-structure. It is not really the common-sense view that is called into question by philosophical scepticism, but only the OT which is part of a metaphysical construction based on the common-sense view.

(5) But at any rate, what our assessment of the appeal to the given implies is that the traditional epistemological task cannot be divorced from metaphysical considerations. The issue between different theories of perception can therefore not be properly discussed or appreciated except as part of a broader metaphysical treatment.

Chapter 12

COMMON SENSE
AND RIVAL ONTOLOGIES

(I) ALTERNATIVE ONTOLOGIES

Our examination of the argument concerning the nature of the given in sense-perception has led us to the conclusion that this argument reflects different conceptions of the 'nature of thought'. It is therefore really a metaphysical argument in which the question of sense-perception is used as the vehicle for the expression of different conceptions regarding the relation between cognition and reality.

In view of the changed climate of opinion among contemporary philosophers regarding the legitimacy and nature of metaphysics, this conclusion is not likely to be regarded as very surprising. But metaphysics has been reinstated in modern philosophy in a number of different ways, some of which accord with what has been suggested by our analysis of the argument regarding the nature of the given, and some which do not accord with our conclusions.

The view concerning metaphysical theories which immediately emerged after the rejection of metaphysics by the 'Logical Positivists' of the thirties was the view that metaphysical theories might have some legitimacy if regarded as merely the adoption of a conventional framework of basic categories. Thus the acceptance of sensible particulars rather than objects as the basic ontological unit of description might be regarded as the adoption of a rival conventional ontology opposed to the one with which we usually operate in common-sense. But since the 'object' ontology was itself merely a conventional framework, the adoption of one or other of these ontologies was to be decided not by what best 'fitted the facts' but rather by considerations of convenience and usefulness. Thus, according to Carnap, the question 'what objects are the elements of given direct experience?' is really a question about words, and is equivalent to asking 'what kinds of word occur in observation sentences?'. The answer to this sort of question depends, according to Carnap, entirely upon one's own choice. The decision concerned the adoption of a conventional framework of description, and no empirical matter of fact was at stake.[1]

This suggestion has striking affinities with the Linguistic Theory of A. J. Ayer which was discussed in a previous chapter. According to that theory, the different theories of perception are merely alternative languages, any of which could be employed to express the facts of perceptual experience. The preference Ayer had for one language, i.e. the Sense-Datum Terminology, rather than its rivals, was due to the fact that according to him it had the advangages of unambiguity of definition, convenience, and so on. But Ayer rejected the Carnap view which made the decision between the different 'alternative ontologies' one of language *only*. While the choice of the 'sense-datum' terminology might be merely conventional, it did not follow that propositions intending to describe the characteristics of sense-data were true only by convention. Sense-data could have properties other than those which belonged to them by definition, and the description of these properties involved a statement of fact rather than the expression of a rule of language.

We have argued before that Ayer's admission on this point constituted the weakness of his verbalist thesis.[2] As a matter of fact it is clear that both Carnap and Ayer, whatever their differences, were able to say what they did about the conventional nature of the adoption of rival 'ontologies' because they both at the time believed that the real basic units of observation were sense-data. They were really Phenomenalists for whom, in spite of their protestations to the contrary, the Sense-Datum Terminology was preferable precisely because it came closest to a description of the real facts.[3]

But even if this were not so and the choice between 'alternative ontologies' were a genuine choice of the conventional sort that they suggested, this evaluation of the nature of the argument about the

---

[1] Carnap's views have been set out in various places in his works. The fullest expression is to be found in his 'Empiricism, semantics and Ontology' which originally appeared in *Revue internationale de Philosophie* IV, 11, 1950 pp. 20–40, and was reprinted in *Meaning and Necessity* 2nd ed. (Chicago, University Press, 1956).

[2] See Chapter 3 (IV).

[3] J. L. Austin makes this point with regard to Ayer alone. See *Sense and Sensibilia* (Oxford, Clarendon Press, 1960) pp. 55–61 and 107–10. But I think examination reveals that it is true of Carnap as well.

given would not correspond to what has been suggested to us by our own previous examination of this argument:

(1) Whatever may be the factors which induce the philosopher to accept one ontology rather than another, it would seem clear that for Carnap and Ayer, the criteria for considering the philosophical adequacy of any particular ontology would be such factors as convenience of use, comprehensiveness, etc. But this would seem to discount the characteristically metaphysical motives which we have discovered to be involved in leading the philosopher to the adoption of his particular ontology. Thus we have suggested that it is a 'dissatisfaction' with the common-sense view of a world of subjects and objects which partly motivates the SDT and the IET. This is what underlies the search for 'certainty'—or so, at any rate, Bradley's theory has suggested to us.

According to the 'alternative ontology' view, this search for 'satisfaction' would be at most a matter of the individual philosopher's psychological idiosyncrasy, having no relevance to the philosophical issues. But this seems patently false. It is just this search for 'satisfaction' which offers an adequate explanation of the argument regarding the nature of the given. Hence the 'alternative ontology' view must be rejected.

(2) Another weakness of the view consists of its implication that the common-sense view is 'conventional' or at any rate to be treated on a par with the rival ontologies. Thus, assuming the OT to be more or less identifiable with the ordinary common-sense view, the issue between the OT, the SDT and the IET becomes an issue between equals, and the fact that ordinary usage favours the OT casts no light on its philosophical adequacy. It may in fact be rejected, on philosophical grounds.

But one of the few really important insights in British philosophy which came to the fore during this century seems to me to be the notion argued first by G. E. Moore and subsequently, in different ways, by other philosophers, that common-sense views cannot be regarded as alternative to rival philosophical theories since the former are the views which we all unhesitatingly accept as forming the foundation of the very possibility of meaningful communication. This is the basis of Moore's famous distinction between the *truth* of common-sense statements and their *analysis*. The common-sense view, according to this, cannot be overthrown by science or philosophy or even refined and instructed by them in such a way as to produce a more accurate and subtle 'enlightened common-sense view'. The common-sense view is not an 'analysis' of the facts at all, and can therefore not be rejected or replaced by a rival 'analysis' of the facts. It represents rather the 'analysandum' of which all the rival scientific and philosophic theories are different 'analyses'.[1] If this thesis of Moore's is accepted then we are faced with the alternative *either* of distinguishing the OT from the common-sense view and regarding it as a suggested 'ontological analysis' of the common-sense view, in which case the 'alternative ontology' thesis of Carnap could still be maintained, *or else* we shall continue to identify the OT with the common-sense view and reject the 'alternative ontology thesis'. The rejection of the 'alternative ontology thesis' is, in the latter case, forced upon us because the only other possibility would be to maintain that the OT was the 'analysandum' and the SDT and IET alternative 'ontological analyses' of this 'analysandum'. But such a view is obviously an absurd one, which is belied by the fact that exponents of the three theories of the given regard themselves as being at loggerheads.

I should therefore suggest that exponents of the 'alternative ontology' view might be persuaded to dissociate the OT from the common-sense view. There would then be, as we shall see, an element of truth in their contention. However, the problem would then remain of explaining the nature or significance of a common-sense view which is other than the OT.

(II) STRAWSON'S VIEW

A view which is similar in some respects to Carnap's but which shows more appreciation of common-sense is the view of P. F. Strawson.[2] This is connected with his concept of 'descriptive metaphysics' as opposed to 'revisionary metaphysics'. While the latter may have been more interesting in the history of thought because of the intensity of the partial vision of the revisionists, it is 'descriptive metaphysics' which has been of more lasting significance. The latter consists essentially of 'conceptual analysis'; but whereas most 'con-

---

[1] See our previous discussion in Chapter 4 (II).
[2] P. F. Strawson, 'Individuals', (London, Hutchison, 1958).

ceptual analysts' have restricted themselves to specific points, 'descriptive metaphysics' aims to lay down the most general features of our conceptual structure. It does so by a close examination of the actual usage of words; but it hopes thereby to reveal the submerged structure which is the basis for the discriminations we make and the connections we establish.

'There is a massive central core of human thinking which has no history—or none recorded in the histories of thought; there are categories and concepts which, in their most fundamental character, change not at all . . . they are the commonplaces of the least refined thinking; and are yet the indispensable core of the conceptual equipment of the most sophisticated human being. It is with these, their interconnexions, and the structure that they form, that a descriptive metaphysics will be primarily concerned.'[1]

This seems to be Strawson's recognition of the centrality of common-sense concepts in our view of the world. He goes on to say that though these deeply embedded concepts are permanent, they are described in an impermanent idiom which reflects both the climate of thought of a particular age and the individual philosopher's personal style of thinking. Hence 'descriptive metaphysics' has to be done constantly over and over again. It is to this task that Strawson devotes himself in his work on 'Individuals'.

In the course of his argument Strawson comes to the conclusion that the 'basic particulars' in our view of the world must be 'material bodies'. The main ground upon which this is maintained is that only material bodies' possess the necessary qualities which enable us to re-identify them as particulars. And this follows from the general character of the conceptual scheme with which we operate, namely, a unitary spatio-temporal framework, of one temporal and three spatial dimensions. Thus 'material bodies' constitute the framework of our metaphysics. The 'private particulars'—sensations, mental events and sense-data—will not serve as 'basic particulars' since there are problems relating to their re-identification. Similar difficulties arise with regard to events and processes. Strawson therefore comes to the conclusion that 'material bodies' are 'ontologically prior' in our conceptual scheme as it is. And he goes on to maintain that we cannot make intelligible to ourselves the idea of a conceptual

[1] ibid., p. 10.

scheme which provided for a system of objective and identifiable particulars but of which 'material bodies' were not the 'basic particulars' of that system.[1]

In saying that 'material objects' are 'ontologically prior, Strawson is in effect saying they are 'given'. However, it should be clear from his method of exposition that their 'givenness' does not consist of any empirically discernible quality. It is not that we can 'discover them' or 'pick them out' or 'point to them' in a way in which we cannot do with events or processes. Their 'ontological priority' is discovered by a logical argument, i.e., by the fact that they are primarily re-identifiable whereas events or processes are only secondarily re-identifiable.

Thus Strawson would probably agree with the conclusion that we have reached in our previous chapter that the argument about the nature of the given was really a metaphysical argument; that the Naive View was quite wrong in supposing it to be an empirical argument; and that the preference of one theory of the given to its rivals reflected an ontological preference. But whereas Carnap and Ayer seem to suggest that the choice between 'alternative ontologies' should depend on convenience of use, comprehensiveness, etc., Strawson makes the choice depend upon the question of the other characteristics of our conceptual scheme and the question of re-identification. In doing so he grants our deeply embedded framework of categories (i.e. common-sense) a certain priority, and it is scarcely to be wondered that he comes out in favour of the 'material object' ontology.

But Strawson's view does not allow us to say much in defence of the SDT and IET. Again, like the 'alternative ontology' view of Carnap, it seems to discount the characteristically metaphysical motives which we showed to be involved in leading the philosopher to the choice of an ontology other than the OT. The 'dissatisfaction' with the common-sense view of the world might well be rejected by Strawson out of hand as an irrelevant idiosyncrasy. But we have suggested, on the contrary, that this is what underlies the search for certainty, so characteristic of a large part of modern epistemology.

Hence we must conclude that Strawson's account of metaphysics does not accord with what has been suggested by our analysis of the argument regarding the nature of the given.

[1] ibid., pp. 38–58

(III) SELLARS' VIEW

An answer to the question of the relationship between the common-sense view and rival ontologies is suggested by Wilfrid Sellars in the thesis that 'what we call the scientific enterprise is the flowering of a dimension of discourse which already exists in what historians call the "pre-scientific age" '. In other words that

'... scientific discourse is but a continuation of a dimension of discourse which has been present in human discourse from the very beginning, ... the scientific picture of the world replaces the common-sense picture; ... the scientific account of 'what there is' supersedes the descriptive ontology of everyday life.'[1]

Thus in accordance with this theory, the OT can be identified with the common-sense view; but this common-sense view may be replaced by a more sophisticated ontology suggested by science. Sellars hastens to explain that this does not mean that the rejection of the common-sense view is a *practical* necessity. On the contrary, there is no need to 'brain-wash existing populations and train them to speak differently'. But, speaking philosophically Sellars is quite prepared to say that the common-sense world of physical objects in space and time is unreal, that there are no such things.

Thus, in Sellars' view, the common-sense view may well be regarded as embodying a primitive ontology (of subjects and objects placed in space and time, i.e. the OT), which is replaced by more sophisticated ontologies with the growth of science. 'Science is the measure of all things. of what it is that it is, and of what is not that it is not.' But the common-sense view may nonetheless be preserved for practical discourse. This gives to common-sense only the priority of being the mode of discourse from which we all start for practical reasons, and which, since for practical reasons it is perfectly adequate, may be retained even by the philosopher.

Sellars rejects the argument that since we learn to describe the world in terms of the categories of the common-sense picture, this gives the latter an unchallengeable authenticity. This is based on the assumption of an 'ostensive tie' between our fundamental descrip-

---

[1] W. Sellars, 'Empiricism and the Philosophy of Mind' first published in *Minnesota Studies in the Philosophy of Science* Vol. I (Minneapolis, University of Minnesota Press, 1956) and now reprinted in his *Science, Perception and Reality* (London, Kegan Paul, 1966).

tive vocabulary and the world. But we may, argues Sellers, learn to use a language without any direct reference to its supposed ostensive element. Learning a language involves a long process of acquiring and manifesting verbal habits in perceptual situations; but the verbal formula (e.g. 'This is green') is not simply a name of a given 'fact'. It is a 'reliable symptom' or indicator of the presence of green objects in standard conditions of perception. And while the correctness of any such particular utterance of this statement requires that its utterer could cite prior particular facts as evidence for the idea that it is a reliable indicator, he need not necessarily have known these facts to obtain. The process of acquiring the concept of green involves a long history of acquiring piecemeal habits of response to various objects in various circumstances. One can have the concept of green only by having a whole battery of concepts of which it is one element.[1]

We may begin our comments on Sellar's remarks by noting, firstly, that they are stimulating, instructive and come very near to the truth. But Sellars seems to me to have given insufficient credit to the fact, pointed out by Moore, that common-sense statements cannot be refuted by philosophical or scientific theories. It may be that Sellars is correct in rejecting the over-simplified view that this is because common-sense statements simply *name* the facts, but his own theory, that the common-sense view is simply the most practical, and its priority and the justification of its retention lie simply in its practicality, does not do sufficient justice to common-sense statements.

It would seem that, according to Sellars, the whole of the common-sense framework can, and, indeed, ought to be, replaced by the more sophisticated scientific description of the world. Thus every common-sense statement is, in a sense, refutable, not directly, but indirectly, through the refutation of the whole of the framework within which it occurs by scientific theory. In that case the sentence 'physical objects aren't really coloured' would be a legitimate way of expressing the indirect refutation, by the discoveries of science, of the common-sense view that 'physical objects *are* coloured'. Sellars in fact does say that this is merely a clumsy way of expressing the rejection of the framework of common-sense.[2] What he fails to appreciate

[1] See Sections 32–44.
[2] ibid., Section 41.

is that if it is the case, as he claims, that common-sense and scientific theory are 'continuous', then the statement is also a legitimate contention expressed in the language of common-sense. If so then can the retention of the common-sense view that 'physical objects are coloured' really be justified at all? Wouldn't it be more accurate to sum up the situation, according to Sellars, by saying that one may continue to *talk* of physical objects being coloured for practical purposes even though this wasn't really true according to science.

But far from legitimizing the common-sense view for practical purposes, this would in fact be to reject the common-sense view. This clearly fails to do justice to Moore's contention that common-sense statements cannot be refuted by scientific or philosophical theories. To the extent that we accept Moore's insight as illuminating, we must reject the idea that common-sense and theory are 'continuous' and that the former can be 'replaced' by the latter. The two are on different *levels*, and are therefore not capable of conflicting with each other. Common-sense provides the analysandum, which scientific and philosophical theory proceeds to analyse.

Sellars treats common-sense, on the contrary, as a form of primitive analysis. This is part of the significance of his saying that scientific discourse is a dimension which has been present already in the 'pre-scientific age'. But this is quite wrong. If common-sense is to be truly legitimized for practical purposes, this can be done only by recognizing that common-sense is not 'primitive science' at all, but rather something quite different, namely, a 'statement of the facts' not, indeed, in the sense that it merely 'names' or 'describes' them, but in the sense that it formulates our everyday experience in accordance with simple universally held categories which are quite adequate for practical purposes.

In fact it was Sellars himself who spoke of these 'practical purposes' as legitimizing the continued use of common-sense. Where he erred was in his apparent supposition that practical purposes can legitimize the use of primitive science. His position seems to be that common-sense is sometimes quite wrong, but we may continue to speak *as if* it were right so long as our purposes are strictly practical. But if we are truly to legitimize the common-sense view we must regard the distinction between 'practical' and 'theoretical purposes' not merely as one between cases when we are speaking in a relaxed and easy-going manner, on the one hand, and cases where we are on our guard, careful and precise, on the other. We must insist that the truth of a statement cannot be considered at all except in the context of the purposes for which it is made. Hence what is true for practical purposes may be false for theoretical purposes, and vice-versa. Commonsense views are adequate and legitimate because they are not offered for theoretical purposes at all, but merely adopted with the aim of expressing the facts for practical purposes. There is no theorizing in common-sense as such. The priority of common-sense lies in the fact that we all share practical everyday existence as the framework within which theorizing activities begin. These activities begin when we start asking scientific or philosophical questions. But we never really leave this framework of common-sense either while engaged in finding theoretical answers to these questions, or even when we have answered them to our own satisfaction. Answering scientific and philosophical questions may lead us to formulate theories of all sorts of complexity, some of them inter-locking, others conflicting, and yet others complementary. But scientific theories and common-sense statements cannot truly conflict, since common-sense is not science, and everyday practical purposes are not scientific ones. The two are on different levels. Theory does not 'replace' common-sense; where it concerns itself with the areas of experience which are also touched on by common-sense, it may be said to 'analyse' common-sense beliefs for scientific or philosophical purposes.

The difference between the view regarding the relationship between common-sense and theory maintained by Sellars and the alternative view that I am suggesting may be illustrated in the following example:[1] Sellars might resolve the clash between the ordinary man's talking of the sun 'setting' in the West and the Copernican astronomer's discovery that it was the earth that was moving rather that the sun, by saying 'The astronomer is right and the ordinary man wrong; but the ordinary man may continue to talk as if he is right, since for practical purposes we are not interested in the real facts and the appearances may serve equally as well.' I on the other hand should insist on saying that the ordinary man is right and not wrong. Only if he were to talk of the 'setting' of the sun in the context

---

[1] See John Wisdom's remarks in 'Moore's Technique', first published in *The Philosophy of G. E. Moore* ed. Schilp, Library of Living Philosophers, Vol. 4 (Evanston and Chicago, North Western University, 1951) pp. 443 ff.

of an astronomical discussion would he be wrong, for then he would be theorizing and offering a primitive and outdated astronomical theory in place of the more developed and reasoned theory of the Copernican astronomer. But in the context of ordinary everyday discourse, where no question of astronomical theory is involved, it is perfectly legitimate and quite right to say that the sun 'sets' in the West.

In distinguishing so sharply between the practical context in which common-sense views are legitimate and indeed irrefutable, and the theoretical context in which quite different answers may be given, we are therefore rejecting Sellars' view of the 'continuity' of common-sense and science, and his notion that science 'replaces' common-sense. But there is still an element of truth in Sellars' remark that 'the scientific enterprise is the flowering of a dimension of discourse which already exists in what historians call the "pre-scientific age"', for it remains true that the conceptual framework within which we express the common-sense facts that form the analysandum of the whole scientific and philosophical enterprise are not entirely free from theory or philosophy. Inasmuch as the common-sense view formed for practical purposes does not, as it were, 'mirror' the facts by naming them but rather organizes certain dominant elements in our experience in the most plausible and convenient fashion, it is to some extent of necessity theory-laden. There *is* a rudimentary ontology involved in common-sense, and so far Sellars is quite right. But this primitive ontology is never offered as a philosophical view; common-sense as such is not interested in ontology. For the purposes of common-sense, i.e. for practical purposes, the primitive ontological elements are quite irrelevant. There may be some thinkers who are tempted to develop these rudimentary ontological elements in order to form a specific philosophical theory, the OT. But if so then this specific philosophical theory must be judged solely on its philosophical merits. It cannot claim privilege by virtue of its special relationship to common-sense. It is certainly not *identical* with common-sense, even though some of its elements form part of the framework within which the common-sense view of the world is formulated.

My view concerning the relationship between common-sense and scientific and philosophical theories may be summarized as the view that common-sense and theory are *complementary* to one another.

(IV) THE COMPLEMENTARITY THESIS ONCE MORE

Two of the factors which seem to have led Sellars to his particular view of the relationship between science and common-sense are (a) a rejection of the positivist conception of scientific theories, which regards them as mere heuristic devices, and (b) a rejection of the complementarity thesis.

The second factor is the more important, so far as we are concerned. Sellars recognizes that human knowledge (which he calls 'discourse') can no longer be regarded as a map, sub-divided into a side-by-side series of sub-maps, each representing a sub-region in a side-by-side series of regions making up the total subject matter of discourse. Discourse must now be recognized to be 'a tangle of intersecting dimensions whose relations with one another and with extra-linguistic fact conform to no single or simple pattern'. But he believes that nowadays 'the grand strategy of the philosophical enterprise is once again directed toward that articulated and integrated vision of man-in-the-universe (or, shall I say discourse -about-man-in-all-discourse) which has traditionally been its goal'.[1]

Thus in spite of his recognition of the poly-dimensional nature of discourse, Sellars seems to suppose that it is still possible and indeed desirable that we should seek in philosophy a synoptic view from a standpoint where we can combine all the perspectives afforded us by the particular sciences. His view of the continuity between common-sense and science is part of Sellars espousal of this goal.

But, as we have argued, the complementarity thesis, while not excluding the possibility of a 'higher' mode of representation which could synthesise all the different disciplines of science, raises the question whether this wider theory need necessarily be sought. Is this higher standpoint worth taking up because of any theoretical or practical considerations?

Sellars with his view of the continuity of common-sense and science seems to be implying that the adoption of an 'articulated and integrated vision of man-in-the-universe' is a goal of theoretical explanations, as well as rising out of the same basic practical considerations which led to the formulation of the common-sense view. It is clear that if we adopt the view concerning the relationship

[1] *Loc. cit.* Section 40.

between common-sense and science that I have suggested in the previous section in opposition to Sellars' view, we shall formulate the matter quite differently, and be led to a much closer sympathy with the complementarity ideal of explanation. For if common-sense is the view adopted for practical purposes, as opposed to scientific and philosophical views which are adopted for specific theoretical purposes, the practical motive may be more or less disregarded in pursuing the different scientific disciplines. There is no need to assume that all our scientific theories must necessarily be combined in a synoptic master-theory. If each discipline pursues its own goal, analysing the facts from its own particular standpoint and using categories formed with a view to its own particular needs, it is difficult to conceive of any particular discipline as being continuous with common-sense in the manner suggested by Sellars. Rather than this it would be more congenial to regard all the disciplines as theoretical superstructures, off-shoots from common-sense for different theoretical purposes. And, moreover, the disciplines 'shoot-off' common-sense in different directions and in different ways. There is, so far as one can see, no one theoretical consideration which would necessitate a re-union of all these off-shoots at a higher level. Is there any practical consideration which necessitates this?

I shall argue shortly that if 'practical' is interpreted in the way it is when we say that the common-sense view is formed for practical reasons, then there is no such practical consideration which necessitates a synoptic unified world view. But there may be another sense of 'practical', i.e. not 'in order to be able to control and make use of the facts', but 'in order to be able to live meaningful and moral lives', in which there may well be a 'practical' necessity for the adoption of some sort of synoptic vision.

But before we continue with this argument, let us recall that in our examination of the argument between the three different theories concerning the nature of the given, we discovered that the argument did not concern itself with the facts (as maintained in the Naive View) but rather involved different conceptions of thought and the mind. And we saw that an explanation of the argument could be found if the 'quest for certainty' so characteristic of the SDT, were interpreted in the light of the rejection of the claim to ultimate metaphysical reality of the common-sense world characteristic of the IET. The argument about the nature of the given was then revealed as in essence a metaphysical argument involving different conceptions of the nature of thought and the relation between cognition and reality. This hypothesis concerning the true nature of the argument about the given is strongly supported by the inherent plausibility of the Naive View of the dispute, which regards it as the attempt by different epistemologists, whose eyes have been opened by their consideration of theoretical difficulties involved in perception, to describe what it is that they *really* see. It is extremely tempting to interpret the argument about the nature of the given in this erroneous manner, which makes it an argument about the real facts. And the fact that it is so tempting can be explained very well by our hypothesis that the real argument concerns the acceptance or rejection of the supposed ontological claims of the common-sense view of the world. In order to show how this is so we may return to our discussion of the relationship between common-sense and science.

(v) WORLD-VIEWS AND MODELS

In distinguishing the common-sense view from that of science or philosophy, we argued that whereas the first 'states the facts' in terms of concepts and categories which, though minimally theory-laden, suggest themselves in order to serve the non-theoretical and practical aim of enabling us to control and make use of the forces of the world in which we find ourselves, the latter arise in order to analyse the facts of the world in the light of specific theoretical considerations. However, we have so far failed to make a distinction between the theoretical considerations which concern the sciences and those which influence the philosopher.

In an earlier chapter[1] we noted the interesting parallel between the different positions taken up with regard to the interpretation of the Sense-Datum Theory, and the corresponding positions taken up in modern discussions of the nature of theoretical concepts in the philosophy of science. Thus in both areas discussion veered from the view that theoretical concepts are conjectures about the facts which subsequent experimentation served to confirm or deny, through a period in which they were regarded not as conjectures about the facts but as 'hypotheses' of a semi-heuristic nature, and arrived at the extreme view that scientific theories were logical

[1] Chapter 3 (v).

instruments usually exemplified by a model, which enabled us to predict subsequent empirical behaviour. We may now ask the question whether philosophical theories are at all like scientific theories, and if they are, in what respects they are alike, and in what respects they may differ.

There seems little point in questioning the legitimacy of the word 'theories' in connection with philosophic views. This use is now firmly established and need not be at all misleading if we take the necessary precautions. But whether we sympathize with the Realist view of the nature of scientific theories, which regards them as attempts to describe the real 'mechanisms' of the universe, or whether we tend towards the Positivist view in accordance with which scientific theories are merely heuristic logical structures and theoretical entities are merely counters whose existence or non-existence is entirely irrelevant to the success of the theory concerned, consideration reveals the fact that neither of these views is in the least bit appropriate to the characterization of philosophical views and the evaluation of the theoretical concepts in philosophy. For it is clear that it is not the formal deduction of facts or events which may be observed, or even the systematic description of facts or events as they are, which primarily interest the philosopher. By no means is he seeking to 'explain' the facts in the manner in which scientists attempt to do this, nor does his view-point entail the treatment of specific theoretical difficulties and problems of the sort with which the scientist is concerned. His interest is centred towards the more pervasive features of the world rather than to particular events or facts, to its *a priori* rather than to its empirical features. And his method, whether characterized as linguistic analysis, conceptual analysis or otherwise, lies in the sphere of reasoning and argumentation rather than that of discovery and description. In fact it is not the facts at all which have been foremost in the minds of philosophers nor even the concepts or categories within which these facts can be expressed, but, I should argue, the illuminating analogy which places the facts in a different light. To be brief I am in full sympathy with those who regard metaphysics as the very essence of philosophy.

A characteristic feature of the unpopularity of metaphysics during the first half of this century has been the widespread attempt to demonstrate that certain classical metaphysical views arose out of trivial, conceptual and linguistic mistakes. This attitude, happily no longer as popular as it used to be, maintained that once a metaphysical view had been demonstrated to be linked with such trivial mistakes, it had been 'shown up' for what it was worth and could safely be disregarded for all posterity.

But I think that those who argued in this way have been intolerantly narrow in their lack of appreciation for the classical metaphysical positions, some of them dating from the earliest times in the history of human thought, which have, after all, been treated seriously by generations of extremely able thinkers.

It has indeed been shown that many metaphysical systems are mistaken not only in details but in regard to the very task which they thought they were supposed to fulfil. Metaphysics—and for this thanks are due to its modern critics—has indeed now been clearly revealed not to be a speculative topography of the intellectual regions or a description of any hidden world of truths. But this does not mean that there is not nevertheless some validity to the idea of a metaphysical outlook, a *weltanschauung*' or world-view. I can only state here very briefly what I believe about this matter. No protracted discussion is required in any case, for similar views have been argued at greater length by several contemporary philosophers.[1]

A world-view is a suggested way of looking at things. It always involves some 'root metaphor', analogy, 'archetype', or model, even though these may never be explicitly spelled out. These models and analogies drawn from limited and circumscribed regions of our experience are applied more widely, and serve as the basis for sets of categories in terms of which we interpret large areas of our experience. When successful these 'root-metaphors' generate relatively wide-ranging world-theories. Metaphysical theories of this sort are far from being trivial. They are certainly not 'nonsensical', and are well worth making. Thus metaphysicians may argue whether the world is like a large intricate machine or rather like a growing plant or organism. These expressions of the classical metaphysical positions known as Mechanism and Vitalism reveal the 'root-metaphors' which underlie the two views. They engender 'synoptic visions', in which we characterize the whole realm of the physical world in terms of familiar models. What is important about these views is that they

[1] See for example S. C. Pepper *World Hypotheses*, 4th printing (Berkeley and Los Angeles, 1961); Max Black, *Models and Metaphors*, (Ithaca, Cornell U.P., 1961); P. Gardiner, *Schopenhauer*, (London, Penguin Books, 1962); etc.

seek to give some special significance to our experience by offering a key interpretative principle. Each expresses a 'world-view', and the adoption of one or other of the positions would involve: (1) a feeling of satisfaction that some insight has been gained about what the world is and how it works, (2) a basis for what could be considered as the right attitude to take up in our practical lives, (3) an attitude recommended for our theoretical activities which might lead to a certain prejudice in favour of one type of scientific explanation rather than another.

When, as in this example, the issue between the different 'world-views' is as clear as this, we may well suspect that both views have a germ of truth which each is exaggerating. Usually the issue is not so clear-cut. But in any case 'world-views' are not mere statements or 'descriptions' of the facts: they offer interpretations of the facts. These interpretations may be very significant for scientific progress, for behaving in certain ways rather than others, or for personal satisfaction. The metaphysical interpretation really makes no difference to the facts. But this does not mean that it merely expresses some irrelevant personal emotion regarding the facts. The alleged dichotomy between the 'descriptive' and the 'emotive' uses of language has long been shown up to be facile and superficial. There are many very different functions which statements can serve, and if an interpretation makes no difference to the facts and has no clear predictive capacity, this does not mean that it might not be very significant in other respects. Insights of the sort that we have been considering in our example can and have served important functions in creating a climate of opinion which helps or hinders the growth of one science or another. They also can have enormous consequence for the evaluation which a given society places upon its existing moral code. It is for this reason that some philosophers have associated this type of metaphysical assertion with ethics and regarded it as 'axiological'. Perhaps this category has some merit; however it is clear that considered as value statements, assertions of this type are quite different from the sort that tell us, for example, that murder is wicked.

Metaphysical assertions of this sort, which involve a model or archetype are sometimes extremely enlightening. I believe that they often represent the highest fruits of speculative thought, for they offer an explanation which *satisfies*. It is to be noted however, that the function of the 'root-metaphor' or model in such assertions is quite different from the function of models in more limited scientific theories. In the latter the model serves primarily as an exemplification of the deductive system or logical apparatus which enables us to deduce descriptions and predictions relating to the facts once certain observations have been made. The logical structure is the backbone of the theory, the model merely its exemplification. It is of course realized that in the actual progress of human thought the models are sometimes more important than the logical structure which they exemplify. But, in principle at any rate, their importance is psychological rather than logical. A fruitful model generates a great deal of scientific research; but the theory is not simply the model—it is what is somehow behind the model.

But in metaphysical assertions of the type to which I am referring, which express a 'world-view', the model is the main thing, and perhaps the only thing. It is when we start looking behind the model for logical structures which it is supposed to exemplify that we create the wrong type of metaphysics, the forbidding systematic philosophic outlook, which looks something like a deductive system, and which acts as a straight-jacket which may prevent us from seeing things as they are. In a 'world-view' it is only the analogy that counts; predictive fruitfulness is more or less irrelevant.

This is not to say that metaphysical views of this sort are never affected by empirical considerations. The philosopher, for example, who considered the universe to be an enormous machine might or might not be convinced of the error of his view by an argument drawing attention to important practical differences between his empirical expectations from machines and the expectations we have with regard to certain regions of the universe. He may be persuaded e.g., that teleological explanations are much more satisfactory in biology than mechanistic ones. But the point to bear in mind is that statements expressing 'world-views', although they have empirical application and have to 'fit the facts' in this manner, are nonetheless clearly distinguishable from empirical assertions which merely draw attention to the facts. Metaphysical assertions of this sort and empirical assertions are quite different things which serve different functions; different motives are involved in their assertion. The confusion of these two classes of assertion has led to confused reasoning and is responsible for some of the blunders with which the history of philosophy is full.

It seems to me that in the case of the argument about the nature of the given as well, empirical and metaphysical motives are intertwined in such a way as to explain why the rejection of the claim to reality of the common-sense world of objects should take the form of an assertion that what is given in perception is not objects.

This can be seen when we have recognized two well-known meanings attaching to the word 'see'[1] to be specially significant with regard to the given. We speak of seeing an object, and also of seeing something *as* having some quality or being like something else. The former expression relates to the objects of perception, the latter to interpretations or judgments. When the ordinary man asks the question 'What is it that we see?' he will, in most contexts, be asking an empirical question to which the answer may be that we see a table, a chair, the side of a cube, and so on. But when, impelled by his wish to deny that the common-sense world is all that there is to Reality, that the common-sense view can by no means suffice for scientific or metaphysical considerations, by his desire to assert that it is a mere appearance of a real world which is different, the philosopher asks the same question, 'What is it that we see?', the sort of answer that would be relevant to him would be 'A mere shadow show', 'A stage', and so on. The question really relates to what we see the world *as*.

It is easy to confuse the two, as their linguistic similarity indicates. And it is because it is so easy to confuse them that the philosopher, who is so inclined, may be attracted by the empirical fact, for example, that an object appears differently from different conditions and under different circumstances. This is an everyday fact and need have no significance. Of course if we are oculists or artists, it becomes important to establish some sort of convention for describing appearances and relating them to the circumstances in which the object appears in these different ways. But for the philosopher, changing appearances have no significance except, mistakenly, to one

---

[1] This distinction is discussed in L. Wittgenstein's *Philosophical Investigations* (Oxford, Basil Blackwell, 1953) pp. 193-214, N. Hanson, *Patterns of Discovery* (Cambridge, University Press, 1958).

who is trying to minimize the ultimate reality of the common-sense world and reject it as mere appearance. The intertwining of the metaphysical and the empirical leads the philosopher to conceive of a sensuous appearance as an entity (in the case of the SDT) or it might cause him to conceive of the object as an appearance on the par with its own sensible appearance, and all of them as appearances of something else(something like this may be what is happening in the IET). But in either case, if I am correct, the primary motive is to dissolve the metaphysical importance of the common-sense world.

Herein lies the strength of the OT. 'When I examine my sense experience', the theorist protests, 'I see neither sense-data nor "immediate experience" but only and always objects'. If he is dealing with the empirical question 'What do you see of the world?', he is plainly right since the word 'objects' is just the one we always *do* use as the basic category to describe the class of empirical things which we perceive. And if he is protesting against the confusion between seeing the facts and 'seeing as', he is right again, though this is not nearly so obvious and may even be disputed. Seeing the world of objects as a mere appearance need not involve the empirical seeing of anything other than the world of objects. The metaphysical insight does not reflect upon the empirically agreed facts, though it may reflect upon our expectations concerning other empirical facts.

But the strength of the OT may also be its metaphysical weakness, for in refusing to be confused it may also be refusing to be metaphysically enlightened. Many would judge the OT-ist wrong if what he is doing is no more than attempting to refuse to recognize the insight that the common-sense view is not the OT, even though it contains some elements of the latter at a pre-analytical level, and that the OT is not the whole of the story. The common-sense view of the world is indeed our starting point; but regarded philosophically, with its conceptual framework systematically developed to form the OT, it is mere Appearance which must be discarded if we are to know Reality.

This interpretation is offered tentatively. From the very nature of the case it must remain in the realm of suggestion rather than that of proof. I cannot demonstrate that supporters of the SDT and of the IET have had anything like this in mind. But I suggest that this is what might have happened, at least in the case of *some* holders of these views. And if I am right, we should have a clear explanation of the fact that a search for metaphysical reality should take the form of a quasi-empirical 'pointing out' of the facts.

But at all events since I believe that the different theories of the given are associated with different world views, and that the issue between such world views may have considerable metaphysical significance, I should like to dissent from the commonly held judgment, both in general and with respect to this case, that if metaphysical views are shown to be connected with trivial conceptual and linguistic errors, they have thereby been refuted. I do admit that many of the attempts to connect such views with mistakes have been successful and convincing. I have myself here tried to show the connection between the argument as to the nature of the given with a particular conceptual confusion – the confusion between seeing *of* and seeing *as*. But believing as I do in the importance and significance of the 'root metaphors' involved in the formulation of metaphysical views, I have come to believe that the reverse of the commonly accepted allegation is often true, and that some of the trivial conceptual and linguistic mistakes are not the *causes* or reasons for metaphysical views but rather *effects* or consequences, which have been produced by the determination on the part of the theorists to maintain and underline their metaphysical views at all costs.

This is what I consider to be the truth about the argument concerning the nature of the given in sense-perception. That there is a dispute between the three theories at the empirical level is not true, in spite of appearances and in spite of any ideas the theorists themselves may have about the matter. The fact that the real issue between the three theories may rest, if I am right, on a fundamental confusion relating to the status of the assertion that the common-sense world is only Appearance, does not discredit this assertion. On the contrary, the fact that theorists have wished to maintain this so tenaciously as to allow it to confuse them concerning what is at stake, is, if anything, a testimony to the strength of their conviction that our common-sense way of describing our empirical experience does not get to the bottom of things – metaphysically at any rate.

This confusion between metaphysical insights concerning the ontological status of the ordinary view of the world, and the empirical facts of perception, is a very common one and of great antiquity.

Its widespread occurrence indicates that if the dispute concerning the nature of the given is reducible to it, as I maintain, then this dispute is certainly more than a mere muddle and has some importance. But this importance consists in the fact that the dispute concerning the nature of the given is not at all an empirical issue, but reflects a quest for ultimate metaphysical reality.

This suggestion, at any rate, provides a consistent account of the issues, motives, and insights at work in the argument concerning the nature of the given in sense-perception.

(VII) SOME RESERVATIONS

Throughout this and the preceding chapters I have been speaking as if the desire to discount the claim to reality of the common-sense view of the world were the *one* conscious prevalent motive on account of which the SDT and IET had come to be held. I spoke purposely in this manner in order to make as clear as possible the explanation I was proposing concerning the nature of the dispute about the given in sense-perception.

But I am well aware of the fact that in practice the SDT and IET, like most philosophical theories, have come to be maintained by individual philosophers for a variety of different motives and considerations, some weighty and rational, others trivial and irrational. Moreover, individual philosophers have usually been influenced not by a single motive or consideration but by a large number of different motives and considerations. So that the most that could be argued would be that the desire to discount the claim to reality of the world of common-sense is an important and pervasive *part*-motive for the holding of the SDT and IET. In fact I do believe that this is the case. However, even in this qualified form the claim is likely to be disputed because it will seem incredible to many readers that some of the well-known contemporary protagonists of the SDT should have been influenced even partly by the desire to discount the claim to reality of the world of objects.

I should like to point out that even if they have not been influenced, even partly, by this consideration, this would still leave untouched the essential point of my suggested explanation of the issue between the three chief theories regarding the nature of the given. For even when the desire to discount the world of physical objects has not been a part-*motive* for asserting the SDT or IET, such a dis-counting of the claim to reality of the world of common-sense has almost always been held to *follow* from the adoption of one of these theories. And this circumstance alone would suffice to explain why proponents of the three theories of the given have regarded them-selves as being at issue with one another, in spite of the fact that analysis reveals that each theory is using the expression 'the given' in a somewhat different sense.

So my suggestion as to the real issue between rival theories of the given, though by no means proven, is at any rate not unplausible.

(VIII) CONCLUDING REMARKS

This I suggest is the real issue in the dispute as to the nature of the given. The argument is revealed as essentially a metaphysical one, involving the attempt to find something metaphysically significant either in or behind the world as it ordinarily appears to us. Reality therefore *does* appear differently to different observers, though this difference is not an empirical difference but concerns only our speculative attitudes, the world-views that underlie our approach to the world. The mistake which gives rise to the dispute as to the nature of the given in sense-perception consists in thinking that this difference is somehow an empirical difference. And the carica-ture to which this dispute most easily lends itself is what we have called the Naive View, which takes the dispute to be a super-empirical one where philosophers 'open our eyes' to what it is that we really see.

It has thus been my aim to evaluate the appeal to the given by examining what at first seemed to be an insoluble philosophical argument, the argument about the nature of the given, and to exhibit how the appearance of insolubility arose largely through the creation of the misleading impression that the issue was in some way empirical. Analysis has revealed that so far from it being empirical, the dispute is a muddle in which the theorists concerned were at cross-purposes. But the fact that these theorists took their argument seriously and regarded their dissension from each other as genuine necessitated a further study of the matter which led to the conclusion that the real issue between them concerned speculative or metaphysical insights regarding the ontological status of our ordinary view of the world.

If the above is correct then the appeal to the given in modern epistemology should correctly be regarded as a product of the metaphysical search for ultimate reality. Epistemology, therefore, cannot be supposed to be an area which can be isolated from metaphysics, or from other parts of philosophy, and treated as a genuinely autonomous region in which logical analysis can by itself make order. The theory of knowledge is no independent and self-con-contained scientific discipline like Formal Logic. What our suggestion regarding the nature of the appeal to the given in contemporary epistemology may have served to reveal is the existence of hidden seams which join epistemology to metaphysics.

INDEX